ting your expertise used will ultimately depend on the level of trust and emotional confidence consultant and client share with one another. After the discussion of new change models, or business processes, or strategy, we finally end up in conversation with a client, and it is what we bring to that conversation that will be decisive.

Consultant As Therapist

There is no discipline that has focused more on relationships than the field of therapy. Every consultant, regardless of the length or depth of the engagement, is a therapist to the client. An untrained therapist perhaps, a reluctant therapist, a therapist with more hang ups than the client, but what else is new? We are therapists nevertheless. So the more we can think like them, the more we have to offer.

Good therapy helps us re-engage in life and deal more directly and authentically with the people, past and present, who populate our worlds. A therapist pushes us to take responsibility for our lives, to stop blaming something outside ourselves for our dilemmas. A therapist also confronts our beliefs and forces us to reframe our experience in a more self- and other-forgiving way. This offers the potential to change our relationships, to make them more open, more vulnerable, and more intimate, regardless of the rational and technical sea in which we swim.

The core skill in consulting is how to contract with your clients, and this is the heart of *Flawless Consulting*. Contracting is about building and renegotiating relationships . . . Exchanging wants with our clients . . . Treating the relationship as central. The hope is that if we can contract well with the client, this will, by example, help them improve their contracts with others they work with.

So contracting is an educational process, much like therapy. The goal for each consulting project is to help the client solve the problem the next time around. Regardless of any ambivalence you might have about therapy in general, or how you recall the time years ago when you went to a therapist who was not helpful, or how determined you might be to solve your problems yourself, or how strong your belief that only

people with *real* problems go into therapy—if you are doing consulting, you need some therapeutic skill.

If nothing else, we all need to know how to deal with resistance, and most of the wisdom about resistance comes from the discipline of therapy. It is from the therapeutic encounter that we learn that resistance is a sign that the client is finally taking us seriously. Resistance and learning are constant companions, and if learning is the goal of your work, then resistance to your ideas will be your constant companion too. Seeing resistance as a natural occurrence, not taking it personally, and learning to simply name the resistance and then be quiet—these are therapeutic skills that will save many of your days. They give resistance its rightful due and do not treat it as something to be "overcome." The wish to overcome resistance is a thinly disguised desire for control. To overcome another is to be convinced that you are right and the other person is wrong.

A good therapist views resistance as a quality in the client that holds the person intact. It needs to be understood and affirmed, especially in the workplace. Much of the resistance we see in the workplace is in response to coercion. The resolution is to stop treating employees as if they don't want change and to work with them in the spirit of invitation. Then their objections will be seen in the context of learning instead of as a way to give us a hard time.

Consultant As Philosopher

There is also a philosophical underpinning to the process of consulting that gives context and meaning to what we do. The ideological questions leading to the skills and steps in the original book are really about the *psychology* of consulting. How to contract with a client. How to engage clients in feedback and give them a clear picture of their situation. How to think about implementation. These are action and relationship focused. The consultant's relationship with the client, the clients' relationships with one another.

All this needs to be enhanced by philosophic insight about our work. We need to understand our purpose, and we need to help our

"Wow! A companion a business owner can't be without! The insights of 30 consultants the caliber of Peter Block is priceless."

—SUE MOSBY, principal, CDFM² Architecture Inc.

"This book is a companion piece for both the desktop and bedside of those who do consulting full time or in their role as leader. The words from the Shakespearean sonnet 'who can be wise, amazed, temperate in a moment, no man,' combined with the image of Davy Crockett going to Congress for the first time describing himself as half of nine things, is what it often feels like to be a consultant. I plan to keep this book close to me to both guide and inspire my work."

—PHIL HARKINS, president, Linkage, Inc.

"No matter how proficient, companies who fail to understand and apply Block's concepts risk operating at the vendor level with their clients rather than at the partner level—a potentially mortal risk in an increasingly strategic marketplace."

—FRED LAMPARTER, director of worldwide training, Ogilvy & Mather Worldwide

"With delight we receive the 'Fieldbook and Companion'. . . . As we encourage our Information Technology professionals to pursue continuous learning, this 'Fieldbook' will be added to their skill-building toolkit. Our IT professionals are groomed to develop core consulting skills which enable our organization to approach the workplace as an arena for relationship building. We've used Block's *Flawless Consulting* guidelines to define the basic consulting skills program."

—CASSANDRA A. MATTHEWS, vice president, Information Technology and CIO, PECO Energy Company

"This is content as rich as tiramisu. I find that I can digest only a small portion at a time; yet I'm always back for more. An indispensable resource for the consultant seeking ideas and inspiration."

—KATHRYN HEATH, director of First University, First Union Corporation

"When it comes to prioritizing my reading, Peter Block is second only to the sports section. In this book, Peter provides different points of view and stories that plunge deeply into the human and organizational experience."

—PAUL ANDERSON, convener, Northern California School for Managing and Leading Change

"Peter's work always challenges me to think about things in new ways and pushes me to take risks I might not have had the courage for otherwise. This long-awaited companion to *Flawless Consulting* is no exception."

—JENNIFER POWELL, human resources manager, Aetna USHealthcare

"Peter Block and his friends have produced an indispensable companion to *Flawless Consulting*. Providing help to others is no easy task, but these philosophical, therapeutic, and artistic essays bring to life the spirit and hope of change practitioners everywhere. Ultimately, they deliver practical insights to the consulting craft."

—**CHRISTOPHER G. WORLEY,** director, MSOD Program, Pepperdine University

"If you're new to consulting, or if you need reinforcement that relationships are the heart of successful consulting, read this book. More experienced professionals will find some real gems along the way like Peter's Twelve Questions. And where else will you find Sufi wisdom, William Shakespeare, and Marvin Weisbord all under one roof?"

—**RICK MAURER,** author, *Beyond the Wall of Resistance*
and *Building Capacity for Change Sourcebook*

"In Peter's characteristically accessible style, this complement to the recently revised *Flawless Consulting* skillfully challenges consultants to learn what moves us toward more accountability and to discover what releases the commitment and passion inherent to the experience of being human.

"By assembling the contributions of multiple colleagues, Peter reinforces his claim that only through the act of choosing our freedom can we effectively support ourselves and help our clients. This is one of the significant ways the book successfully achieves its stated goal of placing consulting practice within a universal human context."

—**GORDON C. BROOKS,** MSOD program administrator,
The Graziadio School of Business and Management, Pepperdine University

"This book is a must read for anyone consulting or considering consulting. Peter has once again broken new ground with *The Flawless Consulting Fieldbook and Companion*. Perhaps the most exciting aspect of the book is that Peter and the contributing consultants all have such a passion and love for their work that surfaces time and again in their writing. They've done an incredible job of sharing that passion and love with the rest of us and rekindling the flames that drive us to serve in the consultant's capacity. It's refreshing to hear their passion and honesty in a world too often driven by greed and political correctness."

—**STEVE GIBBONS,** past president, The Association for Quality and Participation

THE

FLAWLESS
CONSULTING
FIELDBOOK & COMPANION

Also by Peter Block

Flawless Consulting: A Guide to Getting Your Expertise Used
The Empowered Manager: Positive Political Skills at Work
Stewardship: Choosing Service over Self-Interest

THE
FLAWLESS
CONSULTING
FIELDBOOK & COMPANION
A GUIDE TO UNDERSTANDING YOUR EXPERTISE

PETER BLOCK
AND 30 FLAWLESS CONSULTANTS
ASSISTED BY ANDREA M. MARKOWITZ

JOSSEY-BASS/PFEIFFER
A Wiley Company
San Francisco

ISBN: 0–7879–4804–7

Library of Congress Cataloging-in-Publication Data
Block, Peter.
    The flawless consulting fieldbook and companion : a guide to understanding your
expertise / Peter Block and 30 flawless consultants : assisted by Andrea M. Markowitz.
        p.   cm.
    Includes bibliographical references and index.
    ISBN 0-7879-4804-7 (acid-free)
    1. Business consultants. 2. Consultants. I. Title.
HD69.C6 B573 2001
001—dc21   00-010408

Printed in the United States of America

Published by

JOSSEY-BASS/PFEIFFER
A Wiley Company
San Francisco
350 Sansome Street, 5th Floor
San Francisco, California 94104–1342
(415) 433–1740; Fax (415) 433–0499
(800) 274–4434; Fax (800) 569–0443

Visit www.DesignedLearning.com
for more information about workshops,
dialogues, and other ways to build your
consulting ability.

www.pfeiffer.com

Acquiring Editor: Matthew Holt
Director of Development: Kathleen Dolan Davies
Developmental Editor: Leslie Stephen
Editor: Rebecca Taff
Senior Production Editor: Dawn Kilgore

Manufacturing Supervisor: Becky Carreño
Interior Design: Marie Carija
Illustrations: Richard Sheppard
Cover Design: Red Letter Design

Printing 10   9   8   7   6   5   4   3   2   1

To Jennifer and Heather

Blessings beyond measure

Contributors

Dick and Emily Axelrod

Rosemarie Barbeau

Clifford F. Bolster

Neale W. Clapp

Lou Ann Daly

Kathleen D. Dannemiller

W. Patrick Dolan

Phil Grosnick

Joel P. Henning

Sylvia L. James

Jill E. Janov

Henry Johnson

Amy J. Katz

Peter Koestenbaum

Samuel P. Magill

Andrea M. Markowitz

Marie T. McCormick

Elizabeth McGrath

Kenneth F. Murphy

John O'Connell

Charlotte Roberts

Nancy Sanchez

John P. Schuster

David and Carole Schwinn

Paul D. Tolchinsky

Nancy Voss

Marvin R. Weisbord

Margaret J. Wheatley

Contents

Figures and Exhibits

Welcome

I n this time of free agency, outsourcing, and cross-functional work teams, consulting has become a part of everyone's job. Plus, we live in an era in which we are forced to hire professionals to provide the help that we used to seek from friends. It is true in our personal lives, where we have moved away from our extended families and now go to a doctor, lawyer, and financial advisor instead of a grandmother, cousin, or uncle. In our work lives, changes seem to be vibrating at such an increasing pace that we always feel the need for specialized expertise. Some of this need for instant expertise is for reassurance; some is just that we do not think we have time to learn it ourselves.

So, despite all the ambivalence surrounding consulting, it has grown into big business and generally infiltrated our lives. The situation is much like Andy Warhol's quip about fame: It seems that we have gotten to the point where every person will now enjoy fifteen minutes of being a consultant at some time.

A FRIEND INDEED

This book is meant as a companion for people who are doing consulting—that is, anyone attempting to help others effect a change in their lives or work. It is also meant for those who use consultants, for the more we know about the theory and practice of consulting, the better the chance that we will get what we bargained for. A companion can be a partner on a project or someone employed to be of service. The best ones are friends too. The book is intended to be both kinds of companion to you—and also to be a friend to turn to when there is time for reflection.

Companions do at least two things for us. First, they affirm the integrity of our experience. When life is difficult, they remind us that it is life that is difficult; it is not that we are particularly wrong, unskilled, or incapable. They tell us the truth about ourselves that we can get no other way, and underneath their feedback lies an affection that heals more than any advice or suggestion they might offer.

Second, companions can help us change our minds. They give us a deeper way of thinking about our experience. Good therapists are good companions. They give us a different perspective. Artists, visual and literary, are good companions, for they see aspects of the world that we are blind to. They interpret elements of the culture that we swim in, elements that were previously felt but not understood or made explicit. Philosophers are also nice to have around, for they give us a wider view, forcing us to turn the telescope around and shift our focus outward.

So this is the intent of this book:

- To support the integrity of your experience.
- To change your mind about how you interpret your own consulting experience.
- To broaden your way of thinking.
- To bring a manageable dose of therapy and art, philosophy and literature into your thoughts about consulting, and
- To do it in a comforting and simple way.

I hope the book does not sacrifice the practical in its effort to deal with the universal. It includes stories and examples from real life. We have invited thirty consultants to share an experience, opinion, or story with you, as if around a dinner table. A kind of printed-and-bound version of the movie *My Dinner with Andre*. The guest consultants were given no more specific instructions than to speak about what is important to them and to be as vivid and concrete and practical as they can be. For many consultants, this is a great challenge. They were also asked to list the books and other resources that inspire their ideas about consulting, and these are included with each chapter.

The larger intent of this book is to explore how consulting touch-

The Flawless Consulting Fieldbook and Companion

es on the more profound aspects of life and how our service is to translate these insights into our work and the consciousness of our clients. Questions of truth, honor, risk, loyalty, intimacy, and other themes that some might label more "philosophical" than "real world" are the stuff that we yearn to talk about with true friends and wise advisors.

FIELDBOOK AND GUIDE

We have also framed this book as a fieldbook to go along with *Flawless Consulting*, first published in 1981 and recently updated and expanded.

A fieldbook is something you pull out for information and guidance in the midst of action. Walking in the woods, you see a flower you can't identify, so you pull out your fieldbook to learn what it is. In the world of work, you bounce off a difficult business problem, and with time running out, you reach for your favorite fieldbook, and get an idea about what to do—a just-in-time literary aid. Most fieldbooks are derived from a particular theoretical work; they make practical what was conceptual in the original text. This fits with a culture that values the practical above all else.

The problem with writing a fieldbook based on *Flawless Consulting* is that that book is already relentlessly practical. It offers steps, lists, things to say and not to say. To write a guide to make that book more practical would force us into discussing things like body language, how to hold eye contact, or the nuances of group presentations. It would make trivial the experience of both the reader and the writer.

So use this book as both a friend and a guide, something between a book of essays and *Bartlett's Quotations*. You can read it from front to back, or bounce around to follow a particular thread or theme, depending on your mood, or simply dip into it at random.

SEEING MORE IN WHAT WE DO

The familiar and not-so-commonplace themes developed in this book come from the idea that our work finds deeper meaning when we understand that consulting touches questions and problems that are universal and much more central than the specifics of the moment. To take the particular problem facing us, step back, see it more broadly as being part of the human condition. This is also the role of therapy, art and literature, and philosophy. These fields—call them the humanities, liberal arts, or the healing arts—do not find an easy resting place in the conduct of institutional life.

For one thing, the world of work is too often contemptuous of the liberal arts. If we studied the liberal arts, we were quite young, and they were taught for their own sake with no eye toward organizational use. In fact, in the teaching of liberal arts, commerce and organizational life were very often framed as the enemy.

For example, most therapists view the workplace as the cause of human suffering, rather than the answer to it. Literature that presents the workplace as anything but imprisoning or corrupt is very rare. Conversely, it is unlikely that all the books about how to succeed by really trying would ever be accused of being literature. And most traditional philosophers don't acknowledge that the workplace even exists. It is hard to imagine a philosopher like Heidegger writing about how to build support from your boss or how to motivate your subordinates. In fact, when I do a spell check on my computer for the name "Heidegger," it does not recognize the word and suggests replacing it with "headgear." On second thought, the computer may be onto something.

The point is that the realm of consulting suffers from inhaling too exclusively its own breath, caught up in its own practicality. One intention of this book is to bridge this gap in some small way: To breathe some new life back into our practice by taking what we seek in life and bringing it to work.

Every consulting project is a human encounter, even if the content is highly technical. Even in a world of automated interactions and electronic connections, there is always a human being on both ends of every transaction. The human condition sits square in the middle of every computer, every Palm Pilot® and television set.

The essence of consulting is still about relationship. No matter how technical or commercial the consulting work might become, get-

clients understand their purpose, how this moment fits with some larger and more profound intention, and how the moment is grounded in the experience of being human.

The philosophy of consulting brings a stronger foundation to our understanding of our work. If we wish to be clear about purpose, then we cannot be limited by thinking only of our particular, personal purpose or of the goals of an individual project or institution. It calls for us to see the universal drama that is unfolding and speaking to us and our clients through the particulars of our own situation.

This larger view is what is required for authentic, genuine healing. Seeing the larger story, or drama, or archetypal enactment that is taking place through the current event gives us the capacity to then take what we learn at the moment and bring it into every aspect of our lives. Transformation happens when the specific becomes universal. When the crisis gets re-framed into a dimension characteristic of all others who are facing the same reality—the larger human drama.

For example, we benefit when we can see the present situation as an example of the paradoxical nature of human existence. That we and those around us are expressions of our own free will. That we always have a choice to make, regardless of the chains that seem to bind us, and that the choice is always complicated. Both paths in front of us are true; whatever we choose will carry with it some anxiety and guilt, and that is just the way it is. As consultants, our constant task is to confront our clients with the choice facing them and to help them see the choice, make the choice, even if the choice is to do nothing, and to live with its consequences. The insight that this dynamic is inevitable (and life-giving) comes from the philosopher.

Just because we begin to think philosophically does not mean that we veer away from the concrete and the practical. It means that the concrete and practical become luminescent and more profound. It is the experience of deepening and taking our work more seriously and assigning it greater consequence than simply solving today's problem. Work is not just one darn thing after another; it is one darn thing threading its way through all others.

The Images That Save Us

It is difficult, limited as we are by our own experience, trapped by our own thinking, living in our own dreams and memories, to grasp what life can bring to us, to know what is possible, or even to know what meaning to give to our own behavior or the events in our lives. We always need to look outside ourselves for clues of what to make of it. This is where other people's stories, often expressed through art and religion, can serve us—even save us. We hear a short quotation and, despite all the noise of life we are exposed to, it stays with us. An example for me is a statement of Carl Jung's: "What was true in the morning is a lie in the afternoon." I take this to mean that all that I pursued in the first half of my life—ambition, marriage, kids, becoming somebody, acquiring things—will not have the same meaning for me in my later years. The second half of life is about something different. Jung's wisdom allows me to accept a radical shift in my later years—without feeling regret for my younger days, or thinking that my early pursuits were a mistake, or having qualms about leaving behind what was once so important. The idea that the "afternoon is a lie" embodies the inevitability and forgiveness for changes I am drawn toward without really knowing why.

This is how we are served by art and literature, whether the form is short stories or essays, great classical literature, visual arts, movies, fairy tales, or simply a quiet poem by a good friend. Insight about the larger story is also one of the gifts of religion. In addition to testimony about the existence of God, religions impact our lives by the stories, parables, and images that have endured over time. Jesus' forty days in the desert lets us know that there will be times in our lives when we are lost, filled with doubt, faced with attractive but false temptations, thirsty beyond belief. Knowing this is part of every person's story gives us strength to endure these times.

To serve those we consult to, we need our own saving images as part of the way we can have influence. The point is not that these are the particular "saving images" that consultants should be using, but that the wisdom embodied in the arts has been missing from the practical, engineering mind-set that drives most of our consulting.

MOVING ON

These three disciplines—therapy, philosophy, and art—are woven throughout this *Fieldbook and Companion*. The stories and essays themselves focus on what we believe are the thorniest parts of consulting:

- How to handle the risk and anxiety inherent in our work;
- Valuing the emotional side of life;
- Falling in love with questions and ending our love affair with advice;
- How to value the capacities of our clients and stop thinking that focusing on deficiencies is useful for learning;
- Augmenting strategy with experience; and
- The warning signs of trouble and how to think about them.

I hope the book is useful to you. May you find the new friends you meet interesting, if sometimes confusing and challenging, and always present with sincere intent, because their writing is as much an effort to understand their own practice as it is to share what they have learned. I also hope you enjoy this book, let it accompany you into your field, and use it as encouragement for writing your own story, which may be the point of it all.

Quick Guide to Contents
An Index of Concepts, Stories, and Practical Tools

This book is a mixture of concepts and theory, stories, and practical tools and tactics. Each of us needs all of these to develop and express our expertise:

- The concepts and theories help expand or confirm our thinking and, when we are lucky, change our minds;
- The stories give us hope; and
- The practical tools and tactics give us something to do.

Before you begin, here is quick guide to the journey you are about to take. It is like an annotated index designed to help you navigate and understand what is in the book.

CONCEPTS AND THEORY

Because there is nothing so practical as a good theory, concepts help us reframe the work we do and give us guidelines for action. Here are some different ways of thinking, with short excursions into philosophy, history, myth, and literature.

If You Are Looking for Insight on	Try Looking Here
Paradoxes and polarities in our work	Chapter 2: A Sensible Oxymoron, by Andrea Markowitz
The value of fear and risk	Chapter 3: Risk Is Where You Find It, by Peter Block
How the wish for answers interferes with real change	Chapter 7: What Should I Do? by Peter Block
How the new economy changes the nature of our offer	Chapter 9: Changing Focus, by Patrick Dolan
The risk of relying on outside experts	Chapter 10: Be Careful Who You Ask, by Andrea Markowitz
Anxiety, courage, and character	Chapter 17: Talk Is Walk, by Peter Koestenbaum
The nobility of the fool and what therapy can teach us about change	Chapter 20: Nobody's Fool, by Andrea Markowitz

CASES AND STORIES

Case studies, personal experiences, and stories of tribulation give us hope and remind us that we are not alone in our confusion. They also remind us that the person is the product in a service business. Working on ourselves is always the task at hand.

If You Seek Stories and Cases about	Take a Look at
The eternal family triangle of you, your client, and your boss	Chapter 5: Consultant, Flawed, by Ken Murphy
Recovery from colluding with a client	Chapter 12: The Case of Pricilla and the Red Pen, by Andrea Markowitz
The universality of large-group methods	Chapter 15: Resolving a New Paradox with Old Wisdom, by Marvin Weisbord

TOOLS AND TECHNIQUES

Because there is nothing so theoretical as a good practice, take a look at these pieces that feed our desire to add to our inventory of tools and techniques.

If You Want to	Here Is Where to Find It
Create new conversations	Chapter 6: The Power of Conversations at Work, by Joel Henning
Deal with resistance	Chapter 11: Dealing with Resistance, by Phil Grosnick
Use questions for organizational self-discovery	Chapter 13: Making the System Fully Known to Itself, by Jill Janov
Use questions that confront the person	Chapter 16: Change Is in the Details, by Peter Block
Use engagement as a change strategy and do it with large groups	Chapter 30: The Engagement Paradigm, by Dick and Emily Axelrod
Create participation by rearranging the furniture	Chapter 31: Caring About Place, by Peter Block
Build the faith and capacity of large groups	Chapter 32: Unleashing the Spirit, by Kathie Dannemiller, Sylvia James, and Paul Tolchinsky
Use an employee-focused survey to initiate and access change	Chapter 35: Toward a More Participative, Productive Workplace, by Marie McCormick
Use questions that create accountability for learning	Chapter 37: How Am I Doing? How Am I Doing? You Like Me! You Really Like Me! by Peter Block
Reframe client concerns that have the potential to drive you crazy	Chapter 40: Twelve Questions to the Most Frequently Asked Answers, by Peter Block

THE ICONS

Books carry their message through their look and feel as much as through their content. Marie Carija has done the interior design of this book and done it with grace and a determined sensitivity, which is who she is. She has designed a strong and mythic series of images that reinforce the book's themes.

Here are Marie's thoughts about the symbolism of the images.

Part 1: Welcome—The Portal

This is a doorway with the sun beyond. When you walk through the door, are you stepping inside or outside? This image refers to "the light within," within this book, within these writers, within each person. And it also refers to an opening outward to new ideas and experience.

Part 2: No Fast and Easy Way—The Labyrinth

A labyrinth deliberately slows down the journey. Progressing along its path requires attention and allows for reflection. It might be seen as unnecessary complication. But those who have given themselves to the experience over the centuries describe disproportionate rewards: new insight, catharsis, awareness. This image is about doing what you do consciously, always returning to where you began, but at a deeper level.

Part 3: The Complexity of Advice—The Nautilus

The many-chambered shell is structured in the most amazing way. Its complexity is elegant, ideal. This image is an abstraction of complexity at its best. The spiral also comes into play, referring to the dance-like shifting of perspectives that takes place in an ongoing client-consultant relationship. It is also a living creature unchanged since the beginning.

Part 4: The Power of the Question—The Python

The celebrated Oracle at Delphi in ancient Greece was preceded by a dragon called Python who guarded an even more ancient oracle. These oracles exerted a powerful influence over public affairs and personal destinies. The image of the python evokes the mysterious power of the questions addressed to the oracle (and their resulting answers). It is also reminiscent of a question mark. The snake also sheds its skin, which is a classic image of rebirth.

Part 5: Emotions and the Personal—The Lyre

The lyre refers to a story that resonates in the heart: It is the Greek myth of the musician Orpheus who followed his beloved into the underworld where he succeeded in gaining her release by charming Hades with his divine music. Orpheus promised not to look at Eurydice on their way back to earth, but his longing made him look, and she disappeared. Grief-stricken, he scorned the women of Thrace, his home, and they tore him apart. The pieces were gathered by the Muses and buried near Mount Olympus, where a nightingale sings over his grave.

Part 6: Integrating Strategy and Experience—The Eagle

An "eagle eye" is a keen one. It sees very clearly, and from a height where the big picture spreads out below like a chessboard. Strategy requires this kind of perspective and vision. The eagle also connotes power and authority, qualities achieved as a result of experience.

Part 7: Valuing Capacities—The Box

The box within a box within a box is nested, safely packed. The square is the symbol of wholeness, completion. It is a space, a container with volume that can hold everything. It has capacity. The image also reminds me of the Abstract Impressionist painter Josef Albers' reverberating homages to squares of different colors, thereby adding the dimension of the value and conceptual capacities of art. The center box also represents the Inner Kingdom where the soul resides.

Part 8: No Masks No Bargains—The Moon

This moon speaks to the mystery of the night sky, and the power of poetry and the feminine. It is irreducible.

1 No Fast and Easy Way

- Flawless | M. J. Wheatley

- A Sensible Oxymoron | Andrea Markowitz

- Risk Is Where You Find It | Peter Block

- The Journey | Idries Shah

- Consultant, Flawed | Ken Murphy

- The Power of Conversations at Work | Joel Henning

We live in a one-minute culture in which speed is God and time is the devil. Our food is fast, freeze dried and microwaved. Our learning is anytime and online, we read executive summaries instead of books and reports, and we want the answer *now.* And we also want the answer in simple, easy-to-use steps. No pain, big gain. The instinct for speed and simplicity, while useful for mail and information, is an obstacle to wisdom and the reflection required for real change.

In fact, for much of our consulting work, speed becomes a defense against change. To be in a great hurry is to defend against the confusion, doubt, and complexity necessary to create a future that is different from our past. Change is always destabilizing, and therefore it always creates anxiety. Our capacity to serve our clients, then, is always dependent on our ability to deal with anxiety in all its many forms. The emotional cost of doing consulting is to entertain a long-term relationship with anxiety and its unpredictable effects.

Anxiety comes in two forms: Anxiety in ourselves and anxiety in others. My anxiety leads me to think my own toolbox and my own capacities are perpetually incomplete. I travel with five times the amount of notes, overhead transparencies, and small electronics necessary. When I plan a meeting I squeeze four hours of content into two hours of time. I think I have to structure the world, anticipate the resistance, and on it goes. All of these responses to my anxiety interfere with learning and change.

I also have to think carefully about how I respond to anxiety in others. Their anxiety may come in the form of withholding or anger or the most common form. . .confusion. The questions "Where are we? What are we doing? Where are we headed? What do you mean?" are ways clients have of asking us to take responsibility for their experience. If I could develop the faith that their anxiety is a sign that we are touching something close to home, and that touching is essential for real change, then I need to act to deepen their anxiety—treat it as a doorway instead of a disturbance. Give it support and reflect on it. As philosophers, we see the anxiety as a response to the burden of choice, of a life that is ours to choose, a recognition that we are not immortal and time is running out. Our response is to acknowledge and find meaning in its legitimacy.

The Flawless Consulting Fieldbook and Companion

As therapists, we can see the anxiety as a symptom of feelings that are waiting to be spoken. The feelings born of our own history, unfinished history brought into the present. The moment giving rise to the anxiety may be associated with other people or events, or the tension may arise from relationships with those in the room. Much of our most critical consulting work is helping clients in their relationships with each other. Helping them tell the truth to each other, support each other, forgive each other, choose to create a future with each other. Team building in its general meaning is the work of the therapist-consultant.

The artist in us is needed to fully see the client's story, the drama of institutional life. The artist needs anxiety for the story to have meaning. Without a crisis there can be no synthesis, no conflict, no resolution. The artist gives vivid form to the human drama. It is not that the consultant is going to write a story about the client, but that the consultant sees larger, archetypal stories being lived out in the client.

If you want to understand archetypes, you get familiar with Carl Jung. You recognize that literature and movies gain their strength from touching archetypal, universal themes. We need to identify with the archetypal images. We have to realize that Icarus let his ambition fly him too close to the sun and melted him. That Orpheus lost faith in his destiny and looked back to see that Eurydice was still there and thereby lost her. That Ulysses had to return home to where he began and then, on the eve of venturing out into the world, listened to a dream that instructed him to eventually go inward as the final journey of his life. We have to accept that the hero's journey demands refusal and failure before it can be completed. Each of us is Icarus, Orpheus, and Ulysses. We place modesty aside and accept that our journey, and our client's journey, is that of a hero.

Chapter 1
Flawless

M.J. Wheatley

For far too many years
I have wanted to be flawless,
  Perfecting my pursuits,
  I bargained all for love.
For all those many years
I made masks of my own doing,
  Pursuing my perfection,
  I found I was pursued.
And then
one day
I fell
  sprawled
  flattened
  on the fertile
  ground of self.
Naked in dirt
no mask
no bargains

I raised my soiled face
and there
      you were.
I struggled to stand.
Dirt from my body fell
in your eyes.
Your hand reached for me.
Blinded,
your hand reached
me.
There is, in all of us, the place of pure perfection.
We discover its geography together.

About the Contributor

Public speaker, educator, and organizational consultant Meg Wheatley is president of The Berkana Institute and the author of the award-winning *Leadership and the New Science* (Berrett-Koehler, 1992; 1999) and *A Simpler Way*, co-authored with Myron Kellner-Rogers (Berrett-Koehler, 1996).

Chapter 2
A Sensible Oxymoron

Andrea Markowitz

Consultants are always dealing with those aspects of a client's knowledge or experience that they cannot handle by themselves. So by definition we are immersed in situations of complexity and doubt. In this essay, Andrea creates a context for all that follows. The context is one of paradox, contradictory truths, and the impossibility of there being only one answer that is true. Who better a source than Shakespeare, what more bittersweet role model than Romeo? In the modern film *Shakespeare in Love,* whenever the theater owner staging Shakespeare's plays is confronted with how he plans to solve a difficult problem, he replies, "It's a mystery!" Some action plan.

> O loving hate!
> O anything, of nothing first create!
> Misshapen chaos of well-meaning forms!
> Feather o lead, bright smoke, cold fire, sick health,
> Still-waking sleep, that is not what it is!
> This love feel I, that feel no love in this.
>
> William Shakespeare, *Romeo and Juliet*

When Romeo uttered these paradoxical phrases in response to his unrequited love for Rosalind (before he met Juliet), he could very well have been offering a job description for consultants. Our jobs are inherently paradoxical. We wish for clarity and find contradictions. We want answers and find dilemmas. We expose helplessness to encourage hopefulness. We paint the power of suffering to promote fulfillment. We tear down in preparation to build. And we want to be friends to our clients but brand them as the enemy when they resist change—and us.

We serve our clients well when we acknowledge the constant tug of war between opposing forces that are remarkably similar to those Romeo catalogued. Still struggling to break the tradition of patriarchal systems that were modeled after the church and the military, and rounded out with the industrial age's requirement for predictability and reason, we are mindful that we cannot continue our attempts to create "order" during an age in which "chaos" reigns. We try to encourage "healthy" attitudes toward work and life despite the malaise and "sickness" promoted by workplaces in which authentic conversations are rare and telling the truth is a radical act. We try to "awaken" employees to concepts like taking responsibility for their own thoughts and actions while their employers, who do not value consciousness and consider time for reflection as lost production, foster "sleep." But organizational structures that interfere with truth, health, and consciousness, fortunately, are unsustainable and break down over time. We bring our humanity to work.

Romeo's jolting use of contradiction reveals the depth with which Shakespeare understood both the conflicts in human nature and the nature of human conflicts. In his compelling and convincing *Shakespeare: The Invention of the Human,* Harold Bloom explores how the bard essentially created our modern understanding of the complexities and inconsistencies of personality. The essence of Shakespeare's poetic inward glance at our humanity is our ambivalence, the ironic and paradoxical nature of human events. He raised the oxymoron from being a mere literary device or an inadvertent linguistic mistake to a way of capturing the paradoxical quality inherent in each person and in the human condition.

  The Flawless Consulting Fieldbook and Companion

At its simplest, the oxymoron is a phrase that contradicts itself (a popular example is "peace-keeping force"). But in a larger sense it is an expression of what it means to live in modern times. Modernism represents the end of tradition, or a predictable world, one in which you knew from the circumstances of your birth the rough outline of your future. As recently as thirty years ago the workplace was knowable. As a new employee, you knew the steps of advancement and the progressions in salary. You knew that management was in charge and believed that large companies would stay large. But that world has disappeared, and now much of what we deal with is turning in on itself. There are no safe places anymore, if there really ever were. Yet we still wish for predictability and consistency. We want managers to be leaders. We want them to walk their talk and to send clear, consistent messages about their expectations. We believe that leaders should establish a strong mission and values and that change can be cascaded down through the organization. But these wishes are in vain in a world in which the oxymoron has metamorphosed from a figure of speech to a convincing description of our paradoxical reality.

We deal with the complexity of opposites every time we consult. Paradox is built into our roles from the moment clients come to us to seek advice rather than mine the wisdom they need from their own people. This paradox is compounded by the fact that in many cases we inadvertently disable the people whom we were hired to help. The more we try to solve their problems, the more our clients become dependent on us, when our real goal is to encourage self-sufficiency.

Romeo's cry, "O anything, of nothing first create!" conjures up another intriguing and apt paradox in our lives as consultants. Our work requires us to face a kind of emptiness, or nothing, before something new is created. If consulting is about change, then we must face the truth of our current reality, its limitations, its futility, before anything new will occur. If we are truly capable of seeing our situation in a stark and unvarnished way, it creates a void, a nothing, a space for something new to enter.

"Serious vanity" eloquently captures our hubris in believing that we deserve the credit for outcomes that were actually accomplished by the client. Equally ironic is the "lightness" we feel after we have encouraged new conversations and possibilities for organizational members who worked through problems that were inordinately "heavy."

Our "love-hate" relationship with consulting arises from the frustrating limitations of our ability to influence others. Romeo's love did not move Rosalind. Our love and care and hope may not move some clients. There are saving moments when our clients have genuine conversations with one another, when they come to see themselves as powerful, and when they become, in the words of large-scale change consultant Kathie Dannemiller, of "one brain, one heart." But these moments do not alter the reality that paradox and ambivalence are at the heart of the consulting process.

Romeo's tumultuous outcry is a tribute to the complexity of people's relationships with other human beings, a complexity that consultants must address in order to be effective in their work. Paradoxes and conversations are our tools. Through authentic conversations about the extremes of existence, people learn how to make something out of nothing, to extract order from chaos, to inspire hope, and build enduring futures. These conversations invite others to express how they see their worlds today, and what they believe these worlds can be in the future. As Joel Henning, a contributor to this book, says, we must "avoid making conversations a means of manipulation and make them instead events that involve others in deciding how to use their freedom." Paradoxically, when we try to push others toward something, we end up pushing them away from it. Manipulation and force backfire and create resistance. That is why neither coercive nor cajoling language inspires sustainable change. The most effective way to catalyze change is to open it up to discussion and get everyone possible involved in the process. We must engage our clients through conversations that confront them with the choices they have made in the past and the choices they still need to make, and hand them the baton that allows them to be responsible for their own decisions. In this way we help them follow the path of the hero's journey from dependency to choice, growth, and self-reliance.

One of Shakespeare's greatest gifts to us is the insight that our freedom comes from understanding the conflicting nature of our inner

The Flawless Consulting Fieldbook and Companion

world and our relationships. "Loving hate" summarizes the human condition. When we blame our clients because they send mixed messages or do not walk their talk, and when we wish that the world were simpler and more rational, we expose our naivete as well as our unease in dealing with paradox. Mixed messages and the unwalked talk are to be expected. They are part of the nature of being alive. This insight is our gift to our clients, and to express it is to express our affection for them, though our poem may pale slightly in contrast to Romeo's.

For More Depth

Bloom, Harold. *Shakespeare: The Invention of the Human.* Universal City, CA: Riverhead Books, 1998.

About the Contributor

Andrea Markowitz is an independent consultant and assistant professor of industrial/organizational psychology at the University of Baltimore.

Chapter 3
Risk Is Where You Find It

Peter Block

Every conversation about change reaches a moment when eyes close a little, jaws tighten and the client and consultant find themselves looking out the window in silence. It is a silence of discomfort. The feeling is similar to either standing on a cliff or on the end of a diving board. These are moments when the risks inherent in any new possibility are starting to sink in. We are never fully prepared for these moments.

We think we are prepared, but we are not. What we had prepared for was to be right, accurate, insightful, and on target. We had hoped it would be enough to be right, and this is the ground we hoped to stand on. If all we got from the client was disagreement, we would be fine. We are ready for disagreement. We have rehearsed arguments in our head, thought of ways to better overcome objections. This is the rational world, and we know how to win.

Interestingly, and with some disappointment, the wave of disagreement never comes. There are questions, confusion, and other viewpoints, but most of the time, not real disagreements.

As a result, rehearsing the rightness of our position is preparing for a storm that never arrives. The rough weather does come, but it comes not in the form of disagreement. It arrives instead with the declaration that what we propose entails a risk people may not be willing to take. The question of risk is the overriding preoccupation in discussions about change.

NO PAIN, NO PAIN

The fear of risk is initially cloaked in the discussion of reality. "Let's face reality" is the safe ground for the discussion of risk. I am always accused of being unrealistic, too idealistic. This is the irony. Consultants are paid to offer hope. To give voice to the idealism that institutional life tends to destroy. We are engaged to offer hope and then fought for that very reason: We are too idealistic. We are really being indicted for not understanding the risk and danger of what we propose.

The wish on the part of the client, then, is to find a safe, low-risk way to change. The wish on the part of the consultant is to provide it. Unfortunately, neither wish can come true.

We need a way to think about what is meant when people seem paralyzed by risk. What is at stake for them and for us? To think the discussion of risk is a question of reason and logic is a mistake. Risk is about the nature of our experience, a feeling, a statement of who that person is at that moment. It also challenges who *we* are at that moment. The experience of risk, although a feeling, is a fact. It is real. The last response the consultant should choose is to accept the risk at face value and to think it can be reduced or eliminated. Looking for ways to minimize risk is a form of collusion. It is yielding to our own doubt and backing away from our own vulnerability.

Risk cannot be reasoned or reassured away. A strategy that is designed to avoid risk becomes a strategy to avoid change.

An example: The most common recommendation every consultant makes is that certain individuals or groups should begin to talk more honestly and more often to each other. Call it teamwork, relationship building, information sharing, cross-functional dialogue—you name it. Sounds reasonable. The response to this suggestion is most often about the risk involved. Honest conversation is dangerous. Counter cultural. You have heard people say, "When all else fails, tell the truth." So what are we afraid of? How can we as consultants understand the reluctance to tell the truth? We can view it as a problem in skill, do some practice, do some coaching, but this is marginally helpful. We know how to tell the truth. It is its danger, not its mechanics, that prevents us from acting.

The Flawless Consulting Fieldbook and Companion

So if we . . .

- agree with the client that you cannot tell the truth, or have really honest conversation in this culture,
- agree with the client that people need skill development in telling the truth,
- think that this is a problem that can be solved by better definition of roles and expectations,
- join in designing ways to better reward better conversations, and
- think stronger leadership will help,

. . . then we collude with the existing culture.

All of these stances are socially acceptable ways of trying to finesse the risk and deny our vulnerability. They are strategies of postponement, as if we will be better prepared to manage anxiety when we are a little older.

We need a way to understand risk and people's wish for safety. Ultimately the value of our service will be defined by all of us having the courage to face now what we have so long postponed. There is no safe way to do this. If we try to manage the risk, postpone the risk, treat the risk as a problem in skills or structure or lack of clarity, we are engaging in a pretense about the nature of human existence and organizational life. All growth, change, and optimism come from acts of adventure and risk.

THE RISKS WE FEAR

To understand risk we need to look to the philosopher. We need to realize that risk is the experience of anxiety and that anxiety is a natural and inevitable aspect of knowing that we are capable of choosing freedom. Typically people blame the organization for being a high-risk, punitive environment. If management were simply more supportive and the compensation system were more forgiving, then the stakes would be lower and we could act with some immunity. The implication is twofold:

- One is that, until the environment changes, there is little room for bold action. We hold others responsible for our caution. For example, people want to drive fear out of the workplace. I always wonder where we want to send it. Fear is a sign of life, a sign of possibility, so it must exist somewhere. If not in this place, at this time, then whom do we want to deliver it to?

- The second implication is that risk is something that can be managed or controlled. We reach for the financial term "risk management" as if it were a human possibility, as if more political acuity, stakeholder analysis, and campaign manager instinct will hold us safe against harm.

Business philosopher Peter Koestenbaum offers us insight about risk when he describes four fundamental fears that exist in being human: The fears are becoming a fool, being abandoned, being assaulted, and going mad. Each of these takes a deeper cut at understanding what we are afraid of. They also place the question of risk within the individual rather than within the institution. When we can see that risk is our own construction, that it is built into us as a condition of our freedom, we change our stance toward it. It becomes the opportunity we have been waiting for instead of a problem to be solved or a reason to stay where we are.

Being a Fool

To be a fool is to appear naïve, overly innocent. To violate social convention. To lack sophistication. Perhaps to get emotional, to speak instinctively without enough forethought. To hope for what can never be. To be unschooled, ill bred. It is the fear that we may have missed the socialization that others take for granted. The thought that others know a game I have not been trained in. The dread every minority experiences: That the majority has a certain power and grace that we cannot quite comprehend. We want to know what they did not teach us in kindergarten. We hear the glib admonitions, "Don't make a fool of yourself." "A fool and his money are soon parted." "Don't purchase 'fool's gold.'" I thought it was real, but now I find that I have been

taken. Buyer beware. I fear that somehow in my life I missed the point that others saw clearly.

When I stand up, I don't get shot, people laugh.

Being Abandoned

Peers and bosses will withdraw from me. I will become invisible. I'm afraid that I will live my life unseen, unnoticed, and unrecognized—never to have "high potential." To speak and not be heard, to give voice and receive no response. I am the one who had the idea that others got credit for. I am the one others do not remember or pass unacknowledged on the street, the one people look past upon meeting. I have not been an insider, found no one's coattails to ride. My recommendations fall on deaf ears. I keep teaching, and they are not ready to learn. At the end of the class I am conducting, there are half as many people in the room as when I started.

When I stand up, people leave the room.

Being Assaulted

I will be attacked and discredited publicly. The fear of being destroyed. My fatal flaw that I have spent so much effort concealing will be exposed. Management will use me as an example of what they are *not* looking for, and they will do it in a large meeting. It is the vulnerability of projecting so much power on those above us; we fear annihilation. One mistake and it is all over. When the question of what to do with the deadwood comes up, I am the one they are thinking about. My budget will be taken away or decreased. I will be forced to give up more people than my share. The panic at the end of a meeting, when the boss says, "Peter, can I speak to you for a minute?" The call while I'm on vacation that tells me I have to come back to the office as soon as I can get there. The possibility I will be met in the elevator by company security people and told there is no need for me to go to my office, but please report to human resources. Or when I empty my office upon leaving, security people stand there to make sure I don't take anything that wasn't mine. And I was a vice president, no less.

When I stand up, I'm shot.

Being Insane

The feeling that no one else sees what we see, that we are out of touch. People act as if everything is working well when we know this is not true, a denial of the integrity of our own experience. When we are upset or angry, others tell us that we should not feel that way. We attend meetings that are dead and filled with unstated problems and others talk about how productive the meeting was. Management gives presentations that are out of touch with reality, and others are grateful for the opportunity to listen to them. We become obsessed with tension and conflict, think about it in the middle of the night, and no one understands it. We find ourselves over-reacting to seemingly unimportant circumstances. How could they change the schedule and not ask us first? What did they mean by that comment about your group being mostly overhead? The room arrangement is all wrong, and no one else seems to care. We withdraw more and more, dread changes, think constantly of being somewhere else, give up even trying.

When I stand up, I will be taken away.

VULNERABILITY IS A SIGN OF LIFE

These fears are real. They are inevitable. They never go away, even though their intensity might fade. They are signs we are alive and the client is alive. This is the anxiety that signifies that we are human. As consultants, our task is to help clients own these experiences and go deeper into them. It is out of this exploration that we can realize that these fears are inherent in every truly human endeavor, and in every human system—which is every system. Our clients' willingness to act will come from the awareness that the fears are of our own construction.

The cost of not honoring these fears is cosmetic change. Change efforts that are treated as a rational, "objective" process override the personal or existential dimension of our work. The denial of our

humanity is expressed in the technological, science-speak distortion of our language. We distort dialogue by calling it "information exchange." We call lack of relationship a problem of "too little face time." We name intimate conversation "talking off-line." We think that newsletters and websites can solve problems in communication. When we treat anxiety as a problem to be solved and human nature as perfectible, we keep our work on the surface of reality and choose a life preserver instead of the diving board. What is needed is to dive deeper, and this is always a choice in the hands of the consultant. We cannot force others to go deeper, but we can make the dive ourselves and hope others will follow.

The thought that we can manage these fears out of existence is betting on a horse that will not run, for each of these fears and their cousins will, at one point or another, come true. When we pursue our own intentions, our own purpose, make our life truly our own, we *will* be the object of ridicule. We will at some point get shot, others will decide to move away from us, and the act of creativity always carries with it the experience of madness. If they were not reflected some way in our reality, how could we identify with them? To base a future on the elimination of anxiety is the prospect of an unlived life, a life of such safety that our life, our work, will be over before it has begun.

We stand for and are advocates for risk and the dangerous path. Risk is the symbolic experience of death . . . Our mortality. Failures are little deaths. We want to go to heaven but we don't want to die. Our job is to help ourselves and others move toward risk, see it as the life-giving, transforming dimension of our work. It is in the risk that hope resides. Hope was at the bottom of Pandora's box. When consultants agree to reduce the risk, or deny the risk, or treat the risk as a problem to be solved, they agree to a world that does not exist—and support conditions that make real change less likely.

Chapter 4

The Journey

Idries Shah

khtiari relates:

I was sitting in the circle of Sheikh Abbas Ansari one day when a youth came in and asked for help. "I am going on a journey," he said, "and I would be grateful if you could give me introductions to the Sufis of Persia."

The Sheikh inquired as to the young man's route. Then he said, "I am sorry, I cannot give you any introductions." The visitor went sorrowfully away.

As soon as he had gone, the Sheikh started dictating letters to his representatives in Persia, on the route named by the young man.

I wanted to ask him the reason for this extraordinary behavior, but the etiquette of these sessions prevented it.

Several evenings later, when we were gathered together after a contemplation session, Sheikh Abbas said to us all: "If I had told that young man to visit certain of our friends, and that he would be welcomed, he would have been unable to learn, because I would have removed from his mind the determination to struggle without which he could not have benefited from the meetings. I would have given him an increased expectation—which would have been a barrier to his understanding."

I said: "But will he not think he is unworthy and perhaps not attempt to make the journey?"

Reprinted by permission from "The Journey," in *The Dermis Probe* (pp. 42–43) by Idries Shah.

"If he does that, it would be a sign that he is in any case lacking in the necessary resolution, and he would not have succeeded in anything."

I asked: "But will he perhaps think of you as not interested in his welfare, since you refused to help?"

The Sheikh answered: "If he can turn against me so easily, then he cannot in any case learn. He would be like a dog which is refused a bone, and which would snap at whoever refused him, without thinking why."

I said: "It is undesirable for someone to feel gratitude towards another for his help?"

"Gratitude towards another has a limit. To rely too much on the help of another leads to despising oneself and ends in opposition towards that other person. That is one reason why some people oppose those whom they have once admired. They owe them too much."

Chapter 5

Consultant, Flawed
A Story of Eternal Internal Triangles

Ken Murphy

This piece by Ken Murphy could have been placed anywhere in the book. It is a fictional account of a crisis in the life of an internal consultant. The nice thing about writing fiction is that you can tell the truth without having to soften it to protect the guilty. I am concerned that once Ken becomes a famous novelist, he will regret having written this piece out of simple generosity. You will find in the writing great insight into the humanity of our workplaces. I wish more of us had the courage and intelligence to describe the world as it really is.

The story is about being caught in the middle, which is everyone's experience of work. No one is on top—ask a top manager how much power managers have and he will laugh at you. And no one is on the bottom—look at what workers can do when they decide to support or undermine the institution. We have an endless fascination with the plight of middle managers because we are all in the same spot. The benefit in being caught in the middle is that there seems to be no way out, and we are left with several unattractive choices. Then, we finally realize that it is the power that we have given to other people that is causing us the grief. In reality they are powerful, and they can cause us pain, but we take their real power and make it larger than life. Once we realize this, we look at them more closely and see that what we saw as their power was really their own anxiety about themselves, and what we felt as their contempt toward us was more a liberating, luminous indifference. Our freedom comes in strange packages.

Simmons stared past me to the window and opened his mouth to say something edgy. The words were nearly past his too-white molars when he stopped and shot me a pained smile of discomfort, impatience, or maybe both. He shook his head, then reached up and, with a sigh, did a vigorous pinch massage at the center of his single, continuous eyebrow. Emerging from the meditation, he slapped open palms on his knees, tilted forward, and hopped out of the chair and around the corner of his massive desk with an annoyed agility rare in a man his size.

He kept three baseball bats propped up in a small wicker basket next to his credenza. One was an aluminum model that he kept for infrequent games in the park. Another was a bogus Louisville Slugger with his name burned into the wood, a chatchka from some long-forgotten boondoggle. But it was the big one that drew the second looks. It was an ancient forty-two-ounce club allegedly once used by Dick *(Don't-Call-Me-Richie)* Allen to smack a game-winning grand slam while he was still a Cardinal. With its massive barrel and toothpick handle, it looked more suited to Bedrock than Busch Stadium. He picked up the Dick Allen and twirled it in his hands as he focused on the issue. The issue seemed to be me.

"So what'd you say to her?" he asked, as he choked up on the bat and crouched into a compact two-strike stance, or as compact as he could get.

"I told her it was a dumb move," I said, and kept my distance. Not that I thought he'd really hit me, not intentionally anyway. Though, in his present mood, it was just possible he might mistake my furrowed brow for the red-threaded seams of a hung slider. It was a big office, but I had learned from previous coaching sessions that, at 6'5" and gripping a piece of lumber to match, he needed his space.

  The Flawless Consulting Fieldbook and Companion

"Subtle, as ever. What did she say?" he asked, not looking at me.

"She said maybe it was me that was dumb." Among other things. But, hey—this is a top line.

He offered a few check swings, taking the measure of the imaginary home plate glued onto the carpet tiles. "And you ably responded. . ."

"That she could do whatever she wanted, if she was so sure she could pull it off without putting the company at risk," I said, with sufficient weight. I left out the little crack about "going to jail for all I care."

He straightened up and looked at me, as if to say, "And . . .?"

"She said I wasn't being helpful. That she thought I was supposed to be in one of the helping professions. So if I wasn't helpful, what was I?" I think it was rhetorical.

He just shook his head and went back into his stance. He cocked the bat back high and slapped his elbow against his side. His eyes stared out the window in the direction of the Chrysler Building and bored in on the phantom pitcher pawing an invisible mound twenty stories above Lexington Avenue. He tensed, and rippled his fingers on the handle as the ghost hurler shook off sign after sign from the non-existent catcher nestled in the knee hole of the rosewood desk.

"Mikey, Mikey, Mikey. Tsk, tsk, and double-tsk," Simmons said as he lifted his right knee and took a short stride forward. He kept his head down as his wrists flashed through and the big bat came around in a controlled, three-quarter speed arc. It sliced through a perfect plane above the chosen tile and sent a little shock wave out into the chilled office air. The end of the barrel flashed by, within a bent paper clip of a Steuben Glass bottlenose dolphin frozen in mid-tail dance on the bookshelf. He held the follow-through for a split second and glanced over to admire his reflected form in the floor-to-ceiling window. Then he dropped the bat to his side and looked at me, a frown wrinkling the small hedgerow above his eyes. "I'm surprised at you. Really, I am. Have we learned nothing of the craft?"

I hated when he called me Mikey, but I let it go. And "craft." Give me a break. My eye roll had grown so autonomic that he missed it, or chose to. Not that it would deter him. Never one to let a teachable moment pass, Freddie was unlikely to leave it there.

"Tell me, Mikey, my boy. On what basis did you determine the dumbness of your noble client's idea?"

"C'mon, Fred. She wants to can all the career reps—most of 'em, anyway—and back fill with minimum wage contractors. What am I supposed to say? Gee, what a super idea and why hasn't anyone thought of it before?"

"All right. So she at least has a plan. By the sound of it, you have shared your view. What does she think now?"

"I'm not sure what she thinks." Rather, I did not care to *share* what I knew her to think. In fact, I was a little surprised that he hadn't yet received a raving phone call from her demanding a fresh face in the HR jump seat.

"Why would she pursue it then? I mean, this is not a stupid woman. Self-destructive, perhaps? Is that it? Destroy her organization to destroy herself, that kind of thing? Sounds like deep water for the likes of you and me. Better give EAP a call, bring in the shrinks."

I don't like to acknowledge his lame swipes. It only encourages him. "She thinks it's the best way to hit her productivity numbers without skimping on store coverage."

"And you don't."

"C'mon, you don't just ditch a whole sales force, most of them with fifteen, twenty years in, all the trade knowledge, all the contacts, and just back fill with retirees, housewives, and a bunch of college kids trying to figure out which are the gut majors. It's ridiculous. It's . . . it's suicidal. And besides, it's wrong."

"Ah, ha. It's just plain wrong, you say? Hmm. So that's the rub. Wrong." *Damn.* If anything should have been clear from a year of working for the big man, it was his ever-flexible sense of right and wrong.

"And why is it, exactly," he went on, finger in the air, "that she is so wrong? What isn't *she* seeing that *you* seem to see so clearly? And she seems so capable in most things. She didn't get the job because she's adorable, you know," he said, then added under his breath, "not based on my last meeting with her."

  The Flawless Consulting Fieldbook and Companion

That was an admission of sorts. Freddie didn't like going up against Susan Bromley any more than I did. Probably less, as he had more of an organizational aura at risk. It would, however, have been rude of me to point that out in the middle of this current wisdom stream. I took the high road and stuck to the issue.

"I just can't see how it's in any way smart, or fair. It's not . . . the kind of company we are." Or were supposed to be. Or used to be. Or claim to be. I refuse to answer on the grounds of confusion.

"*Fair*? There's shrewd business insight for you." He shook his head, pondering the dim bulb standing before him, looking in vain for the toggle switch that might let him make a player of me yet. He didn't seem to look very hard. "So how did you leave it with her? Tell her you wouldn't lift a finger to help her evil scheme if she were the last client on earth? Which, in your case, come to think of it, is actually sort of true." He smiled, as if lighthearted job threats were just fun stuff between buddies. He did have a point though.

"Well, based on our last discussion, I'm not sure she's that anxious for my help. Look, Fred, the fact is that she's a menace. You know it and I know it. I don't know what the hell to do with her."

"That may be true. But then, she's *your* menace, isn't she? Unless, of course," he smiled, "you'd like *me* to carry the ball on this one, go have a talk with her, make her see reason. That is, if the two of *you* just can't seem to find a way to connect."

Uh huh. Right. Unless, of course, something more pressing comes up, like a haircut. I blew out some air and looked at the ceiling, in search of a snappy, confident comeback. Nothing.

"No, don't think I want to do that."

He seemed relieved. "Okay, then how about we make a proper job of it, hmm? Build the logic stream. You're her counsel, the business partner, the organizational wizard. Let's see some wizardry. Dazzle her with your expertise and insight. If you can't tell me why she's so wrong, how the hell are you going to tell her? I'd throw you out, too."

He sat back down and snapped open the *Journal.* I leaned casually in the doorway and watched for signs of latent desire to coach me toward higher levels of impact, but Freddie Simmons started to hum. Humming was the nonverbal signal that this audience was over. He sat back in his chair and spread the paper out in front of him, a newsprint barrier protecting the remainder of his day from any further pesky subordinate inadequacy.

I cleared my throat, but the paper didn't even ripple. I took a step or two into the office, shuffling to be noticed. Still no sign of interest. He wasn't about to make a move, and I suddenly realized that I didn't at that moment have the stuff to do what I really wanted to do, which was rip the damn newspaper from his face and make him talk to me, make him give me more than the empty "go get 'em" crap that I usually left with. I should have done just that. But I didn't.

Instead, I slid off the door jam, walked slowly back to the elevators, and thought about my next inevitable contact with Ms. Susan Bromley. The doors whooshed open and the mail cart guy (I can never remember his name) nearly ran me over as he roared out of the elevator like a triple-crown winner at the Preakness. He stopped short and watched with detached but mild concern as a package leapt off of his cart and bounced across the marble floor. It sounded fragile. I could relate.

"Whoa! Damn," he said, looking down at the crumpled package. "That ain't good, man." He took in my equally unplaceable face and smiled. "But hey, how you doing today, chief?"

"Great," I said, "just friggin' great."

While I had come fairly clean with Freddie Simmons, I will admit to brushing somewhat lightly over the color and hot drama of the actual episode in question. Susan Bromley's insinuation that perhaps *I* was dumb was, in fact, the most charitable thought expressed in the last twenty minutes of my strategic business partnering session with the recently appointed and very formidable senior vice president for sales, consumer products division. The fact that the whole sorry mess played out in full view of her cowering staff—well, I guess I forgot to mention that too.

It was not what one would describe as a classic client interaction. Out of nowhere, in the middle of postings, she dropped her plan on me as though she was Lex Luthor and I was some thick-necked henchman from the old *Superman* series, the one with George Reeves. I think my programmed response was supposed to be along the lines of "Aye, aye, cap'n" as I amble off to mindlessly execute her dirty deed. Her staff, brave men all, just looked at each other, opting to wait (wisely?) until they reached the relative solitude of the john before expressing their august opinions to each other. Not me. After just a month of working with sales, here was a chance to make a difference *and* announce my value-added presence, killing two goals with one issue. On top of that, I was fresh from digesting an inspiring little piece of train reading on "Constructive Confrontation" in part two of the *Journal*. Without hesitation, I let her have the full force of my candid reaction. In retrospect, I should've read the whole thing.

My counsel, such as it was, had apparently missed the mark. That much was clear when she labeled said counsel "tantamount to a personal attack on her leadership." I was still pondering the uncommon use of "tantamount" in the middle of a staff meeting when the offensive shifted to her end of the table. The other sales leaders leaned back in their chairs and watched invective go forth and back like baseline ground strokes at the French Open. I could do little more than defensively keep the ball in play, and that just for a while. What did I say? What did I do wrong?

Her last word out the door was that shot about the helping professions. And it was a shot, no question. That hurt. She made me feel as if I was some kind of nurse, or a diet center counselor. Not that there's anything wrong with being a nurse. It's just that, in my world, nurses rarely achieve salary grades above the single digits. I am *not* a nurse.

It was classic Bromley, though, totally in line with the word on the street. Driven, humorless, all business, all the time. Somebody once asked her what she liked to do on weekends. "E-mail and expense reports," she said. It was this single-minded focus that had fueled her rapid ascent from product manager on a brand that was a perennial dog before she got it to her current lofty perch, in just four skimpy years. Add to this picture some well-honed disdain for staff types, whom she perceived as having "no skin in the game." "Damned coffee drinkers," I heard she called them—I mean *us*. My shaken predecessor claimed that she had playfully nicknamed Human Resources as the "Department of Sales Prevention." From all reports, she was not one to be trifled with. As a bruised trifler, I now knew.

She was good, no issue there. You had to respect what she had done with what had been mediocre, dead, or dying businesses. Admire even, if you could get past the *semper fi* front she affected. Susan Bromley hadn't made the cover of *Fortune* yet, but it seemed only a matter of time. She was organized, and then some. I imagined what her garage looked like. Every rake, broom, and hammer hanging on a peg rack in front of its painted outline. Extension cords all wound neatly around whatever the hell they wind around. She once let slip that she awoke naturally at 4:30 a.m. (her words, exactly—*awoke*, for God's sake! I mean, *who* talks like that?) and probably looked pretty good doing it. College dress size, I'm almost positive. And strong, wiry even. I'll bet the Stairmaster groans in anticipatory fatigue when it sees her coming.

You had to respect her, and I kinda wanted to like her when I first got the spot. Maybe even vice versa. But it wasn't working out that way. I'm sure it wasn't her main objective, but she intimidated the heck out of me. And I wasn't alone. The sales senior staff was still feeling the whiplash from her surprise replacement of Bud D'Addario. Bud was a legend who had effectively retired over ten years ago, but shrewdly chose to stay in his job until just last March. When Bud's physical form finally vacated the premises, in came tropical depression Susan, from *marketing* of all places.

Many revered heroes of the previous regime were quickly found wanting by the fierce winds of her early evaluation. Of the nine fellows who once collegially bent an elbow with ol' Bud, only four remained. Three were canned outright, one was demoted to a trade relations spot running customer golf outings, and the last was "offered" a once-in-lifetime international opportunity to open a new import office in a frigid depot just south of the Ural Mountains. If that's not actually Siberia, it's in driving distance. All in nine months. Not that she was all that wrong about any of it, but, *man*. Like I said, candor around the staff table was a little thin of late.

All of this swirled in my cooling brain as I sat at my desk and watched the sun set over the mighty Hudson and the vast, contiguous acreage of flat-roofed warehouses that stretched to the Jersey Turnpike and beyond. My eyes vacantly scanned the settling crimson smog for inspiration. Then, there it was, on my bookshelf, just creeping into the corner of my eye. My official Churchill "Never Give Up" coffee tankard. I spun it around to see Winnie's meaty mug growling up from the mug, his stogie pointing upward to victory. "Be ye men of valour," said the caption on the handle. Hmmm. So be it, I thought as I swung my feet decisively off the desk and planted them firmly on the floor.

May tyrants quake.

Still, it was with some hesitance that I lifted the receiver and punched in the five digits that would re-connect me with the bad dream that was Susan Bromley.

I was sure she was out of town. Voice mail seemed the perfect medium for my narrowly focused communication goals. Leave a quick message about wanting to set up a follow-up meeting, then high tail it for the train and take the whole evening to plot a revitalized round two. With that plan in mind, it was with choking chagrin that I heard her somewhat human voice pick up at the other end of the line. Rattled, I thought for a second about hanging up.

"Hello, Michael," she said. *Damn.* I had forgotten about the new phone system that shouted the name of the caller in one-inch neon letters. The element of surprise, so critical in the use and abuse of office telecommunications, had fallen victim to this latest enhancement. Since its installation, no one under salary grade twelve could get anybody to answer calls from them. A long moment passed before I could get a grip and answer. I didn't want to talk to her, not here, not now—but there was no way out.

"Susan! Hi! Mike Blair here. I—I didn't expect to catch you in. It's great . . . that you're in, I mean." Smooth.

"I got an early flight from Chicago, so I came back to the office." It could have been my imagination, but she sounded irritated just having to explain her unexpected presence to the likes of me.

"What can I do for you, Michael?" A note of weariness crept into her voice.

"I thought we might get together tomorrow afternoon to revisit the manpower stuff. I've got some ideas that might offer some alternatives." Or will have by then, surely.

"Really," she said, as she seemed to consider the odds of that being true. "That would be nice, but I'm afraid I can't do it. I've got an early flight to Tampa. But . . . let's see . . ." She went silent for a second, and I could hear her fingers tapping out the empty sound of electronic calendar consultation. "I've got some time right now."

"*Now*? Now would be, uh, perfect." *Oh, mama.*

"Fine. I'll be here for a while. Come on over whenever."

"Be there in two shakes," I said, and started to quiver.

The halls seemed colder and emptier as I made my way over to the elevators and up to the sales floor. Most had gone home, and the cleaning crews had begun to materialize from out of their hidden lairs. The mausoleum tone of the building at night suited my mood as I paced off the shrinking distance. It was just as well there was no one else to talk to. The conversation in my head left few openings for intruders.

Calm down, for God's sake. Deep breaths. Deep and slow. Exactly what was my problem, anyway? What was it that was so anxiety-generating in a little chat with Bromley? What was the worst thing that could happen if it went badly (again)? Lots, came the answer. Quickly, I shut the door on my inner voice as it started to suggest deeply tangible worst things, realizing that this was not helpful. The goal for round two was simple. *Engage* her in mutual exploration of options. *Legitimize* the issues of the employee stakeholder. Most important, *avoid* a repeat of rancorous round one.

Her overhead fluorescents were off, and the office seemed a touch spooky, divided as it was into somber pools of light surrounding various table and desk lamps placed with purpose about her ample workspace. Susan was at her desk, head down, running a pencil down a column of impossibly small numbers on a weekly share report. I knocked, an upbeat rat-a-tat-tat.

She looked up without expression, then looked right back down,

The Flawless Consulting Fieldbook and Companion

and waved me in as she continued her microscopic examination. I plopped into one of her armchairs with exaggerated composure, as my mind searched for the right opener. I reached for knowledgeably casual.

"Last week's shares, huh." Yes, if there was any doubt, I can read *upside-down.*

"Yes. Not a pretty sight."

"Right, right. Looked a little soft in the southeast, from what I could see," I said, having overheard that insightful tidbit from one of the Market Research people in the copy room. In truth, I was about as conversant with our share summaries as I was with early editions of the *Talmud* in the original Hebrew. But cut me some slack—I'm a people person.

She sighed, leaned back in her chair, and flipped the report onto a neat pile of paper next to her blotter. She looked at me for a long moment, as if just awakening to the fact I was there.

"So, Michael. What do you want to talk about?" I opened my mouth to answer, but she filled in, "I figured that you'd said it all yesterday."

Okay then, there'd be no warm-up ceremony, no good-natured re-engagement banter. "Well, I didn't want to leave it like that," I said. And what's more, I wanted to suggest, perhaps you, Ms. Bromley, cap'n, ma'am, have re-thought your position? Perhaps you've seen the wisdom of my arguments and found yourself able to look past my clumsily aggressive presentation? Wasn't that just possible?

"No?" she said. "Could've fooled me. How did you want to leave it? Does this mean you've decided to help me do this?" Then again, perhaps not.

"Well, yes and no. I came to see if we could rationally look at some different approaches to getting your costs down." Oops. Citing irrationality was a poor opener. I could see the edge forming in her voice before she spoke.

"I *have* looked at it. And I have a way, thanks very much. What I need is help executing. What I don't need is more second-guessing from the safe seats." Staff shot, low and outside.

"It's not second-guessing when you haven't done anything yet.

It's called partnering. I'm trying to partner with you here." On my knees, can't you see I'm trying to partner?

"I'm pretty beat, Michael. Was there anything new you wanted to cover tonight?"

"Well, yes. I want to strike a deal with you. I want you to hold off on your initial plan and let me work with you on scoping out some alternatives. Come up with some tactics that would be less disruptive to the sales force than your current, uh, plan."

"I see," she said. She seemed to mull over the offer for a moment. "So you didn't *actually* bring any ideas along with you tonight."

"Well, no, not exactly," I said hesitantly. "Maybe an unformed hunch or two. I thought we might collaborate on generating options, you know, two heads better than one, that kind of thing."

"Uh huh, got it." she said tersely, and picked the share report up off the pile and let it drop with a smack on the blotter in front of her. "Good night, Michael."

A chill struck deep within my core, and the chair seemed to grow impossibly large around me. My body felt smaller and smaller, and I could swear that my feet could no longer touch the carpet. I sat there, metaphysically swinging my feet in empty air, wanting to roll into a defensive fetal position, and wondered what to do next. I watched her go back to her columns, acting as though I was just a cloud that had come and gone through the ventilation system. I shrank so fast that I felt like I might disappear into the genuine leather of the captain's chair. At the very bottom of the well into which I had fallen, a small voice offered an option. It said calmly, "Call her on it."

"You, uh, you just dismissed me," I said, with a matter-of-fact tone that belied the churning whirlpool inside. She looked up, said nothing, but gave me a squint that said, "So?"

"I mean, not as in 'this meeting is over,' but you dismissed *me*, like as a human."

She dropped her pencil and sat back. "Sorry?" she said, as a question, not an apology.

"Just now. We were talking, sharing reasonably intelligent adult discourse, and then you shut off and erased me like I was junk e-mail."

The Flawless Consulting Fieldbook and Companion

"Well, I'm sorry you felt that way. I merely meant to—"

"Call it a hunch, but I'll bet you do that with your staff." I felt blood returning to my limbs, and sat forward in my chair. "Do you? Do you do that with your staff?"

"Now look, Michael. It's late. I have a lot of work to do yet tonight. I am not going to sit here and be analyzed by—"

"Who said anything about analyzing you? I just want to talk. That's why I came here tonight. I want to talk about what you need—for your business, for your team—for you, in fact. I am here," I said—and stood, arms spread in humble offering—"to help *you* pursue *your* success. And to do that . . . we need to be able to *talk* with one another. Openly. Honestly. Like . . . partners." I searched her face for signs of mutual desire for dialogue, but all I saw was a narrowing of her pupils and a slight flaring of her nostrils. She slammed down her pen and took no notice as it bounced across the desk.

"Okay, partner. You want to talk? Really talk? Fine! Have it your way." She spun around in her chair and reached across her credenza for the little button that came only with offices at her level. She punched it with an angry flourish, and her large oak door silently swung shut behind me. "Now. Let's *really* talk, *partner*. What else is on your mind?"

Ignoring the challenge in her eyes, I plunged on, trying to sound professional while searching the ceiling for a star to steer by. "Well, okay then. How about we start with your staff? Good," I said, answering my own question. "Let's talk about them for a minute. How are you feeling about the interactions, the, uh, alignment you've been getting?" Alignment was usually a good thing to probe in organizational matters, as it could mean whatever the listener decided it meant.

"All right, how about them? Why don't you tell me? You have eyes, you're in most of my staff meetings. What's your learned assessment of our dynamics?"

"Well, to be honest," I said, and bit my lip, as every time I said that I sounded like my next offer would be a great deal on a whole life policy, "the atmosphere does seem a bit strained. I don't think they're comfortable with being very open in the group."

"Is that right? My, I hadn't noticed." Even in my stressed state,

I knew this immediately as sarcasm. "Tell me more. To what do you attribute this condition? Anything in particular jump out at you?"

"Well, there are many factors that could contribute." I mentally thumbed through my favorite team diagnosis models. "There has, for example, been a lot of change in a short period of time, for one." I didn't care for the tentative way my voice faded and jumped an octave at the end of my observation, but what're you going to do?

"The biggest change being me. I assume that's where you're going."

"Well, sure."

"I'm not Bud D'Addario, am I?"

I choked out a nervous laugh. "No, I think we can safely say that you are *not* Bud D'Addario. Which is not a bad thing," I said quickly, recovering. "I mean, it's mostly a good thing. Bud—Bud was long past ready to go. You represent a big change from him, that's all. I mean, you're decisive, smart, a little aggressive, perhaps, and a—"

"A woman?"

"Well, yeah, that's true, too."

"You don't suppose some of our communication issues have anything to do with the fact that I'm a woman in this spot, do you?"

"Here? In your group? No, I don't think so. They—I don't think they're the kind of guys, uh, people, who let something like that influence them one way or another."

"I'm not talking about them."

"No? Then wha—"

"I'm talking about you."

"Me?"

"You."

It was my turn to flare a nostril. "Now, just what the hell is *that* supposed to mean?!"

"Michael, you're reasonably astute. You might have noticed, the conversation in that staff meeting changes—freezes, in fact—whenever I walk in the room, and it's not just the normal boss stuff. And you, partner, are part of that chill. You seem to have as hard a time talking to me—really talking—as any of them do. And you don't even report to me."

The Flawless Consulting Fieldbook and Companion

"Well, I—"

"And as long as we're being so honest, I'd have to admit that I'm disappointed in that. I thought you would be different, maybe grow into an ally on some tough work that had to be done. But so far, I don't think you are different. Just younger."

"Now, wait just a second," I said too loud, vibrating between anger and anxiety. "I think I know something about this. For God's sake, I'm a certified diversity facilitator! To even suggest that I have some kind of gender issue with you is . . . I think it's absolutely ridiculous!"

"You do, do you?"

"You're damn right I do." Ha-*rumph.*

"Okay. Do me a favor. Look me in the eyes."

"Excuse me?"

"Right now. I want you to look at me in my eyes. You never look me in the eyes. Neither do they. C'mon, look at me."

"Okay, okay," I said, "but this is silly." I looked into her eyes. And looked away.

"C'mon. You can do it. And relax. I'm not coming on to you, for Pete's sake."

I struggled to hold her gaze, but could only last what must have been seconds. I was embarrassed. I think I turned a color. Vividly.

"See what I mean?" She stared in a second longer, and then sat back in her chair. "Okay, you're off the hook. I'm just making a point."

"A *point*? What's your point?" I almost shouted, trying to mask the feeling that I had just been caught at the train station wearing my pajama bottoms.

"How can we be these great partners if you can't look me in the eyes for more than a few seconds?"

"Hey, I don't know what you're getting at, but—"

"Yes, you do," she said, and the light from her eyes flashed with the righteous conviction of unerring certainty. Her judgment hung in the air between us like a sword. My body squirmed under its weight and threat, searching for a way out even as the point pressed more insistently against stretching skin. I waited for the final thrust that would finish this conversation, and me along with it.

Then, suddenly, she seemed to soften. "But it's late. You don't need me busting your chops, and I'm too tired to keep it up. Sorry if I made you uncomfortable," she said, in a semi-sincere tone that I hadn't heard before. She considered me for a moment, as if from a distance, and sighed. Then she leaned in and closed the gap. "Michael, you really want to help me on this thing?"

She was being real here; I could tell. My indignation and embarrassment melted away with the sincere offer peeping out from within her question. My nostril returned to its normal aperture, and I felt a weary relaxation come on. She did need help. And I did want to help her.

"Yes, I really do."

She kept looking at me with a wrinkled forehead. She seemed to weigh each word I said, adding up the visible level of sincerity and determination contained in each. She started to nod, slowly. "I believe you do. But how?"

I thought. Hard. About how, and when, and where. What was the line about nothing sharpening the mind so much as the prospect of being hung in the morning? Miraculously, thoughts came.

"Well, for starters, let me dig into the actual problem more than I have. I've got a rough feel for the budget targets, but I could use a deeper look at your coverage patterns now and what they might look like under straight reductions. We could get with the strategy group to gen up some competitive coverage information—I'm pretty sure they have it just sitting around." I thought further. "Then, we could get a few smart people out of the field—maybe a diagonal slice that reaches way beyond your staff—and get them to look at the facts along with us. You and I would frame it, of course, so you're not asking them to tackle more than you mean to, but my bet is that a group like that will uncover one helluva lot more options—and have a better feel for the pros and cons—than by you just working through it alone."

"I don't know. I'm not sure I want anybody else knowing much more about this. I don't want a panic on my hands."

"Susan, I hate to break it to you, but your well-oiled staff ain't exactly the CIA. My bet is that it's all over the place already, and not in the way you'd want it." I kicked myself for reverting back to tone, but she seemed to be thinking about the point, and not the snarky manner in which it was delivered. I pressed on. "Besides, give your field people some credit. Especially the reps. They know what's going on. They see what's happening to volume and share—long before anybody in this building does. You don't think they know what could happen if it doesn't turn around? They're thinking about it—and talking about it. Believe it."

"You're probably right."

"And, they're the ones who stand to lose the most. They could be damn creative—and productive—in figuring out ways not to."

She tapped a pencil against her chin, her chair facing the dark windows, and squinted in thought. Then she turned back to me, resolved.

"Tell you what. Tucker and I are doing market checks in and around Atlanta and Charleston next week, to try to figure out what's going on down there. Why don't you join us? You could get a better sample of what we're dealing with, and we could use the down time to scope out how your diagonal piece might work."

"That's *slice.* Diagonal *slice,*" I corrected, ever the proper jargonist.

"Whatever. And Tucker's got some good people in his region. Maybe some of them could take part in your plan. What do you say?"

Wow. "I say, that would be great." Sonofagun, I thought, it really would.

"Good," she said, satisfied for the moment. We didn't shake then and there, but I felt the unmistakable stirrings of a contract coming on. It felt good, and tension didn't drain so much as slowly evaporate from my body, like sweat on a breezy June day in the sun. We were going forward, sort of together. Complete with the upbeat promise of a genuine, honest-to-God next step. What had I been worried about anyway? Silly, silly.

I rose to leave, feeling good. She stopped me.

"Hey, Michael. While we're being so open, I've got another question for you." A slight smile played on her lips. "What's the deal with you and Fred Simmons?"

"The *deal*? I'm not sure what you mean."

"I mean . . . how come every time I see you with him, you act like some kind of doofus."

"Excuse me?" I said, again. Check that self-satisfaction—we're going back in.

"You know. You get all quiet; you let him do all the talking, even when it's boloney. I ask you a question, and he answers. If you say anything, you look at him before you say it, and after. How come you don't just say what's on your mind? For a while there, I was beginning to think there wasn't much to you." She leaned forward over the desk and stared in once more. "What's that all about, anyway?"

I instinctively backed away and averted my eyes. "Hey, give me a break. The guy's my boss. What do you want from me?" I said, nervous laughter fading quickly into the carpet. Indeed, must we go back to *me* again here? We were doing so well.

She sat back and folded her arms. "I want to hear from you, that's what. If we're going to be really work together, that is. You're smart. I know you've got some courage—misdirected at times. You wouldn't have taken me on in front of the staff the other day—or even come over here tonight—if you didn't. I'd just like to see it when he's around, that's all."

"Hey, look. You know Fred. He's—he's just . . ."

"Just what?"

"Jeez, I don't know . . . you know, he's—"

"You ever talk to him about it?"

"Hey, I talk to him all the time—more than I care to."

"No, I mean about this, about how you work with him. Like you came here to do with me. You ever do that with him?"

"Susan, all due respect, but you don't know Fred like I do. Trust me, the last thing Freddie Simmons wants is for his little Mikey to give him any crap about. . . ."

"Well, let's just see, shall we?" she said, as she picked up the phone. "You have me curious now."

She hit the speed dial button second up from the bottom as a muted scream froze in my throat, and died there. She held my eyes as she spoke into the receiver with an energetic cheer that clashed with the late hour.

"Fred? Susan Bromley. Hey, I'm glad I caught you, late as it

The Flawless Consulting Fieldbook and Companion

is. . . . Do you have minute, or are you running for a train?. . . Great. Michael and I were just sitting here going over. . . . No, it's nothing like that. . . . You do? . . . Super. . . . We'll be down in just a second."

She hung up the phone and smiled. I returned a chilly facsimile.

"You know," I said, "I thought for a brief moment back there you might even be starting to like me."

She laughed, got up from behind her desk, and grabbed her coat off the hook behind the door. "Of course I like you, Michael. That's why I'm helping you out. No time like the present to face your demons." She opened the door and waved her hand with exaggerated grace. "Shall we go?"

I hesitated at her portal. "And do what, exactly?"

"Tell him what you want. Just like you so smoothly did with me. Piece of cake."

I started to form reasoned objections deep in my throat, but she was halfway to the elevators before I could say anything. I trailed after her and got in just as the doors closed. I started to ask her just why we had to do this now, but she just looked up at the numbers and whistled an old Janis Joplin tune— "Piece of My Heart," I think it was.

Freddie was standing behind his desk, glancing down at a copy of the latest news clippings thrown together by Corporate Affairs. He still held the bat, twirling it between big hands. Susan cleared her throat, and he looked up.

"Susan! Great to see you. Working a full day, are we?" he said, with a laugh.

Susan just nodded, started to say something, and then threw a theatrical glance at her watch. "Oh! Hey—I just realized—I gotta run. If I miss this train, the next one's not for an hour." She turned and gave me a little shoulder punch. "Michael, I think you can take it from here. See you in Atlanta," she said with a smile, and disappeared down the hall.

Simmons watched her go, a hint of surprise on his face. A subtle grin formed at the corners of his mouth. "Well, well, well. Just what did *you* do to deserve that playful little poke? You caved; am I right?"

I started to explain, then suddenly realized that I was here for something else.

"Fred, would you put the bat down for a second? There's something I want to talk to you about."

"Sure, Mikey, why not? I was on my way out, but I always have time for you."

I bristled inside, and then caught it. No more. Swing, batter. Swing.

"First off, Fred, it's Mike. My name . . . is *Mike.*"

"Huh? Wha—? I say something wrong? You getting all sensitive all of—" I held up an open palm and cut him off. I took a deep breath.

"Look, it's just Mike."

For More Depth

Further Reading

Lansing, Alfred. *Endurance: Shackleton's Incredible Voyage* (2nd ed.). New York: Carroll & Graf, 1999.

Lee, Harper. *To Kill a Mockingbird* (40th anniv. ed.). New York: Harper-Collins, 1999.

Leonard, Elmore. *Get Shorty* (Reprint). New York: Dell, 1991.

Lovell, James, & Jeffrey Kluger. *Apollo 13* (Anniversary ed.). Boston, MA: Houghton Mifflin, 2000.

Manchester, William. *The Last Lion*: *Winston Spencer Churchill: Alone, 1932-40* (Paperback reissue, Vol. 2). New York: Dell, 1989.

Manchester, William. *The Last Lion: Winston Spencer Churchill: Visions of Glory, 1874-1932* (Paperback reissue, Vol.1). New York: Dell, 1994.

O'Brian, Patrick. *H.M.S. Surprise.* (Reprint). New York: W. W. Norton, 1994.

Tuchman, Barbara W. *A Distant Mirror: The Calamitous 14th Century* (Reissue). New York: Ballantine, 1987.

Further Training

Staff Consulting Skills, Designed Learning. www.designed learning.com.

About the Contributor

Ken Murphy is senior vice president of human resources for Philip Morris U.S.A.

Chapter 6

The Power of Conversations at Work

Joel Henning

One way to think about change is that the way to change a culture is to change the conversations. If we want to help create a new future for a client, then it will happen in the most concrete way when we are catalysts for a new conversation. One way we are faced with the risk inherent in learning is in the anticipation of a conversation that we have not had before. In many ways, our cynicism or pessimism comes from having the same conversations over and over again.

Joel was one who first understood that cultures change through changing their conversations. In this article, Joel shares his deep understanding of the meaning of conversation. Conversation is not simply about communicating with each other; it is a way that we define reality and define who we are. The work of consulting is to evoke among our clients the capacity to deal with each other in a courageous and more direct way.

A peculiar e-mail was sent to the Senior Management Team of the GoodJeans Company on the 4th of July.

The author was never identified. The timing of the e-mail suggested that it was written in response to preliminary recommendations detailing difficult changes authored by the senior management team. These findings had been released the week before in a series of meetings with employees. The news was bad. The meetings had not gone well.

The team developed the recommendations in response to an unexpected, significant, and prolonged business turndown. They were doing what management teams do in these circumstances—scanning the environment, cutting expenses, reducing head count, rearranging structures, re-engineering processes, and searching for techniques to manage all the various constituencies impacted by the changes they would propose. These techniques included uncovering threats, scheduling meetings, seeking gurus, selecting programs, soliciting sponsorship from leaders, appointing teams, defining goals, designating targets, determining timelines and budgets, designing training sessions, inventing slogans, distributing coffee mugs, pens, plaques, and posters, soliciting "buy-in," issuing mandates, demanding compliance, and conducting evaluations. I was consulting to the organization as they worked their way through this downsizing process.

Our techniques didn't work. When we rolled out our grand plans during our meetings with employees, we were met with indifference, objections, ridicule, and hostility. We were dumbfounded and angry.

None of us imagined that the success of our work would hinge on grasping what was written in the e-mail. Here's what the memo said:

The GoodJeans Company

To: The Senior Management Team
From: Me
Date: July 4th
Subject: Some Thoughts on Change

Before you ever see me, before you conceive of ways to understand me, before you ever name me anything, I find

The Flawless Consulting Fieldbook and Companion

myself in the world with choices to make and a future to create. Before I am a name or number, an employee, a part of the process or system or a manager—before I am anything you may say about me, I am in the world deciding what to make of my life. I decide what to make of you and your plans for me. I decide what meaning you will have in my life. I will decide for myself the future I pursue and your place in it. These things are not in your hands. You cannot demand my commitment or passion, or determine my destiny. I choose or reject these things for my own reasons.

The e-mail provoked considerable curiosity from team members. Comments like "Huh?" and "What's this about?" were typical. Almost everyone concluded that the comments were too odd to clearly understand. The strange e-mail was soon forgotten and dismissed as irrelevant. The author was disclosing; we were not listening. Time, frustration, and failure would change that. Lost in an instrumental mind-set, ignoring the reality of personal freedom, seeking packaging techniques to get "buy in" from the masses, we forged ahead. We believed that change was only an issue of empowering management to rearrange things while making the other people feel good about it. How little we knew.

My thoughts about change now were inspired by what the team and I came to learn from the e-mail message and this consulting experience. The learning transformed our understanding of how change occurs and what is fundamental to proposing and sustaining it. It taught us the importance of individual freedom in grasping how things work. We learned to recognize and appreciate the power of the ordinary person to change the world, and the impact of words and conversations in creating the reality we call work, life, and culture.

HARD LESSONS ABOUT FIRST- AND THIRD-PERSON PERSPECTIVES

At the time the team and I were planning for organizational change, we were oblivious to the individual's power to determine success or failure in their hands no matter how slick management's theories and plans might be. If people want change to fail, all they have to do is say,

"No!"—be it with a fist or a smile, with a loud voice or silent resistance. It is that simple!

We were also oblivious to our exclusionary approach to change. We didn't consider the ramifications of the "third-person perspective." We wanted employees to "buy in," "sign up," "enroll," or "get on board" with our plans. These phrases represented how limited our interest was in them and communicated an implicit wish that they simply comply with what we were designing for their lives. But, as we learned, we could not create sustainable change by adopting a utilitarian viewpoint and demanding compliance with a smiling face.

Organizational change looks very different when you look at it from the third-person perspective, rather than from the first-person. From the third-person perspective—*he, she, it,* and *they*—we see roles, costs, tasks, systems, structures, and processes. From this perspective, grand plans are created to re-engineer the organization in hopes of improved performance. The view is instrumental—people serve as the means, or as agents, for implementing someone else's plan for their future. The team and I were embedded in an instrumental perspective. We ignored the will, intelligence, and intentions of the people for whom we were designing a world. We were foolish.

People decide for themselves the meaning of change. They resist or welcome it based on the meaning they confer on it. In the end, organizational change only succeeds if the individuals impacted choose for its success. If they bring the outlook of a cynic, bystander, or victim, change will falter and succumb. How can success be built on a foundation of hopelessness, detachment, and helplessness?

If change is seen as the chance to gain advantage over others, it is put in jeopardy. The welfare of the whole is lost in a sea of individual ambition. To dismiss, ignore, or ridicule the outlook and power of individuals is foolhardy and ill-advised. Success and failure are in their hands.

So the first lesson we learned was:

- We had lost or denied the first-person perspective—*I, me, we,* and *us*—in thinking about people, organizations, and change.

Our second lesson was a natural extension of the first:

- We needed to learn how to talk about change from the first-person perspective.

We were superb at creating words and language to talk about organizations and change from the third-person perspective. We failed to do the same for the first-person perspective. We understood the language of design and understood little about the language of personal engagement. If we wanted to create sustainable change—change based on each person choosing accountability for making things work—we needed to change the way we engaged people. We would have to change our conversations with them. The challenge was to speak with the voice of the artist and poet, inviting intimacy and involvement. Forsaking our preoccupation with control, consistency, and predictability, we would have to embrace and enter an unpredictable world in which freedom is sacred.

This unpredictable world of engagement makes sound business sense. Hard truths face organizations every day. Primary among them is the absolute necessity of achieving positive results. Whether results are market share, return on investment, cycle time, or some other measure, the demand for results is unequivocal. Every organization must create more value than it consumes. This is not an epiphany. We all know it. The urgent question is always, "How do we create this value?" In search of answers to this question we rack our brains, go to meetings, hire consultants, and create management schools.

There are three factors that consistently appear to forcefully impact the capacity of an organization to succeed in achieving results. The first is the ability of the organization to give original and unique responses to its customers. The second is the capacity of the organization to create new knowledge and apply it successfully to products and processes. The last factor is the ability of the organization to create a workplace in which each person chooses accountability for making the entire enterprise successful.

To create new knowledge, to grant all customers the exception they want, and to encourage everyone to choose accountability for the whole requires each person to make the business his own. This means throwing oneself into work with hands, head, and heart. Such leaps of faith do not occur because they are demanded. They only occur when they are personal acts of choice.

These strengths cannot take root and flourish within a management strategy committed to control, consistency, and compliance as the "primary" way to run things. The heavy hand of demand simply will not create an organization that's distinguished by resourcefulness, inventiveness, or imagination. Consolidating power and issuing orders falter. A few deciding for the many, while holding people accountable, mandating programs, doing performance reviews, and crafting corporate visions—all of this comes up short in creating the passion, artistry, and dexterity to succeed.

If we want to give birth to a workplace that chooses, supports, and sustains individual accountability, we must do at least three things. First, we must engage people in radically different ways. Second, we must forsake our utilitarian thinking about change in favor of inviting engagement as the means of creating change. And, finally, we must deliberately let loose the reins of power and commit to a broad and deep distribution of business literacy and accountability throughout the workplace.

So the third lesson we learned was:

- Sustainable change would require us to give up programmatic intervention and engage the will, freedom, and intelligence of the people with whom we worked.

THE POINT AND PURPOSE OF ENGAGEMENT

Engagement is about inclusion. It requires us to seek and invite commitment and forsake the heavy hand of management demands. It is an affirmation of faith in the capacity of each individual in the organization to contribute toward positive change. It is the first step toward using the first-person perspective in creating a future and sustaining change.

Engagement draws on the power of conversations—the common and conventional talking we do with one another. It is in our conversa-

tions that we create and disclose to those around us the future we are pursuing. Through our conversations we invite, demand, or manipulate others to join us in creating a future. In our conversations we define who we are and what we choose to become, individually and together. Conversations create, disclose, invite, and sustain the culture in which we live!

These conversations can happen in bars, boardrooms, cafeterias, and offices, in training classes and on factory floors. They can occur in formal deliberation about weighty matters and as small talk in casual settings. The participants are you and I, along with customers, vendors, managers, workers, and others who come to work.

Finally, engagement is about choices—about what each of us chooses to believe is real and worth pursuing in work and in life. It is expressing our individual freedom and what we think is possible for others and ourselves.

Individual worth, ordinary conversations, and the first-person perspective are not the issues I used to talk about in my consulting work. I ignored them or thought of them as irrelevant. Instead, I talked about large-system change strategies, organizational designs, empowerment, and restructuring processes. The instrumental mind-set was never far from my thinking and lips. But the peculiar July 4th e-mail triggered a fundamental transformation of how I understand change.

My fondest hope is that you will affirm and validate the relevance of this thinking in your own experience. It is also my wish that you can see how it makes business sense and provides new and powerful possibilities for understanding and action in your own circumstances.

ENGAGING CHANGE AT THE STREET LEVEL: THE FIRST-PERSON VIEW

When whole-system models are a necessary part of looking at large and complicated organizational change, a third-person perspective is useful. We could not function in a complex community without the language, concepts, and models that let us look at the whole. They are powerful and necessary. They help us see things clearly.

However, when we take these abstractions and symbols to be concrete reality, they can distort and obscure. Words, concepts, and models are ways we talk about life. They are not life! Talking about life is not the same as living life. Life is not lived in an abstract, detached, and disembodied place. It is lived on the street, with all its uncertainties, messiness, and contradictions.

The street view is an alternative to third-person views of work, organizations, and change—the view from the top. Viewed from the top, the individual is reduced to a footnote or deleted altogether. You and I become objects—he, she, it, or they—manager, blue-collar worker, executive, employee, professional, or union member. The third-person perspective can do away with "you" and "I" altogether. We are no longer "you" or "I," or even "he" or "she." We are insignificant parts of a process or system that needs fixing. The temptation to embrace an instrumental view of people is almost irresistible if the only way we see and talk about people is from the top. When we are lost in this thinking, our conversations about personal freedom, worth, and meaning become foolish and irrelevant.

ENGAGING OTHERS ON THE STREET

What then does it mean to choose engagement over an instrumental view of people and change? It means, above all, a radical redefinition of how we understand people, language, and our own purposes.

From an instrumental point of view we use language for effect. People are the means or agents of achieving an outcome that someone else designs. Getting others to participate in creating and sustaining a future of someone else's choosing is the goal—this is what "signing up" and "getting on board" mean. The key question is: "How do I make this happen?" Words and conversations are used as techniques to shape and move others toward ends of my choosing. Selling, promising, bartering, and threatening are all examples of instrumental conversations.

The ends and means of the instrumental viewpoint are alignment and compliance. Contact with others only has meaning in light of my agenda and goal. I pay attention to those people who are important to the outcomes I strive for and ignore those I see as irrelevant to what I

value. From this point of view, engaging people only has value if it contributes to the ends I pursue. In this context conversations are not an invitation for engagement. This is why in so many instances the promise of employee participation is a fraud—and participation is used as a technique to achieve alignment and compliance.

To choose engagement over utility in relationships creates a very different picture of reality. Language is used for disclosure. The other is not an "it" to be shaped and manipulated. Others are free to make choices, seek their own futures, pursue meaning, and create their own worlds. Engagement recognizes that others were not born to fit in a world of my choosing—any more than I see myself as existing to fit in a world of their choosing. They are just as capable of seeing me instrumentally as I am of seeing them that way. So the key question is not: "How do I get my way?" The key question is: "How do we each employ our freedom to work together and create a worthwhile future?"

Words and conversations are not techniques to manipulate others to achieve my ends. They are the way we invite one another to disclose heart, mind, and soul and pursue mutual commitment to a future of our joint creation. Conversations are the event during which we confront as a group or organization questions of meaning, choice, accountability, and where we seek to build a community based on choice. Through the eyes of engagement, freedom is not an enemy that is threatening a world built on the pillars of control and consistency. Rather, the exercise of freedom is the only road to create a sustainable future for which we all choose to be accountable.

It is true that the world of engagement is messier, unpredictable, frequently conflicted, and unceasingly frustrating. At times the apparent quiet, serenity, and organization of utilitarian thinking becomes very attractive; unfortunately, for the most part, it is an illusion. The noise of freedom has gone underground.

Looked at in the short term, there is no question that strategies of engagement frequently seem to fail and that instrumental strategies often seem to work. The larger question is: "Can strategies of change and transformation based on seduction, manipulation, and fear create anything of sustainable worth?" Or put another way, "Can any worthwhile work be done if freedom and meaning are denied or seen as irrelevant?"

Changes of the Heart

The pursuit of engagement in conversations is not just a technique. It is also the intention:

- To recognize and publicly acknowledge others as whole human beings, fully capable of exercising their freedom, defining meaning, and choosing for accountability.

- To build community and purpose based on commitment and consent over compliance and demand.

- To resist care taking, prescription, overpromising, and threat as the means to managing relationships.

- To abandon barter as the primary means to create and sustain relationships.

- To choose telling the truth, confessing doubts, extending forgiveness, and seeking reconciliation over retribution as the means for creating and sustaining relationships.

- To persist in the face of indifference, rejection, hostility, or ridicule.

- To live with doubt and ambiguity about outcomes.

- To confront issues of stance in yourself and with others.

HOW WE ENGAGE

If we want to change how we think and what we do about engagement, it is likely we will have to change how we talk. What follows is a preliminary effort at developing answers for questions of how to engage. It is neither comprehensive nor complete, but it is a beginning, as are the following questions:

The Flawless Consulting Fieldbook and Companion

- "If I want to pursue engagement as the means to create and sustain relationships, organizations. and change, how do I do it?"
- "How do I avoid making conversations a means of manipulation and make them instead events that involve others in deciding how to use their freedom?"
- "How would I justify pursuing my work in this way to the powers that be? What are the business reasons for it?"
- "What do I do if others will not go along?"

Stance Fosters Engagement

The power of our conversations is in conveying to others what we think is—and what we believe will be. When we speak we disclose our stance, our version of life. We use conversation to solicit others to join us in seeing it that way. It is powerful stuff! The stance we carry colors what we pay attention to within an event and what we expect from it.

Stances are usually formed from experience. For instance, over time each of us experiences disappointments. When disappointing experiences are transformed into a conclusion that life is disappointing, experience has solidified into a stance. I then expect events and life to be disappointing. Occasional moments of joy, celebration, or intimacy are seen as the exceptions to the rule. I project into the future life as I expect it to be. I prepare myself for a future I have created through my projection.

Once formed, stances are powerful. They influence how we see the possibilities of life and how we invite others to see what is possible. Yet stances can be changed.

There are three primary stances: Life As Disappointment, Life As Indulgence, and Life As Creating Worth. Of these three stances, only Life As Creating Worth fosters engagement.

Life As Disappointment

From this stance I view life as fearful. I am vulnerable and helpless, held hostage in a life that is unjust and discouraging. The preoccupation is with what I expect from the world. I consistently predict that the world will respond to me with indifference, disapproval, or rejection. I know that the answer to my deepest wishes is "No!" I anticipate failure in love, work, and relationships. I try to barter with the world in good faith and am betrayed. I seek safe harbors in leaders, lovers, ideologies, and withdrawal, knowing all the while that, in the end, I will be disappointed. I participate in life as a bystander, cynic, or victim. I boast about how well I endure and suffer in a disheartening and unfair world. Not only do I see my own Life As Disappointment, I see others in the same light, either as victims or oppressors living in an unjust world.

Life As Disappointment ends in spiritual suicide. The cumulative weight of constant disappointment becomes unbearable despair. The spirit withers and dies. I lie down in the graveyard before my time.

Life As Indulgence

This stance is self-interest run amok. I choose to believe all people and events are intended to serve the ends I value. My preoccupation is always "What's in it for me?" I pursue wealth, privilege, and status. From this stance I lay claim to omniscience about how things are and how they should be. I pursue the power to make it so, always putting my welfare and myself at the center.

The world is viewed instrumentally. People and events only interest me to the degree that they threaten or provide opportunities to gain personal advantage. The common good is a secondary consideration. I pursue and develop relationships based on bartering and on the advantage they may provide me.

Engagement cannot be pursued if this is the starting place. From this stance engagement only has value if it is useful in gaining advantage.

Life As Creating Worth

To see life as the opportunity for contributing to a common good without the expectation of something in return is a Life As Creating Worth stance. The preoccupation is with what I offer others. I pursue generosity in service of sustaining, enlarging, and increasing the possibil-

The Flawless Consulting Fieldbook and Companion

ities of life. There is no assurance of success, appreciation, or recognition. Creating worth persists in the face of disappointment and discouragement. This is a stance taken without barter. It is chosen as an act of faith.

From this stance I work to do that for which I have passion. Knowing I am accountable, I pursue the possibility of liveliness, joy, giving, and compassion as the intention and practice of my life. I forsake surrender.

The end of this stance is to "lie exhausted," as George Bernard Shaw put it, "on the scrap heap," having chosen to be a "force of Nature instead of a feverish selfish little clod of ailments and grievances complaining that the world will not devote itself to making me happy."

Stance and Conversations

Stance is a central issue if we want to engage each other freely in deciding what futures we will create in building relationships and community. Conversations are the means by which we convey our stance and recruit others to join us. If we describe our workplace as disappointing, unjust, and insensitive, it will be so. We make it so by naming and characterizing it in this way. If we describe others as helpless to change anything, we contribute to making it so. If we always depict work as impersonal drudgery where the only value is personal advancement and a paycheck, we will make it so. If we depict employees as limited and in continual need of care taking, we will make it so.

This story makes the power and relevance of stance apparent. It occurred at TheNewsCompany Corporation. I was working with one of the large city newspapers—*The Voice*—owned by TheNewsCompany Corporation. Like many newspapers *The Voice* had fallen on difficult times. Circulation and revenue were down, and costs were going up. The corporate owners at TheNewsCompany were not happy.

I had agreed to do team building with the senior managers of *The Voice.* In preparation for the two-day off-site event, I had interviewed the ten members of the management team. For background information I had also gone to the corporate offices of TheNewsCompany to interview the senior managers who had oversight responsibilities for *The Voice*. With few exceptions, there was general agreement about two things: One, *The Voice* was in serious trouble and in a "financial free fall" with no bottom in sight, and two, Jack Flack, the publisher, was managing things badly—very badly. Executives from TheNewsCompany regularly collected disparaging stories from *The Voice*'s senior managers about Jack's incompetence. They eagerly carried these to Jim High, the CEO of TheNewsCompany. They didn't have to pull teeth to get the stories; people from *The Voice* were eager to contribute. By the time I became involved, Jack's job was clearly on the line.

Of course, Jack knew nothing of this. He fully understood the difficult issues he and the newspaper faced with the "folks" at corporate. He assumed, however, that the people he worked with at *The Voice* were supporting the efforts being made to turn things around. He also assumed that they were telling him the truth.

These were the unhappy circumstances facing the "team" when we convened for a two-day team-building session. I was not looking forward to it.

During the first day the group talked about their relationships and the future. It was minimally useful but did not confront or acknowledge the collusion between members of the team and the executives at corporate. I had a sleepless night.

The morning of the second day, I was due to give feedback to the group about what I had learned during my visit to TheNewsCompany headquarters. I anticipated that what I had to say might bring the team building to a premature end.

I pressed forward: "The people at corporate are unhappy, very unhappy, about the performance of *The Voice*. They see this paper floundering, with no credible plan in sight to turn things around. They see your relationships in shambles. They are most disturbed about you, Jack. Your job is on the line. There are no more chances left." I went on to name some of the specific business issues: Union negotiations, loss of circulation, advertising strategy, and employee morale.

Then to the most difficult problem: "What makes all of this particularly upsetting to senior management at TheNewsCompany is that this group has no plan. When Jack goes to Metroplace to report a plan, the very next day people sitting at this table undercut and attack it. It becomes only Jack's plan or no plan at all.

"The executives at corporate told me that none of you will tell Jack what you really think because of his temper. 'There's just no way to talk to him! He won't listen!' Almost everyone I interviewed at corporate told me identical 'Jack stories.' There are about six or seven of them. They are all negative, and they all were collected from people sitting at this table. In short, that is where things stand. Does anyone want to comment?"

Jack was the first to respond: "You mean that for the last year I have been talking to Jim and the others down there about our plans while everyone here was tearing them apart when they talked to corporate. Do any of you have any idea how foolish I feel?" He seemed stunned. It was the voice of someone betrayed, abruptly realizing he had been living in a fictional world for the last year. He looked around the table and fell silent.

Denials, confessions, justifications, and accusations followed from others for the next fifteen minutes. I thought it was a good time for a break. I went to the cafeteria to get away. I was sitting in a booth pondering what to do when Jack slid into the seat across from me.

"Do you mind talking?"

"No, not at all," I responded.

He looked at me. Jack is a proud man, almost aristocratic. He enjoys the station and status of being the publisher of one of America's premier newspapers. Looking like a fool did not rest easy with him. This was a very difficult moment. His voice was calm and even: "I feel so stupid. I have no idea where to go from here."

"I'm sorry all of this happened. I don't have any pithy advice. What are you thinking?"

He paused for what seemed like five minutes. "I could call it quits and tell Jim and the group, 'Okay, I get it. I give up. I'm out of here. Who needs this kind of craziness and deception?'"

I imagined myself taking that course if facing the same circumstances, "Yes, you could do that. I think anybody would understand. I hope you give yourself some time to think about it before you make any announcements. It's impossible to reverse if you change your mind."

Again there was a long pause.

"I could go back up there and take their heads off. I have some stories about every one of them that the people at corporate could add to their horror story collection."

"You could, but my guess is it would reinforce everyone's view that they can't talk to you—you know, the 'temper thing.' I know that it might be satisfying, in some ways justified, but I am pretty sure it will not help anything—for you or for them."

He pushed himself back from the table and started to get up. Just before he stood he looked at me and said, "Or I could go back up there and start all over with them—from the beginning. I don't know what I'll do." Without waiting for a reaction, he thanked me for listening and headed upstairs.

The meeting started again with Jack saying, "We can't continue like this—this intrigue is going to kill us all along with this paper! We've got to find a way to tell the truth to each other. I know my temper is a problem, and I'll do my best to catch myself and stop it. I am asking you to help. Tell me when I'm doing it. You've got to stop excusing yourselves for not telling the truth. We can't live with it anymore. I want to start from the beginning and forget about the past. I hope each of you is willing to start over. I realize each of you has to decide for yourself. I don't want to rehash what happened earlier. That's my offer. I'd like to hear from each one of you."

In that moment Jack taught me about stance—its power in conversations, and its impact on business. He could have returned from lunch seeing Life As Disappointment—unfair, unjust, abusive, full of betrayal. He could have surrendered and resigned. It was tempting and seemed justified to take such a position. In so doing he would have invited everyone in the room, including me, to join him in that stance.

He could have returned full of anger and retribution, escalating the fear and apprehension already in the room. He could have put the

The Flawless Consulting Fieldbook and Companion

wrong done him at center stage, adopting a stance of Life As Indulgence. The data also seemed to justify that stance. Self-righteous anger and retaliation were fitting under the circumstances. Again, if he had done that, Jack would have invited everyone in the room, including me, to see the world and these circumstances from this viewpoint.

He did neither.

He chose starting over—beginning again. It was an act of faith in Life As Creating Worth. The act of faith was to choose the action that contributed to the possibility of healing and reconciliation—the rebuilding of relationships and community. There was no promise of a return. In fact, at that moment, there was little reason to believe there would be any positive response at all. The greater probability was that his attempt would be met by silence, indifference, or quiet ridicule. He did it anyway. And in so doing he invited everyone in the room, including me, to see the possibility of Life As Creating Worth. The subsequent resurrection and recovery of *The Voice* began on that day and in that meeting.

Naming the issues, confessing doubts, confronting, and changing stances are practical activities in conversations based on engagement. They contribute mightily to building relationships, community, and a worthwhile future.

THE CORE SKILLS OF ENGAGEMENT

Conversations aimed at engaging another require both intention and technique. The commitments listed in discussing the "changes of the heart" are all issues of intention. Here are some skills, methods, and techniques that are useful for encouraging and creating conversations of engagement. The list is neither complete nor comprehensive. The point is to get practical.

Telling the Truth.   Telling the truth is the foundation of engagement. Without disclosing the truth as we know it, nothing else is possible and engagement will fail. When we offer spin, distortion, omission, or lie as a substitute for authenticity, we create worlds we cannot believe in or sustain. Even more damaging, we affirm our belief that relationships cannot bear the simple light of truth. To tell the truth with goodwill is an absolute affirmation of faith in relationships.

Self-Disclosure. Asking yourself or others to fully engage in work with hands, heart, and mind is impossible without offering and encouraging discussions about feelings and issues of the heart. Choosing and inviting emotional transparency creates authentic relationships and integrates the person with work.

Framing Choices. Framing choices is the alternative to prescription, care taking, and other techniques that try to "get people to do something." Naming the choices you see for yourself and asking others to do the same makes issues of freedom, accountability, and meaning immediately relevant and compelling.

Extending Goodwill. Goodwill is not a feeling. It is an intention. To choose goodwill toward another is to offer a contribution to the person's success and the success of whatever joint ventures you are pursuing. Goodwill does not require you to like or love the other. Goodwill bases the relationship on commitment to contribute, even in the face of disappointment.

Taking and Supporting the Other Side. Extending understanding to others by publicly embracing their positions is one of the most powerful ways available to deepen a relationship, validate the value of the other, and move the conversation. It is the alternative to arguing, attacking, and treating the other cosmetically with statements such as, "I understand, but. . . ."

Naming the Difficult Issues. Unnamed and unresolved resistance, conflict, and cynicism debilitate organizations, draining them and their members of energy, optimism, and the belief that they can deal with confrontation. Avoiding, denying, and rationalizing the issue rarely fixes anything. Publicly naming these issues with goodwill and inviting engagement are central to getting "unstuck."

Acknowledging Doubt, Anxiety, and Guilt.
Confessing doubt, anxiety, and fault does not come easily to any of us. No one welcomes anxiety, vulnerability, and responsibility for harsh realities. Yet nothing speaks louder for the value and power of accountability. Nothing does more to encourage the same act in others. If we want everyone to embrace accountability for the whole, for change, and for the creation of a common future, acknowledging doubt, anxiety, and guilt is a fundamental skill.

Making Promises and Offering Guarantees.
Few of us are eager to abandon or close all escape routes. Nothing in organizational life is quite so rare as someone who insists on offering accountability and giving guarantees. The skill to do this in forming work relationships with peers, customers, and other constituencies is one of the most powerful tools available for using conversations to change the culture.

WORTH AND WORDS AT WORK

Change is inevitably and inescapably about each of us, one at a time. It is a truth that is easy to miss in a world so saturated with our abstractions—paradigms, strategies, models, programs, and techniques. Change incessantly and persistently reminds us we are vulnerable and at risk. Change also instructs us about impotence. For the most part, we do not control the changes we face in our lives, only the way we take them in and respond. It may be that the idea that people are free and the architects of their own futures spawns too much anxiety in a world in which control, consistency, and predictability are so dominant.

From aging to the death of someone dearly loved, from falling from grace to falling in love, changes keep coming at us like ocean waves. Too much has been written about organizational change. Its inevitability has been pronounced so frequently that just mentioning the subject causes even the most eager listener to lapse into a sort of daze. Markets change, products become obsolete, new competition appears, costs go up, and more is always required. Accepting it is not the difficult issue. Understanding the relevance of it to our lives and grasping the choices it creates for us—that is what is important. Each of us will choose a stance.

The Difficult Conversations

Not all conversations are occasions for significant engagement. However, there are some that are particularly good opportunities to involve others in powerful conversations about work, relationships, accountability, and the future.

Proposing Change.   Shifting markets, increased competition, cost pressures, mergers and acquisitions, the introduction of new technologies, and other changes create ideal openings for conversations based on engagement.

Creating New Beginnings.   When things have gone badly, when projects or new ventures have failed, when relationships are conflicted and stressed, any time things need to be "fixed," significant opportunities for engagement are created.

Confronting Stance.   When organizations or individuals become lost in helplessness, hopelessness, cynicism, detachment, or exaggerated preoccupation with status, privilege, and entitlement, critical moments are presented to invite changes.

Seeking an Exception.   Control and consistency are major preoccupations in most organizations. They cause almost everyone to seek safety, approval, and permission from people in powerful positions. When an individual or group wants to march to the beat of a different drummer, powerful opportunities are created to engage and confront issues of accountability.

Initiating Endings.   Coming to terms with "ending things" is one of the most onerous tasks at work. The possibility of closing a plant or department, the potential resignation or termination of an individual, or the threat of losing a valued customer or vendor creates moments that invite authentic engagement.

Dealing with Performance.   There are few things in organizational life that create as much anxiety and as many complaints as performance reviews. When cast as a parent-child dialogue, these discussions are rarely satisfying to anyone. Group or individual performance discussions create powerful opportunities to change the culture by changing the conversation.

Say the organization makes serious efforts to change. Everyone in the company is aligned and committed. The change is initiated and seems to be working. Yet six months later everything is back to where it was a year ago, or something totally unexpected has been created. The goal of the transformation has failed. A few posters with their change mottoes still hang on the walls, but in everyone's mind, the company is once again the same old company it has always been.

A year later, some new change program, even better than the last one, comes along and everyone gets excited about it. The organization's leaders try it, give it their best shot, but six months after the new program kicks off things are back to business as usual.

What went wrong? People diagnose the situation and scratch their heads, puzzled about the cause of the failure. Some blame it on upper management, others blame it on the rank and file, still others blame the training staff or the consultants—and of course some claim that the new methods were flawed.

These efforts do not realize their potential because we ignore the "street" perspective. We have thought about the change with words and phrases such as "sponsorship," "systems," "alignment," and "enrolling employees." The voice of the first-person perspective is not present.

When looking at the future, each of us will take a stance born of disappointment, the pursuit of advantage, or creating worth. Nothing I do can replace or substitute for the starting place—finding myself in a world with a stance and future to choose. No matter what I name others or am named myself, no name, notion, or concept will rob or relieve me of the freedom and responsibility for taking a stance and pursuing a future. No one changes you or me. Cultures, organizations, strategies, techniques, programs, visions, values, or leadership do not transform us. In the end, we choose to change ourselves.

For More Depth

Further Reading

Heidegger, Martin. *Being and Time: A Translation of Sein und Zeit.* Joan Stambaugh, trans. Suny Series in Contemporary Continental Philosophy and Culture. Albany, NY: State University of New York Press, 1997.

Further Training

The Conversations Workshop. Henning-Showkeir and Associates, Rupert, VT.

About the Contributor

Joel Henning's consulting and training firm, Henning-Showkeir and Associates, is in Rupert, Vermont. His 1997 *The Future of Staff Groups: Daring to Distribute Power and Capacity* (Berrett-Koehler, 1997) is a classic on the staff role in complex change.

2

The Complexity of Advice

There is nobility in the willingness to consult. It is an offer of service, help, even love. Consulting embodies the wish to make a difference in the life of another. This wish is matched by the willingness of the client to seek and accept help. The act of receiving, of being vulnerable in the eyes of another, is an act of love in its own right. It is a sign of strength and faith to request help, a prayer in its most personal form. Just as asking a friend for help is a sign of trust, bringing in a consultant is an expression of confidence and hope.

The fundamental question, then, is: "When is help helpful?" The answer too often is that it is not. There are times when the help becomes interference, defended against, a disappointment on both sides. This is a question this whole book addresses, and the chapters in this section take particular aim at advice-giving as the risky business it is.

What is fundamentally corrupt in the process is the idea that one person knows and the other does not. That one human being can speak wisdom to another, and that this delivered wisdom, right as it may be, will lead to change. These beliefs are popular but misguided. Tim Gallwey, author of the *Inner Game* series of books, has it right. He understands that learning comes from within. It is a function of deep reflection and awareness to see that what we need to learn, in all but the most technical and informational areas, already resides within us. Our task is to increase awareness, pay closer attention to purpose, and see clearly the effects of our actions. He believes that change can be facilitated and coached by another, but help will never come in the form of advice or recommendations. In fact, it is our instinct to control ourselves and others, expressed in the act of giving advice, that actually interferes with change. The phrase that expresses this idea most cleanly is "Learning is rediscovering what you have always known."

Now, there is the argument that people do not know what they do not know. This is true. There is information, and technical knowledge, and history, and a thousand other things that I need to understand. But we are talking here about giving advice, making recommendations that lead to change. This is different from the process of teaching. Teaching is fine and noble, but the question is

The Flawless Consulting Fieldbook and Companion

whether it leads to action. The argument for teaching is most often a rationalization for maintaining control and believing that wisdom resides with the service provider rather than with the student or client. When we are in the position of getting others to change their behavior, we have lost faith that what is needed for action always resides in the learner. What passes for useful advice is most likely the act of imposing a certain way of thinking.

What is needed by the client is help in reflection. Powerful questions instead of powerful answers. Despite what the client is asking for. What leads to real change is not action plans, but some combination of courage and free will on the part of the client. It takes nothing less than a willingness to engage in an inward journey, plus the recognition that there is a price to be paid for an alternative future—for our clients and for ourselves.

Chapter 7
What Should I Do?

Peter Block

Of all the expectations that clients have of consultants, none is more institutionalized than the idea that the consultant will give advice, usually packaged in the form of recommendations. This expectation is worth exploring, for most advice and recommendations go unheeded. The majority of reports from study committees, oversight efforts, and consultant diagnoses show that such recommendations end their useful life the moment they are written. Perhaps the reports and recommendations were useful for the consultant's learning, but they rarely result in real change for the client.

What is even more puzzling is that most advice is generally on target and delivered with sincere goodwill. Consultants are very careful about the advice they give. They take into account the needs and capacities of the client. Consultants work hard in learning the business of the client, so the recommendations are usually relevant and hold the promise of utility. The more extreme recommendations are usually filtered out before being reported. Plus, most clients' first response when they receive advice is to say, "Well, I'm not surprised."

Further indication that the advice is to the point is that employees of the client organizations usually feel that the advice from the consultant was what they, themselves, had been recommending all along anyway. What this shows is that the difficulty clients have in acting on advice is not because of the content of the recommendations.

The limitations of advice are more about the expectations of the client and the behavior of the consultant. It is the advice-giving process itself that leads our recommendations to carry their own seeds of futility.

THE CLIENT

If we were the client and were honest with ourselves, we would acknowledge that the advice we want is more in the nature of affirmation than confrontation or innovation. As a client I want low-risk, low-cost, easy-to-implement recommendations. I want a turnkey operation. I want to be able to put the key in the ignition and have the car start every time. Years ago my friend Neale Clapp said that when we go into therapy to seek advice, what we want is confirmation, not change. I think he was right.

We say we want change, we say we want innovation, but what we want is something new that does not carry a price tag. We do not want to pay the price of questioning our basic beliefs. We do not want to change our basic thinking or our way of behaving.

What most requests for advice seek is a better way to control other people. The most common request for help begins with "How do we get those people to . . .?" And you can finish the question any way you please. Beginning the request with "How do we get those people to . . .?" means two things.

First, I want more control. To "get someone to" is to control. The request for this brand of help usually comes after a long period of using every means of controlling others at our disposal. What is desired is a mystical new control device that can be smoothly inserted into an already high-control environment.

This is most visible in the public arena. Every time there is a disaster, or misconduct, or a problem that defies solution, the outcry is for stronger controls, better oversight, stiffer penalties. Despite the fact that there have been controls, oversight, and penalties in place for years.

If the project is to exert more control over other people, you can bet that if you give the clients what they ask for, they will value the recommendations, but little change will happen. The reason is that most often the disease that is afflicting the institution is that it is already over-controlled. Perhaps not controlled in an oppressive way, but in a more subtle way. Control is most exercised by the people who are defining reality. Who decides what is needed, what is wrong, what is true, what kind of solutions are sought? The answer points to those who are exercising the more subtle form of control. Even the decision of what kind of consultant to bring in defines the nature of the solution—and limits the solution to another version of the practices that have led to the current situation.

In addition to wanting advice to increase control, most clients define the problem outside themselves. The problem is "those people." The wish for advice usually does not seriously include the client's own way of thinking and acting as the subject for inquiry. The words of self-discovery may be present, but the deeper willingness to name ourselves as a significant part of the problem is very rare in an externalizing, non-reflective culture.

A vivid example was the re-engineering movement, a high-cost, high-promise endeavor where even its own advocates acknowledge that 70 percent of the projects never came close to fulfilling their promise. The common element across most re-engineering efforts was that those signing the checks for the change rarely included their own job or role as a subject of the investigation and change effort. This symbolizes the self-defense that is inherent in most efforts to help.

Another example is the incessant quest for "how." We have all read ten books on change, all with at least ten steps to achieve it. And yet we still want to know how. This unquenchable thirst for "how" drives the consultant to answer: "This way. . . ."

Advice and recommendations then become acts of collusion with client defense against really changing the future. This is why fads are so dominant, and why many of us feel drowned in the stream of answers. We have now moved through the eddies of Quality, Empowerment, Participation, and Re-engineering. We then can turn right and be pulled by Market Discipline, Customer Obsession, and Portfolio Options, then make another shift into being up with the information age. SAP (don't worry what it stands for, the name may be more about us than the product) rides on the illusion that having all the data we need at our fingertips will make the ultimate difference. If we are asking the wrong question, then we have to live with an unsatisfying answer. When our client's question is "how?" we are tempted to give an answer that seems practical and operationally sound. And the recommendation stays on the shelf.

THE CONSULTANT

Chris Argyris was my professor in college. For over thirty years he has persistently advocated telling the difficult truth and being always willing to put your own behavior under scrutiny. Each time we are unwilling to question our own premises, feelings, and attributions, we in effect are engaged in an unconscious act of control, even manipulation. His recent book, *Flawed Advice and the Management Trap*, partly focuses on the incongruence of the consultant. He points out that help is denied when consultants are unable to be a living example of the very advice they are giving the client. And, worse yet, when consultants are unaware that they are not taking their own advice. Do as I say, not as I do.

Chris takes laser-like aim at the lack of honesty and integrity that characterizes much of our effort to help. Instead of facing our clients squarely with what we know and see, we engage in techniques and devices to bring others to our points of view. We do this to avoid conflict, the discomfort we feel in violating another's expectations of us. For those of us working as internal consultants for the organizations that employ us, we end up confronting those people who have our future in their hands. No easy task.

Our lack of self-awareness, our caution in the face of disapproval, and our willingness to constrain our advice to the safe level of rational action and business processes all contribute to the futility of advice. Clients do not really want to confront each other, and we often do not want to confront our clients. An example of this is the number of times I was invited to do team building with a group and told the group needs to "work better together." After a little probing, it turns out that the boss or a powerful member is very angry at one other person. Rather than face that person directly with their disappointment, they called for a more generic and palatable team-development process, which made it everyone's problem, when in fact it was two people who could not get along.

The Flawless Consulting Fieldbook and Companion

The key is for consultants to be willing and able to face the fundamental and most troubling questions facing our clients. These are most often emotional issues; they involve problems of control, integrity, vulnerability, and relationship, and they represent an arena no one enters lightly.

Our reluctance to confront our clients with their own personal contribution to the problems they face meets with their wish to look far outside themselves for answers. This combination results in change efforts that ultimately disappoint.

OUR COMMON CULTURE

We search for the external answer, one that gives comfort to our desire for the safety of reason and helps explain why we all, consultants and clients alike, keep going through ever-shorter cycles of looking for what's next, the Next Big Thing. It is not surprising that we end up feeling afterward that we have just been through another fad. For two decades now we have been longing for changes in our organizations and for that long have passed through a long series of the "perfect answer." Why do we so often experience new ideas as fads? Why is the promise of a new theory so enticing, and then why does it breed so much cynicism? Some might say that we find a new theory, implement it, and go on to the next one, but we in fact move on to what's next long before the last big thing has been internalized.

KEYNOTE SPEAKER AS UNIVERSAL SOLVENT

This wish for the safe and emotionally low-priced answer is always there—the wish for the ultimate advice, from a religious leader, a political leader, a heroic military leader, an archetypal figure to embody our hopes. One symbol of this fervent seeking is the Keynote Speaker.

If you are organizing a conference, you have to promise a well-known speaker to get people to show up. If you don't offer a big-name speaker, backed up with a menu of medium-name speakers who know what you don't, then no one comes. This is good for the prosperity of the speaker, but questionable for the learning of the participants. What is ironic is that the speaker is the draw, yet when you ask people what was most valuable about a conference, the answer is usually what people learned from other participants. In fact, there is a consistent, after-the-fact disappointment in the keynoters.

Bill Pfeiffer, who used to organize large conferences, once told me that the bigger the name of the speaker, the more people are willing to be disappointed. Give us a name personality and our expectations are low. Let someone we have not heard of speak to us, and they fall under an unrelenting scrutiny. We choose celebrity and entertainment over learning. So why do we make this choice? One reason is that the act of sitting and listening to a speech is in itself a defense against our own transformation. Rather than face my own accountability for the frustrations I face, I hold to the wish for some magical resolution to come from the lips of another.

The Keynote Speaker is a symbol for my belief that there is an answer to my problem and someone else has it. It is a secular wish for the experience of God. It embodies the tension between seeking advice from another and trusting my own experience. We enter wanting advice and leave valuing experience. The wish for a speaker is our collusion with the wish for sizzle over steak, style over substance. It is not that the speakers are not good; it's just that within the structure of their speeches, all they can offer is a long list of clever "chicken soup" solutions that, upon reflection, are swallowed but never fill us up.

So much for my advice to avoid advice.

For More Depth

Argyris, Chris. *Flawed Advice and the Management Trap: How Managers Can Know When They're Getting Good Advice and When They're Not.* New York: Oxford University Press, 1999.

Gallway, W. Timothy. *The Inner Game of Work.* New York: Random House, 1999.

The Flawless Consulting Fieldbook and Companion

Chapter 8

Four Communities

Idries Shah

A Sufi master on a journey saw a number of people struggling to haul a crocodile out of a river. Seeing that the animal was not dead and could kill some of them if they got it on shore, he cut the rope which they had attached to it.

The people seized him and beat him, crying: "Dressed like a Sufi, he is a hypocrite as well as a wrongdoer, for Sufis only do what is good."

Some time later, he came upon a group of dervishes who thought that by action they would attain "being." He told them that their "being" would come through inaction. They put him to flight.

Subsequently he settled among a school of Seekers who were contemplatives. He realized that they needed action, so he told them: "'Being' comes through action."

They followed his guidance until one of the dervishes happened to call upon a friend, after which he came back and told them: "This man is a fraud and an opportunist. He used to preach 'Being comes from inaction' and was thrown out for it. So he tries the opposite argument."

So the Seekers expelled the Sufi master.

He found another group of people, and said to them: "'Being' comes sometimes from action and sometimes from inaction."

They answered: "If you had only told us to act when it was time to act, we would have done so. And if you had told us not to act when it was time for inaction, we would have done

Reprinted by permission from "Four Communities," in *The Dermis Probe* (pp. 24–25) by Idries Shah.

so. As it is, you are confusing us, dividing our concentration. Give us one dogma at a time."

He had to part company with them.

These were the first four communities with which he worked.

It is rumored that he is now living in a fifth.

The Flawless Consulting Fieldbook and Companion

Chapter 9

Changing Focus
Consulting in the New Economy

Patrick Dolan

No one has dramatized the damage and dysfunction caused by rigid organizations as compassionately and vividly as Patrick. He has made famous, even notorious, the staying power of the steady state, the system in place. Also, when he works with a client, he makes a deep commitment and fully joins the fray. So when he shifts our focus, which he does in this short essay, we need to pay attention. If the new forms of work require finding glue, instead of dissolving what we see, then consulting skills will in fact become everyone's task.

This profession of "change consultant," at its best, brings a conscious and deliberate tension between the organization itself and the people who work in it and for it. Ordinarily we are hired to help in the area of organizational improvement by somehow forming a better, a sounder, connection with the organization's people. More information, stronger voice, proper autonomy, and responsibility have to accompany good structures and processes for anything substantial to occur. There are, of course, many elements of the old organizational model that throw this relationship off, and our work early on is often simply to bring that information to the attention of the leadership and begin to address the damage it has done. We have to do this *before* we try to move to better technique and processes. Hard, a little risky, but straightforward enough.

With the rubric of "contracting" in *Flawless Consulting*, Peter made explicit this first "touch" with the client and suggested deepening the relationship and the work. "Put into words," he suggests, "what you are experiencing with the client as you work." This, of course, is one of the simplest ways to drive the two unknowns of client and consultant toward a more authentic relationship. To make the emotional world explicit, early on, is to attempt to unpack what is usually a flawed relationship from the beginning—one of false promise, control, and money, loyalty versus honesty. Not to be able to control the consultant's freedom, knowledge, access, or voice creates deep ambiguity in the relationship from the beginning as well. To draw out these issues is the meaning of "contracting" here.

To move through these issues for the good of both organization and people, most of us have developed maps in the maze. Personal economics, fear, acceptance, and rejection are all demons that haunt these trails. Clients who want implementation of hard, lean techniques seem simple enough to deal with. Those who want help manipulating are as well. But those who want improvement and know that people have something to do with it—and want help doing it—are more challenging. They have been our real clients.

Historically, when we found tension between the people and the organizational structure and processes, we had the comfort of knowing that they came linked together. The large consulting groups entered the practice from accounting for the most part and wrote the consulting equation much more heavily weighted for the organization. You bought them for headcount reduction and hired the rest of us to repair the damage. Until now.

My practice has changed abruptly, and I can see it clearly not only in the new e-world organizations, but in the old organizations (the best ones) as they start their own e-journeys. The inversion principle is that knowledge is the business and electronic "holding" of it allows one to rethink and redeploy all the pieces of it, including place, processes, and people. They are no longer linked physically or operationally, and hence they are not linked morally in the same way either.

So the organization/people links—and their fit and authenticity—have changed drastically and still are changing. But I find that only a small portion of the organizations I encounter grasp the change. The labor unions deny it. The people experience it suddenly, brutally, and without much context or meaning. If we have been trained to help somewhere in this relationship, and "contracting" with the organization has been our way to understand its needs, the peoples' hard corrective data, and the stance and skills we bring to the equation, what now?

In a conversation with Meg Wheatley recently, she proffered that the best we can do at this moment is "bear witness." If you have a high profile and are clearly on the "outside," that may work and surely has value. But the internal consultant must find new contracts, new conversations, and a new work to merit continued presence.

The new direction seems to me to require thought in the following areas:

Less Inside and Outside. The organization and its boundaries will have less and less meaning. The complexity of work will be mirrored by a complexity in relationships to the enterprise. The "whole" will not be a corporate entity as much as an integrated series of activities, operations, and services performed by many different groups, held together much as a blueprint visually holds all the elements of a building. The terms "employee" and "subcontractor" describe an old boundary simplicity that is changing in front of us. The so-called "enterprise" will reach far back in the supply chain and reach far out into a series of customers.

Less Control. The blurring of boundaries leads one to think in terms of long intellectual chains, not separate hierarchies. Control chains will be replaced by hand-off activities controlled by the information chain. Horizontal will replace vertical, and those who knew how to contract with hierarchies—even as we muted them and repaired their damage—will now find organizational slippage and pathology in the lack of linkage, integration, and commitment to one another.

Less Cohesiveness and Teamwork. Our old problem was huge, unyielding bureaucracies, and our skill was to "unstick" them and lift their offensive effects so individuals could claim freedom and responsibility. My guess is that our future practice will come off of a pathology of sloppiness, missing links, failures of promised commitments—in short, a lack of cohesiveness and teamwork.

These new realities will mean new challenges for all consultants, especially internal ones. The purpose of our work will be—if it isn't already—not unsticking but *resticking* the organizations we consult to. We will still be consulting "flawlessly"—helping our clients with finding authentic linkages, developing trust among individuals and groups, and building communities of work by using rational blueprints, but with deeper fundamentals of mutual respect, common purpose, and promises kept.

About the Contributor

Patrick Dolan and his associates in Leawood, Kansas, specialize in giving new direction to labor and management through cooperative approaches to large-system change. He is the author of *Restructuring Our Schools: A Primer on Systemic Change* (Systems & Organization, 1994).

Chapter 10

Be Careful Who You Ask
Perils of Wisdom

Andrea Markowitz

Literature, religion, and mythology are filled with advisors in the form of witches, guides, prophets, and angels. In this article Andrea refers to these and links them to modern forms of consultation. There is, however, a significant difference between traditional wisdom and professional advice. Traditional wisdom is a voice from the spirit world. It is the voice from a higher self, from the many faces of God.

These eternal messages are meant to teach all humankind. We cross over a line when we endow expert professionals with this kind of power. We would do well to give less power to the professional and perhaps to reflect more deeply on that advice that has become timeless and was offered with the intent of love rather than as a means of economic exchange.

A consultant met with a group of clients who assembled to discuss problems that arose from a merger that brought together two very different organizational cultures. During the discussion, the group members frequently referred to the chaos and frustration that resulted from continuous clashes about how to manage people and how to accomplish the work. Toward the end of the discussion, a particularly distressed client implored the consultant, "What are you going to do to change things around here?"

Change, a.k.a. *transformation, reorganization, growth.* No matter what consultants call it, many employees look at it with both desire and dread. They want a particular aspect of their work life to be better, but shy away from the responsibility of making it better. They'd rather depend on someone else, such as a management consultant, to lead the transformation of their workplace. And why shouldn't they, with so many historical precedents that have conditioned people to think they need to hire "experts" who are "more knowledgeable" and "more powerful" to lead or save them?

FROM MYTH AND HISTORY

We can trace precedents that encourage people to be dependent on authorities at least as far back as the Bible, with its examples of kings who seek the advice of wise men and prophets before making decisions about war and peace and of prophets who promise that humankind will be delivered from their earthly suffering by a Messiah. Ancient Greek tales describe heroes who consulted the Oracle of Delphi before embarking on adventures that would change their lives and who, without the intervention of gods and goddesses, would not have successfully overcome the difficult obstacles that they encountered in their journeys. Medieval fables, parables, and fairy tales feature witches who predict fates, fairy godmothers who help children escape from the clutches of wicked stepmothers, and elves who come to the rescue by performing magic for maidens in distress. During the Renaissance, Shakespeare's plays moralized about the consequences of ignoring the prophesies and counsel of witches and fools.

While these stories, myths, fairy tales, and literary works teach us to have hope, it is a hope that is compromised by individual helplessness. Their examples lift our spirits with a promise of a brighter future, but suggest that we cannot achieve such a future on our own. Rather, they imply that we need someone wiser and more powerful than ourselves to make the promise a reality.

Many of these tales involve an economic transaction. They teach us that we are expected to repay our advisors for their efforts on our

behalf. In the Old Testament, the Pharaoh rewarded Joseph for interpreting his dreams by freeing him from prison and slavery. Some priests of Apollo at the Oracle of Delphi, presumably to encourage larger donations and repeat business, were accused of deciphering prophesies in ways that would appeal to wealthy and powerful patrons (Wilson, p. 45). The royal fools in Shakespeare's plays received gold coins from their patrons for their clever insights. In the fairy tale "Rumpelstiltskin," the magical elf demanded compensation before he would come to the rescue of a poor young woman whose father bragged to the king that she had skills worthy of being the queen. The king put the woman to the test with three seemingly impossible tasks. If she did not accomplish them, she would die. Rumpelstiltskin suddenly appeared and offered to carry them out—the first for her necklace, the second for her ring, and the third for her first-born child.

THE EDUCATED EXPERT

Every culture, ancient and contemporary, has had its medicine men, sufi, gurus, rabbis, and priests. With increasing opportunities for secular education, during the European Renaissance, a small percentage of privileged males, and later females, had opportunities to become experts in special fields such as the sciences, medicine, and law. By the late 1800s, a university education was accessible to the Western middle class, and today a university education is becoming increasingly available to every social class, worldwide. With education comes the expectation of wisdom in a specialized field. With wisdom in a specialized field comes the expectation of a career. And with the career comes the expectation that the specialist will be compensated for his or her advice.

The capitalistic 20th Century bred a growing reliance on the counsel of professionally educated and trained specialists, such as lawyers, doctors, psychologists, architects, and organizational consultants. Now anyone who is interested in experts' advice can choose between seeking their opinions individually or listening to them on endless radio and television talk shows that tell people how to better live and love.

Until recently many patients did not question a doctor's medical diagnosis and prescribed treatment. Many clients did not question a lawyer's trial or settlement strategy, or a psychologist's interpretation of their thoughts and behaviors. Many families allowed architects to design uncomfortable homes. Many citizens and politicians allowed city planners to create sterile neighborhoods. And most organizational leaders allowed their consultants to take responsibility for motivating their employees.

With such a rich tradition of laypersons relying on experts to guide them, it should be no surprise that many managers and employees still ask what the consultant is going to do to make things better for the organization. People in organizations, like practically everyone else, have learned to depend on experts to take care of the thinking, interpreting, planning, and doing that are required to achieve desired results. They have been conditioned to believe that the direction of influence and responsibility flows from the consultant to the client.

Beginning with the first organizational consultants in the early 1900s, both clients and consultants took it for granted that consultant-experts should do the work and be accountable for the outcomes. While the consultants investigated the problems and planned interventions, clients would focus on their business's day-to-day operations. And they would come to know little or nothing of the processes that the consultants used to identify problems and come up with solutions.

But this total reliance on experts resulted in undesirable consequences. If another problem were to arise, the clients would not have learned how to confront it themselves. They would still be dependent on the consultant to fix their problems. Dependency on consultants intensifies clients' insecurities and creates feelings of helplessness. And, as many organization managers and change practitioners have observed, the dependency-building consultant-as-expert model is a disenfranchising way to effect change. Today, we have begun to realize that clients who are removed from the problem-solving process and solution generation are not very likely to accept ownership for the problems or the solutions, and this lack of ownership makes them likely to resist implementing change.

PARTNERSHIP: THE PROMISE AND PERILS

An alternative to being an expert is to become a partner. Partner-consultants ask, "How can we support organizations through a change process in a way that requires the clients to accept responsibility for both the problems and the solutions, and in a way that discourages the client from developing an unhealthy dependency on us?"

The goal of a partner is to help clients achieve a new level of understanding that enables them to recognize the sources of their problems and find their own solutions. Partners begin this process by confronting clients with the nature of their problems. Often, the clients already know the nature of their problems, but either they don't realize they know it, or it is so threatening that they won't openly admit it without being provoked.

Partners and their ability to provoke are to organizations as grains of sand are to oysters. They irritate the system, and the system reacts by protecting itself from the irritation. In the process, the system transforms the irritation into something that is prized and valued—a pearl for the oyster, and new wisdom for the organization.

Of course, imparting different ways of thinking about and interpreting reality is not an easy task. Organizations with any history have imbedded patterns of thought and action that feel "right" to the organization members. It is difficult to get people to recognize and change these habits. To help organization members become aware of their dysfunctional patterns, consultants may need to confront them with hard-to-face facts about themselves.

Partnership is the most difficult consulting paradigm to practice and the most difficult to sell to clients, who expect their money to pay for a more tangible service than having a consultant confront individuals and groups with their personal and organizational shortcomings. It is also more difficult to sell this model to consultants who believe it is their responsibility to fix clients' problems and who derive a great deal of personal and professional satisfaction from taking credit for doing so. It is also harder to know when your job is done—the point at which you can confidently say to people in the organization, "You are now ready to be on your own."

Professional codependence is another potential difficulty for partner-consultants. In *The Careless Society,* John McKnight observed that institutionalized caring becomes a commodity when it hides economic issues "behind the mask of love" (p. 39). In other words, professionals who see their clients as being in need of expert care often overlook the fact that they, the caring professionals, are *creating* needs in order to justify their own existence and make a living.

The professional caregiver's codependence on the client often results in such dysfunctional practices as viewing the client's so-called "need" as a "deficiency." For example, change consultants who frame a client's need as a "deficiency" rather than as an "opportunity for growth" may *anticipate* and *seek* problems where there are none. This attitude is not only disabling in that the clients are labeled as defective, but also in the dependency-creating assumption that clients need the knowledge, skills, and tools of experts in order to solve their problems—to get rid of the deficiency. These professionals further abet their client's dependency by asserting that they, not the client, will be the judges of whether or not the intervention has been effective and whether or not the client needs more help.

Consultants who attempt to avoid unhealthy client dependencies and codependencies will find it is not an easy task. Care providers, like mothers, may experience the conflict of wanting to both protect their children and save themselves from becoming overly involved in their children's lives. Albert Memmi compared care provider-client relationships to a sculpture by artist Henry Moore in which a mother is gathering her children to her, but at the same time she pushes them away out of fear that they will devour her. Likewise, Memmi suggested, care providers must defend themselves from their clients, even at the risk of being labeled as uncaring. If they don't, they will lose themselves in their provider roles.

MINING THE EXPERT WITHIN

A long tradition of reliance on the advice of experts has conditioned many of us to believe we must depend on authorities to take care of the thinking, interpreting, planning, and doing that are required to solve our problems, whether they be large or small. But we create our own disabling effects when we blindly rely on experts. Instead of building our confidence and independence by solving problems on our own, we intensify our insecurities and make ourselves dependent on a stranger. When we minimize our ability to think for ourselves we don't try to help ourselves. But no one knows us as well as we do. No one can advise us as well as we can advise ourselves.

This does not mean that people should not reach out to others when they need help. We are not islands. We do need support from other human beings. But in addition to support from others, we need to learn to support ourselves, to do the work that makes us as expert as we can be in decisions that have an impact on our lives.

For More Depth

McKnight, John. *The Careless Society: Community and Its Counterfeits.* New York: Basic Books, 1996.

Memmi, Albert. *Dependence.* Boston, MA: Beacon Press, 1984.

Wilson, Damon. *The Mammoth Book of Nostradamus and Other Prophets.* New York: Carroll and Graf, 1999.

About the Contributor

Andrea Markowitz is an independent consultant and assistant professor of industrial/organizational psychology at the University of Baltimore.

Chapter 11

Dealing with Resistance
Having the Right Conversation in Difficult Situations

Phil Grosnick

We all talk about resistance to change as if it were a law of nature. True, we all have feelings about change, but when we talk about "overcoming" resistance, we approach it as an enemy instead of as an ally. In this article, Phil details a way to embrace resistance and use it as a step toward a more intimate relationship with a client that is wide enough to contain our fears as well as our hopes. The context is to focus on the conversation as the mixing bowl for what we plan to create.

Also pay attention to Phil's voice. He writes in the first person and speaks to you, the reader, as he would to a client. By reading this you will know what it feels like to work with Phil. He consistently makes a choice about his own reactions and behavior, which allows him to stay with the client emotionally. This is more than a writing style; it is a stance in life that places the consultant on an equal level with the client. It creates a world in which each player is in the business of learning, and the learning takes place as we go. This creates a balanced power between consultant and client, a relationship of political equity. This stance may be as important as any particular style or skill that the consultant brings to the table.

One of the hardest things for me to accept as a consultant learning the craft was that difficult meetings with clients weren't necessarily "bad," and that easy meetings weren't necessarily "good." Here is a story that illustrates the point.

I was called in by the vice president of marketing in a large corporation to diagnose the reasons behind the poor morale in his department. Let's call him Ray. My data collection revealed that Ray was the primary cause for the low morale. He was treating his employees badly, which included berating them in public and telling them that they didn't know as much as they should. When I met with Ray to give him this feedback, he became enraged. He stood up, leaned over his desk, jammed his finger in my face, and with veins and eyes bulging shouted, "Where do you guys get off? You are the third consultant to come in here and tell me I'm the problem!"

If I hadn't been so frightened, I might have asked Ray how many of us it would take to get the point across, but instead I raised my hands as if his finger were a gun and said, "Ray, you're yelling at me."

Without missing a beat and without lowering his voice, Ray said, "It's not you, it's those #*%$ kids I have to work with! They come in here with their MBAs thinking they know so much! I've already forgotten more about marketing in my thirty years on the street than they will ever know!"

Ray didn't calm down when he said these things. He didn't slow his pace. The meeting was at a high emotional pitch. Ray and I were having the right conversation, but someone else observing the meeting might have thought things weren't going very well.

Ray was telling me how out of touch and distant he felt from his direct reports. In as calm a voice as I could muster, I told him it sounded like he was talking about his children, and he told me that was exactly how he saw them. We stayed with this conversation for a long time, more than half an hour. Ray told me how different and old he felt, but the gentler tones only came near the end of our conversation, when Ray felt completely understood. It was only then that we could begin to discuss changes that might improve the morale in the department.

By the end of our meeting I was exhausted. It was one of the most difficult meetings of my consulting career. It was also a very good and productive one. I was learning about dealing with resistance.

REVEALING RESISTANCE

In consulting, resistance is the indirect expression of real concerns. Put another way, clients are not always open with consultants when expressing what's on their minds. I might go to a meeting to talk about doing work with a client, and all of a sudden the client is yelling at me, changing the subject, or questioning the methods I used to reach my conclusions. Some clients will talk about anything but what is really bothering them. When this happens, not only are we not talking about the substance of the work we need to do together, we are also not talking about their concerns about proceeding with that work. And we have to talk about their concerns before we can proceed with that work.

If clients who have doubts about proceeding could use direct language to discuss their concerns, we could do some problem solving. Or at least I could communicate my understanding and validate the legitimacy of their concerns. Unfortunately, we human beings are not so rational. We protect ourselves from difficult issues by avoiding them, even when we know disclosure would allow others to offer assistance and support.

As consultants, we can best apply our expertise in facilitation and managing interactions when we identify the feelings and issues that are motivating the resistant behavior in the room. When these feelings and issues are hidden from us, we struggle in the dark. The point of dealing with resistance is to have concerns and feelings expressed directly and to support the client in coping with them.

facilitation managing interacti

Begin with a Good Faith Response

The first step in dealing with resistance is to respond to the client's behavior with goodwill, treating their reactions as totally legitimate. For example, in the contracting phase I give a good faith response by offering business reasons for the requests I make and by presenting a reasonable explanation for what I want. So when clients question my need to develop my own view of their situation, I give them a straight answer with goodwill, such as: "I need to assess whether my expertise will have a real impact on your business objectives before I make you a promise to deliver results. The only way I can find this out is to get my own data on your situation."

Resistance doesn't occur only in contracting meetings. When collecting data I find interviewees reluctant to share information—and even more reluctant to tell me why. When this happens, I make good faith attempts to legitimize the client's hesitancy by rephrasing my questions to make them clearer or more specific. Another good faith response would be to reassure the client by explaining the reason for my questions and by reiterating how the data they provide will be used.

Feedback meetings are not immune to resistance either. If a client questions my data because I am an outsider, a good faith response might be: "It's true that I do not know the operations of the unit as well as you do. The data I gathered gave me *this* picture of your unit. Why do you think this was reflected in the data?"

Often, resistance goes away when the consultant gives a good faith response because it clarifies things for the clients and validates their needs. In other words, their concerns are addressed. But sometimes the concerns are deeper and the resistance continues. Continuing to provide good faith responses probably won't win the day in these conversations, especially because consultants tend to lose their patience and their interpersonal skills as they feel obligated to increase the number of good faith responses.

So here's the rule of thumb: When dealing with resistant clients, offer no more than two good faith attempts.

For any technique or model, there is always an exception to the rule: Being yelled at is the exception to using two good faith responses. At best, I attempt to let them vent. I move more quickly to naming their behavior. I do not begin by offering two good faith responses. My clients tend to realize the inappropriateness of this kind of behavior without any help from me, often apologize almost immediately, and start telling me why they did what they did. I am grateful when they do this and find it easy to not take the attack personally and to respond with goodwill as the conversation continues. But when the resistance persists in spite of my good faith attempts, the next step is to shift the conversation to naming the resistant behavior.

Next, Name the Resistant Behavior

The clearest and most powerful way to name the resistant behavior is to simply describe it. When I said to Ray, "You're yelling at me," I was naming his behavior.

The naming statement is only the beginning. This is where the work starts. Naming doesn't set you free—it starts the new conversation that the client and consultant need to have. The conversation begins with what is happening between the people in the room, and you hope it will lead to what is driving the resistant behavior. This is a necessary conversation. This is what needs to be talked about. This is also a difficult conversation.

In my nearly twenty years of employing this technique, I have yet to experience a client who responded easily to my naming statements. Only in my fantasies do I hear them say, "Thank you for calling attention to my non-productive behavior. I have been waiting all my life for a nice person like yourself to confront me so I could open up about what is really on my mind." What usually comes back at me is a bit more edgy, more confrontational in tone, and exactly the information I need from them.

An example I have often used when training consultants involves a client of mine who asked me to provide customer service training for all of the employees in his organization. I knew that training was a solution to a problem and began contracting to get my own view of the situation to assess the best use of my expertise. The client kept offering excuses for why that would be difficult and unnecessary. I responded with two or three good faith alternatives and reasons for his objections.

Eventually I said, "Dan, you are choosing a solution without data to back it up."

Dan's response was: "You headquarters people always come out here wanting to make mountains out of molehills! You can never do anything simply. You use up our resources for your own projects and agendas and never listen to our side of the story!"

My response was simple. I just summarized the emotional content of his outburst: "You have had some bad experiences with people like me."

Dan and I spoke for a long time about his experiences with visiting staff people. It was only until he felt understood and decided that his fears would not be actualized in my work with him that he was willing to give me some latitude to diagnose the situation properly. By the end of our meeting, I was exhausted. It was one of the most difficult meetings of my consulting career. It was also a very good and productive one.

FOUR GUIDELINES FOR EXPOSING CONTENT AND EMOTIONS

All consulting meetings have three levels that need to be managed, and all three need my constant attention. They are *the content, the client's emotional reaction,* and *my emotional reaction.*

When I name a client's behavior, it is only the beginning of the important conversation between us. The heart of the interaction is taking her side by validating and understanding her concerns. I have to do this while managing the content of the meeting and my emotions as well. I have found that the best way to manage my emotional reactions to all types of resistance—evasive answers, angry outbursts and even silence—is to do the following:

- Realize that this difficult conversation is the right conversation—the one we need to have;
- Let go of my need to defend myself;
- Remind myself that I am there to engage the client and maintain goodwill; and
- Care enough to want to hear what the client has to say.

Here is a story that demonstrates how I use the four guidelines you just read.

The Flawless Consulting Fieldbook and Companion

This time it was a contracting meeting. I had already met with one member of the organization who apparently thought enough of me to schedule a second meeting with her boss, Valerie. From almost the moment we were introduced, Valerie began firing questions at me about my credentials, background, and methodologies.

I responded as I was taught in school and answered the questions to the best of my ability. But the pace didn't let up, and so I said, "You're firing a lot of questions at me. You're worried about my credentials."

Maybe this wasn't the perfect naming statement, but it did change the conversation. Valerie fired back: "I know what you're doing! I know that technique! I have a master's degree and can do anything you can do!"

I let go of my need to defend myself, and I moved psychologically toward Valerie by affirming her expertise. I told Valerie that I was sure she could consult and that it was obvious she knew exactly what interpersonal skills I was using. She told me I was "damn right," and said again that she could do anything I could do for her organization. I offered goodwill by telling her I understood "what" she was saying and asked her to tell me "why" she was saying it. She said it was because "people around here think you have to be an external consultant to have any credibility." I demonstrated that I cared about what she had to say by empathizing with her and discussing her situation for more than an hour.

In the end, we agreed to work together, with me in a shadow role and Valerie getting the visibility and credibility she craved. If I hadn't cared about what Valerie had to say, I would not have gained her support. Without her support, I would have had a very difficult time in her organization. By my understanding her frustration about being passed over and taking her side about doing the work herself, we reached a collaborative agreement that benefited everyone, including the organization.

TAKING THE RISK

Is it necessary to deal with client resistance this way? I believe that taking the risk results in superior consultations. If you believe as I do that the relationship you establish with the client is the primary vehicle for your influence, then exposing and supporting real concerns is essential. When I look back on my least effective consultations, most of them went off without a hitch, but nothing of substance happened. The meetings and conversations were smooth. Things went easily, and the results were minimal.

I guess good consulting can be easy, but for me it usually means hard work and difficult conversations. The irony is that I have to be willing to risk the very relationship I am working so hard to salvage by describing the difficult issue in the room. That's the only way I can get to the point at which I can extend the understanding that strengthens that relationship into one based on trust, collaboration, and commitment.

For More Depth

Further Reading

Block, Peter. *Flawless Consulting: A Guide to Getting Your Expertise Used* (2nd ed.). San Francisco: Jossey-Bass/Pfeiffer, 1999.

Block, Peter. *Stewardship: Choosing Service over Self-Interest.* San Francisco: Berrett-Koehler, 1993.

Henning, Joel P. *The Future of Staff Groups: Daring to Distribute Power and Capacity.* San Francisco: Berrett-Koehler, 1997.

Further Training

Designed Learning, Staff Consulting Skills Workshops. www.designedlearning.com.

Gestalt Institute, Case Western Reserve. www.gestaltcleveland.org.

Pepperdine University, MSOD program. www.pepperdine.edu.

About the Contributor

Phil Grosnick is president of Designed Learning, Inc., Fanwood, New Jersey, and is heavily involved in the firm's Staff Consulting Skills Workshops.

Chapter 12

The Case of Pricilla and the Red Pen

Andrea Markowitz

We end this section on advice with lots of it. Here is a story in which the consultant is faced with a group flooded with helplessness, anger, and despair. The story underlines the complexity of the consultant role and shows how a consultant can take on the pathology of the client and ultimately work herself out of it. It is impossible in human affairs to get it right the first time, but we always have the possibility of recovery. Being able to see our own complicity in events that do not go well may be our only salvation. It demonstrates that our own learning and change are critical to doing the work well.

The story also takes an interesting pause to consider the power of symbols. Our work is highly dependent on the power of language as leverage for change, and the images we choose have great capacity to change a social system. We need to be able to speak metaphorically and use images that emerge from each local situation.

With the statement, "And what *really* bugs me is that *red pen*," Carmen opened a floodgate.

"Yeah, that red pen." The other five production assistants nodded vigorously, agreeing that the red pen was a major issue.

"What's the problem with the red pen?" I asked.

"Well, *she . . .*" Carmen nodded toward Pricilla, their manager, who was sitting across from me at the conference table, "she always uses a red pen to mark what's wrong with our assignments."

"I love my red pen," Pricilla responded.

"Well, we hate it," retorted Nancy.

"Well, how else am I supposed to mark up the mistakes on your advertising copy?" challenged Pricilla.

"Why don't you use a different color pen, like purple?"

"Or green?"

"What's the difference?" Pricilla looked incredulous. "My teachers always used red pens to grade my papers. I didn't mind at all."

"That's the problem," Carmen explained, "You're not our teacher and we're not your students. We're *adults.*"

Pricilla raised her eyebrows. "I know you're adults. So why should the color of the pen matter?"

"What do you love about your red pen?" I asked.

"It's got a nice point. And it's fatter than my other pens. I like the way it feels in my hand." Pricilla held it up to emphasize her point.

"Does the same pen come in different colors?" I probed.

"Probably. I don't know." Pricilla didn't appear to care, either. "I don't see what's wrong with red."

"Red is the color of anger," Mitch explained. "It's aggressive. Perhaps you could use a color that doesn't symbolize anger."

Nancy focused everyone on another aspect of red. "It's also the color of *blood.*"

A short discussion followed about what color ink Pricilla could use instead of red. Pricilla was quiet. The rest of the group agreed on green, although someone in the group objected because green suggests "envy." But most agreed green was a "peaceful" color.

Pricilla reluctantly agreed to use green ink for the next two weeks.

I had been asked to meet with Pricilla's production unit of an advertising agency because the creative director was concerned about mounting complaints concerning her management style and escalating "personality conflicts" between Pricilla and a few of her assistants.

The Flawless Consulting Fieldbook and Companion

Pricilla herself told me she frequently had to "write up" three of her employees for problems such as absenteeism, lateness, and insubordination, and these employees kept going to their ombudsman with charges against Pricilla for unfair treatment. Actually, these problems were not new—Pricilla had a long-standing reputation for not caring about her employees and for being very rigid and stubborn about how things were done in her department.

When I met with the group again, I was eager to learn how the green pen was working out. I greeted them with the usual "Good morning, everyone." Their unenthusiastic reply signaled that I was in for another struggle. "Well," I continued to smile, "what has changed since the last time we met?"

Seven pairs of eyes looked at me. No lips moved. "Hasn't anything changed?" I pushed.

Someone mumbled, "Nothing."

"Well, I know *one* thing that changed," I ventured. "Pricilla corrected your copy with *green* ink instead of red."

The assistants' eyes rolled, but their lips were frozen. Pricilla was perfectly still.

"Well, didn't she?"

One assistant bravely but barely shook her head.

"Pricilla, didn't you change to green ink?"

"Well, I did for a few days, but then I went back to my red pen."

"Oh?"

"The green one was too skinny."

"Couldn't you have found a fatter green pen?"

"It would take a while to go through purchasing."

"How about if I give you the money for a green pen? What could it be, a few dollars? We could go to a store right after this meeting."

"Okay, if you want to. But I don't have time to go to the store."

Six pairs of eyes followed our conversation as though it were a tennis match. Now it was time to put the ball in their court.

"How do the rest of you feel about Pricilla not using the green pen?" Silence.

"No feelings? No comments? No opinions?"

Carmen, who had initiated the discussion about the red pen at the last meeting, sighed, "It doesn't matter any more. I've gotten over it. It's just a pen. I'm just here to do a job. I just have to learn to accept it. I've got to work on myself and my own attitude."

"What about the rest of you?"

Finally Bev said something: "I'd like to talk about the problem with the computers. We are wasting time and money because they are too slow to handle the amount of copy we have to get out in a day. We also don't have enough printers to support us when we're all working on projects at the same time."

Bev waxed on for a good fifteen minutes about the equipment woes—how she tried to convince management that they would save money in the long run with improved technology, because it would prevent the backlogs and breakdowns on the existing equipment. And how the people in the department would meet their deadlines with less stress.

Pricilla explained that *her* boss refused to approve the purchase of faster computers or more printers or copiers.

Bev said, very politely, that she wished management would listen to employees more. She surprised everyone, including herself, when she ended with an energetic admonition, "We're the ones who do the job. We know best what equipment we need. We're people, not machines, and we can't make our quotas and deadlines if we don't have the equipment to do it."

"Go, Bev!" Her fellow staffers' support lasted a half a minute or so. Then silence.

"What else would anyone like to talk about?" I ventured.

Silence. And more silence.

"Well, if no one else has anything to say, I'd like to return to the subject of the red pen."

Signs of life and anticipation appeared in six pairs of previously dead eyes.

"Pricilla, I'd like to tell you how I would feel if I were one of your staff and you broke your promise to change to a green pen. I would feel as though you didn't care about me, as either your employee or as a

The Flawless Consulting Fieldbook and Companion

person. I would feel like you didn't respect me enough to follow through on a promise that you agreed to in front of your entire group."

"Well, it wasn't that," insisted Pricilla. "The green pen just wasn't working for me. I missed my red pen. And my staff didn't notice some of my corrections when I used a different color. So I'd get the work back and I'd have to highlight the corrections they missed."

Oh-come-on eyes rolled in unison around the table.

"And you should have heard all of the other people in the building who are used to my red pen. They've been asking, 'Pricilla, what happened to your red pen? It's just not the same without it!'"

"So you have a reputation throughout the organization for using your red pen."

"Yes, and I'm proud of it. I just don't see why I should change pens."

"It's *symbolic!*" exploded an exasperated Melissa.

"Of what?" challenged Pricilla.

"Of you telling us we're wrong and you're right. Of you always getting your own way. Even when we're right and you're wrong, you won't admit it."

"Yeah, remember when you insisted that I spell 'whether' as 'weather?'" Mitch's voice was low, but animated and emphatic. "I looked it up in the dictionary and showed you the difference between the two words, but you made me use 'weather' anyway. Then you changed your mind and said I could correct it, but I had already reproduced one hundred copies with the wrong spelling."

A thought occurred to me. "All of you have worked for other managers. Some of you still occasionally work on assignments for other people in this organization. And these other people must mark corrections on your work."

"Ye-es." Their voices lilted up as they wondered where I was going with this.

"Do any of them use red ink to make the corrections?"

"Ye-es." More lilting.

"Does it bother you when they use red ink?"

"No-oo."

"Why not?"

"Because they don't pick on every little thing."

"They don't tell us to change the typeface that we chose to a typeface that *they* prefer."

"Yeah, it's just a personal preference. It's not like it's right or wrong. If Pricilla doesn't *like* the typeface, she makes us change it."

"The other managers let us be creative. They only correct things that are really wrong, like spelling and grammar. She makes us do everything her way."

I think everyone was at the same time taken aback and relieved by these rapid-fire explanations. Everyone except Pricilla. So I asked, "Pricilla, what would you like to say?"

"Well, it's true that sometimes I just don't like the typefaces they choose, but sometimes I change them because they're hard for me to read. If I can't read them, other people probably can't read them either."

"And for certain advertising campaigns the clients insist we use a specific typeface," added Bev.

"Well, as long as we choose typefaces that are easy to read and they are acceptable to the client, why can't we choose our own typefaces?"

"Pricilla, what do you think about that?" I asked.

Pricilla's hesitation betrayed her reluctance to hand over the reins. She finally resigned, " Okay. Fine with me."

"Okay!" It was time to build consensus. "Then can we all agree that for the next week Pricilla will allow her staff to choose the typefaces for their assignments, as long as they are readable, and as long as they comply with the needs of specific clients?"

Nods all around.

"When I meet with you at the end of the week, we'll discuss how it went."

And thus began another chapter in the journey of triumphs and frustrations for a well-meaning but controlling manager, her complaining and disenfranchised assistants, and their naïve consultant. It was catalyzed by a symbol: the red pen. Everything that was threatening about their manager was captured in the symbolic meanings that this simple,

The Flawless Consulting Fieldbook and Companion

common writing instrument conjured and conveyed. It had the power to create a coalition and incite a rebellion—not because anything about the pen itself was inherently threatening, but because of the assistants' perception that its user was intentionally using it against them.

WHEN A PEN BECOMES A SWORD

Why did a red pen become the symbol of this group's oppression and the key to their liberation? Pricilla either consciously or unconsciously used the pen to symbolize her power. The red pen's symbolic power follows an illustrious tradition. In mythology, Zeus used lightning bolts to symbolize his indomitable image. In real life, Winston Churchill and Franklin Roosevelt exploited their walking sticks. The public knew better than to take the sticks as signs of weakness, especially when these men banged them on the ground or pointed them emphatically into a crowd to punctuate the force of their words. Pricilla's power was her red pen. She carried it with her everywhere she went in the organization, and wielded it lavishly.

Symbols are vital in finding a common and idiosyncratic language for people to talk about the subjectivity of their experience. Symbols serve as a shorthand for feelings that are otherwise difficult to talk about. The group's feelings of oppression were too hard to talk about directly, so they needed to focus on an object to depersonalize their frustrations with their manager. Pricilla had blatant non-verbal behaviors that cut off her assistants when they tried to offer their opinions or question a procedure or assignment. When I pointed out these behaviors to Pricilla in front of the group, the subordinates excitedly acknowledged them at once, exclaiming, "Yes, that's exactly what you do!" They did not feel safe enough to initiate discussions of Pricilla's suppressive nature with her. Openly attacking Pricilla's red pen posed less risk of reprisal and alienation than openly attacking her mannerisms. So instead they depersonalized Pricilla's peremptory style by attributing the root of their problems to the red pen.

The color, shape, and utilitarianism of the red pen also were fitting symbols of the group's struggle. In traditional symbolism red is associated with blood, wounds, death-throes, and sublimation (Cirlot, p. 53). The red ink in Pricilla's pen communicated to her assistants that she was out for their blood, insensitive to their pain, and determined to affirm her right to be the boss. The pen's shape became a sword and a wand, symbols of power and control. Pricilla used her red pen like a sword, slicing away at her assistants' morale as she cut through their work, taking away the little bit of autonomy they could have had in their jobs. She treated her assistants like adversaries instead of like the *support* staff she wanted them to be. Ironically, she then wondered why they were so antagonistic toward her.

Jung (1993) described a symbol as "the outcome of a definite view of life endowing the occurrence, whether great or small, with a meaning to which a certain deeper value is given than to pure actuality" (p. 345). The subjective value of symbols was also noted by J. E. Cirlot, who suggested in his treatise on symbolism that "Symbolism *adds* a new value to an object or an act. Once it is brought to bear, it turns the object or action into an 'open' event. . ." (p. xiv). The red pen became an "open event" when Pricilla's assistants discussed how Pricilla's use of it made them feel. And it became a catalyst for transformation when they asked Pricilla to stop using it against them.

The fact that the group members did not feel threatened when other managers used a red pen reminds us that context defines meaning. Every group has its own shared meaning, built over time though patterns of interactions. These shared meanings are the group's reality, the group's truth. The pen is benign, but the meaning it has for people is everything. This is true of every aspect of a group's culture. It is not the action of management or of employees that is crucial, but it is the meanings people give to the actions.

What is true for a group is also true for individuals. Not every individual in the group felt as strongly about the red pen as Carmen did. She had stronger feelings about the red pen because she had stronger personal issues with Pricilla. Carmen may also have had stronger issues about power and control (others' administration of them and her lack of them) than others in her group. Yet once Carmen mentioned the red pen, everyone in the group related to it as a symbol of Pricilla's autocratic style. Including me, the consultant.

The Flawless Consulting Fieldbook and Companion

Red pen = Pricilla's authoritarianism. Symbols are shortcuts to shared language, shared meaning. Like the members of the proverbial club who laugh at a joke by number, bypassing its recitation, organizational members bypass the explanation of a symbol and go straight from symbol to understanding. The members of this advertising production unit will never have to explain to one another the meaning of the red pen. Nor will they ever have to analyze it again for themselves.

Symbols then become tools for our work on individual and group development. Every group develops its own symbols. Consultants can benefit from consciously attending to the symbolic potential of phrases that resonate with the group. Symbols help the group extract meaning from their circumstances and help people find their voice, which is a primary objective of consulting. But a symbol alone is not enough to move individuals and groups toward growth. Most important is how consultants define their advice-giving roles when working with groups. Our wish to give advice betrays our own need to control our clients, to have a stake in a specific process and outcome. It also leads us to take sides, sometimes subtly, sometimes not. This is why we all have to look at ourselves more closely.

CONSULTANT HUBRIS

Although we, as consultants, want to help a group develop its capacity to work well together, we have to be careful not to become too invested in their progress. Pricilla and Carmen and all of our clients are ultimately the ones who will decide when they are ready to reconcile. We cannot move individuals, groups, and organizations from one stage to another and should know better than to presume that we are responsible for the progress that clients make. We should also know better than to presume that our guidance will result in automatic improvements from one stage to the next. We are no more responsible for the group's improvements than for its setbacks. When we attribute a group's progress or discouraging reversals to our interventions, we are guilty of hubris. Who are we to take so much credit for the outcomes of such complexity?

Consultants join a drama already in progress. The group's or organization's patterns of relationships are well-established before our production due to her absence and that she "had no complaints" about how her assistants handled their jobs while she was gone. And for the first time in the two weeks that she had been back from the workshop, Pricilla thanked her assistants for taking care of the department in her absence.

I was thinking to myself that my consulting skills must be skillful indeed to have affected such positive changes in Pricilla. Within minutes of my self-congratulations, however, Pricilla had a confrontational exchange with Carmen and Mitch, and Pricilla shut down. She announced that she was not going to change her management style and that was the end of it. This "caring" stuff wasn't for her. She declared that she supervised people's jobs, not their feelings. Everyone was here to do a job and "feelings" were irrelevant to getting the job done. Like dominos her assistants shut down, too. One by one they shrugged and said they didn't need these meetings anyway. Everything was fine. And even if everything wasn't fine, nothing was going to change, so why bother?

I was stunned. At the time I was too stunned to speculate about what could have happened to evoke Pricilla's about face and the group's shutting down. I affirmed Pricilla's "right" to be authoritarian in her management style, admitted that no one could force Pricilla to change, and asked the others in the group how they would deal with Pricilla's refusal to be a more participative manager. Some assistants said nothing. One assistant said she would look for another job. Two said they would pray for comfort and the ability to cope and that they would work on changing their attitudes toward Pricilla. All of the assistants looked like wounded deer.

With some distance from the meeting, I began to speculate about what had happened. Earlier in the meeting Pricilla had made a remark about complications in her own life. Perhaps she currently had too much personal emotional turmoil to deal with and could no longer exert the additional energy she needed to deal with her assistants' neediness. Or perhaps Pricilla's personal angst had to do with her manager's recent decision to reorganize Pricilla's unit so that now Pricilla would be supervising fewer employees. Pricilla must have known that in her

The Flawless Consulting Fieldbook and Companion

arrival on the scene. We may arrive with pre-conceived notions of what constitutes dysfunctional and healthy relationship patterns and choose to apply those theories of organizational behavior that we believe will be most helpful in fixing the current situation. During our consulting process we superimpose theories that have been developed by *past* experience to *present* and *future* events. Although our theories are not necessarily static, neither are they typically in a state of flux that keeps pace with an organization's ongoing changes. We are in a continual struggle to keep up with the changing natures of our clients and their organizations.

And so it was with the red pen. I had originally concluded that, after an initial setback, Pricilla was well on her way to incorporating more employee participation into her management style. As you will recall, in my first meeting with the group, Pricilla submitted to her assistants' request to change from red ink to green. In the second meeting, she admitted that she tried the green pen for a while, but she wasn't happy with it so she reverted back to using the red one. In the same meeting Pricilla agreed to try green ink again. In the next meeting she acquiesced to the group's wish for more autonomy in their choice of font style. In the meeting that followed she consented to try to get in touch with her "caring" side. And she continued to use green ink to make corrections on her assistants' work.

In return, Pricilla's assistants had agreed to encourage her to follow through with her changes by acknowledging their appreciation. They also agreed to improve their lateness and attendance records. With each consecutive meeting, the assistants spoke more freely in front of Pricilla. But while some said that they noticed improvements, Carmen and Mitch continued to complain about their manager.

I was especially excited when Pricilla showed signs of becoming more trustful of her assistants. Pricilla announced in a meeting held before her week-long trip to a production workshop that she had decided not to give her assistants "to do" lists as she had in the past. She also decided not to call the office to check up on their performance while she was away. At the first consultant and group meeting following Pricilla's return, she admitted that there had been no glitches in organization gossip would have attributed the cut in her staff to her reputation for being unable to supervise people properly. And Pricilla had another reason to feel slighted. Her manager had recently chosen to be assisted on an important project by one of Pricilla's assistants, thereby skipping over Pricilla, whose position rightfully placed her in line to assist the manager.

Now a different picture of Pricilla's pre-vacation behavior emerged. Pricilla had been making what her assistants and I considered "progress." I had applauded myself for suggesting the right things to move Pricilla "in the right direction." I was especially excited that Pricilla appeared to now "trust" her staff enough to go away for a week without micromanaging from afar. But the changes Pricilla made in attitude and behavior may have had nothing to do with either trust or my influence. It was possible that the real reason why Pricilla abandoned some controlling behaviors was her anguish over how her own manager was treating her. Maybe she was angry and therefore decided to throw less of herself into *her* job.

There could have been a number of other reasons for Pricilla's reversal that a consultant could neither have foreseen nor controlled. I began to understand that there were and would always be both hidden and unhidden forces that had more power over my clients' decisions than I could ever hope to have. So what good am I? What can I do? What can any consultant do?

According to some schools of thought, I could have recommended that Pricilla be fired. The president of the company had communicated his desire to have all of his managers become more participative in management style. Pricilla refused, ergo fire her. But then I'd be doing precisely to Pricilla what I did not want her to do to her assistants—I'd be giving up on building a relationship with another human being.

Another option would have been to encourage Pricilla to become more participative in style through peer pressure. I could have recommended that she be sent to a management workshop at which she would be the only person from her organization. While surrounded by strangers who were learning together about the benefits of a more considerate management style, Pricilla might become more receptive to it.

The Flawless Consulting Fieldbook and Companion

However, when she returned to an organization in which the majority of managers were still autocratic and in which participative management was not rewarded by her manager, she would be likely to abandon what she learned and resort to old habits.

Ironic, isn't it? Here I was, contemplating how I could best manage Pricilla. Bolstered by expert support for participative management in journals and books, I tried to get Pricilla to see the error of her authoritative ways. I didn't see at the time that I was exhibiting the same need for control that I condemned Pricilla for having, and that my controlling behavior was every bit as counterproductive as Pricilla's. I still had a very important lesson to learn.

CONSULTANT GUILT

Ask almost any OD consultant why he or she decided to become a consultant, and invariably you will hear the words "desire to help others" in the answer. Somewhere in that desire to help, however, consultants can get lost in their own needs to advise and control. There are very fine lines between helping, advising, and controlling. Therefore, before we can attempt to help people like Pricilla and her assistants, we must determine where we ourselves stand.

Before I could continue helping Pricilla's group, I needed to confront personal demons that were interfering with my fairness and empathy. I had to deal with my own anger and frustration over my lack of control, which was directed at both Pricilla and myself. I was angry and frustrated with Pricilla for not caring about her assistants' feelings. I was angry and frustrated with Pricilla for not embracing my message that participative management is a good thing. I was angry and frustrated with myself for allowing my personal dislike of authoritarian managers to affect my attitude toward Pricilla. And I was angry and frustrated with myself for feeling impotent in my attempts to change Pricilla and her antagonist, Carmen. I also colluded in defining Pricilla as the problem. She was a problem, but not "the" problem. Carmen was just as stubborn as Pricilla. She was righteous in her own stance and unwilling to see any integrity in Pricilla's stance. Carmen kept a perfectionist's eye on Pricilla, and any small regression sent Carmen back into despair.

When I admitted to myself that my negative feelings toward Pricilla were getting in the way of helping her and her group, I was able to replace my hostile feelings toward Pricilla with empathic ones, just the thing Carmen had been unable to do. At first I found it difficult to have empathy for Pricilla. I liked and admired her honesty, her focused dedication to her job, and the way she stood up for herself while her subordinates complained about her and events related to her supervision in their meetings. I even admired Pricilla's ability to detach herself from her assistants' accusations about her behaviors. But I could not get past Pricilla's unyielding need for control. My personal aversion to controlling bosses led me to identify with Pricilla's subordinates and to allow myself to be sucked into the role of the subordinates' advocate. I went over the line when I offered to buy a green pen for Pricilla after she did not keep her promise to change to green ink. I was letting everyone know that I was taking the assistants' side against their boss. Instead of remaining professionally neutral, I had become furious. How could Pricilla not keep her promise? What kind of manager was she? What kind of person was she? How could she be so dishonest?

But Pricilla was not being dishonest. By staying true to her red pen, she was staying true to herself. She had always been clear about who she was and what she expected from her subordinates. They chose to dislike her strict rules. So were they the ones with the problem? Should they have been more concerned about their own performance than with the way Pricilla controlled or communicated the process?

Pricilla thought so, and she was right. My negative response to high-control behavior had led me to undervalue the integrity of Pricilla's position. In an individual interview with me, Pricilla had said, "I wonder what people think their jobs are. Is this a meeting place where you collect a paycheck, or do you come here to be of use to someone and provide a service? I sense some of my staff have the attitude, 'I'm here, but I'm not doing anything.' I don't like to see my staff idle." She also mentioned problems with her assistants being absent from work too frequently, disappearing during working hours, spending too much

The Flawless Consulting Fieldbook and Companion

time on personal telephone calls, and being dishonest when explaining to her why they missed work, where they disappeared to, and to whom they were speaking on the phone.

Of course the assistants disagreed with Pricilla's perception that they were ever "idle." They argued that they did all of the work they were assigned and did it within their deadlines. They felt that they kept getting more and more responsibility and had fewer people to do the work. Most agreed that "There is no pleasing Pricilla." And through grapevine gossip the group members surmised that neither Pricilla's manager, nor people in other units in the organization, appreciated how hard they worked, and that they even singled out this unit to use as a scapegoat for production problems in the agency. Some of them expressed the wish that Pricilla would speak up to the rest of the organization in the unit's defense.

Some assistants did agree, however, that they were evasive when questioned on their whereabouts during and outside work hours. They felt their personal lives were none of Pricilla's business. These same assistants seemed to be unnecessarily fixated on what others, including their manager, did and did not think about them and their unit. They appeared to be hyper-vigilant in their search for others' statements about them that could have deeper, more slanderous meanings. They also appeared to be hypersensitive to negative feedback. In some of our meetings I tried to help them to see that in their defensiveness they tended to create problems where there were none. They invariably blamed their defensiveness on Pricilla's communication style: She was too bossy, she always criticized, and she rarely complemented their work. Slowly, I began to see that the assistants were too sensitive to feedback and too quick to read negative intent where none was intended.

Carmen especially didn't like being told what she "should" and "should not" do, or what she "had" to do. She had frequent shouting matches with Pricilla, both during consultant-led meetings and at work. A recurring theme of these conflicts was the need to "be my own person." For example, Carmen told Pricilla, "I don't like it when you say to me, 'You've got to . . . .' I don't *have* to do anything. You don't control me." She also mentioned that she had problems with the word "control" when used in the context of management behavior, preferring instead to have managers who "inspire" or "encourage."

Ironically, Carmen was also the one who said on a regular basis, "I can't keep letting this stuff get to me. I have to work on myself—my own attitude." Yet her attitude continued to be antagonistic. So we come back to the question: Was Carmen the one with "the problems"? Yes. But so were Pricilla, the other assistants, and myself. The implications seemed overwhelming. How could I possibly handle everyone's problems, including my own? How could I work through Carmen's inappropriately hostile responses to Pricilla's managerial personality? How could I help the other assistants who were less critical of Pricilla, but just as disappointed in her refusal to become a more participative, more caring manager? How could I help Pricilla understand that, just as there is nothing inherently wrong with being an autocratic manager, there is nothing wrong with being a caring one too? How could I keep myself from falling into the trap that assumes my consulting skills are the direct cause of an intended effect?

TEACHING VERSUS AWARENESS

An insight into what I might do to find a different way of thinking about the complexity of my consultation with Pricilla and her assistants comes, surprisingly, from a book titled *The Inner Game of Tennis*. Author W. Timothy Gallwey's method for improving one's tennis performance applies just as effectively to improving one's consulting performance. Gallwey observed that performance improves by eliminating the tendency to judge what we do and by replacing it with the choice to observe our technique with detachment. For example, to naturally improve your backhand:

> The trick is not to *identify* with the backhand. If you view an erratic backhand as a reflection of who you are, you will be upset. But you are not your backhand any more than a parent is his child. If a mother identifies with every fall of her child and takes personal pride in its every success, her self-image will be as unstable as her child's balance. She finds stability when she realizes that she is not her

The Flawless Consulting Fieldbook and Companion

child, and watches it with love and interest—but as a separate being. (p. 36)

This passage suggests that as consultants we need to refrain from identifying with our clients. We cannot view their triumphs and failures as a reflection of who we are—or even of what we do. We can watch them with love and interest, but must remember that they are separate beings.

Gallwey also distinguished between *making* something happen and *letting* it happen (p. 36). In order to let something happen, such as hitting the tennis ball exactly where you want it to go, you must abandon control and judgment, and call on trust. Consultants too can learn to let something happen and *forget ourselves,* lose our tendency to judge, and have trust in our consulting process. We can increase our own awareness of what is and, as we become more aware, hope that this will transfer to the high-awareness/low-judgment capacity of the client. What is critical is our confidence in the capacity of our client. Both we and the client will *naturally learn* to do what we need to do and to become what we need to be (p. 49).

So in the case of Pricilla and the red pen, I lost opportunities to let the group grow because I tried to make something happen. Although it was my directive from upper management to change Pricilla from an authoritative manager to a participative one, my method was tarnished by my own ego and by my stake in adhering to a predetermined outcome. I openly expressed to Pricilla and the group that it was wrong to be authoritarian and that it was right to be a participative and caring manager. I didn't trust Pricilla or myself to *let* change evolve through learning, partly because I did not know better, and partly because I wanted the credit for getting Pricilla to change.

Gallwey's explanation of the tennis player's need to receive credit for success works for consultants as well:

When you try hard to hit the ball correctly, and it goes well, you get a certain kind of ego satisfaction. You feel that *you* are in control, that you are the master of the situation. But when you simply allow the serve to serve itself, it doesn't seem as if you deserve the credit. It doesn't feel as if it were you who hit the ball. (p. 72)

When consultants try to control the situation and the results are positive, we enjoy ego satisfaction. We feel that we have rightfully earned our pay. Yet if we simply have a picture of an intention and combine that with a non-judgmental awareness, we might lose something in our pride, but we will have been of greater service. We are not the ones hitting the ball, but we are part of what ended up in a good shot.

When I felt that I had failed to hit the ball, I took time to lick my wounds. A month went by before I met with Pricilla again. This time I met only with Pricilla and Carmen to discuss their interpersonal conflict. And this time I did not have an agenda. I was resolute to "let it happen."

But it already had happened. Carmen reported that since the last meeting she had changed her attitude toward Pricilla, and Pricilla agreed that their relationship had improved. Carmen said she didn't let the little things get to her the way they used to. Pricilla agreed again. Pricilla explained that she could now give Carmen negative feedback about her work and Carmen could deal with it as a request to be more accurate rather than as a personal criticism. When Carmen asked to be excused from the meeting, I agreed, but only after asking whether she had truly changed her attitude or had just given up. She said she had truly changed.

Another surprise was in store for me. Pricilla admitted that despite her public outburst that she was not going to change, she had changed a lot. She said she had backed off from confrontations with Carmen. She also explained that she no longer expected perfection from her assistants and had even begun sending out reminders to help them complete their tasks more accurately, concluding, "You can't expect them to remember everything. You have to be willing to help."

Pricilla then explained why she managed people the way she did. She said she had been with this advertising agency for more than twenty-five years. When she first worked there all managers were authoritative and everyone adhered strictly to personnel policies. More recently, most managers had become more lax about rules, such as signing in and out when entering and leaving the building and dress codes. Even though creative people in advertising are usually given more leeway in dressing for work, Pricilla felt that sometimes they went

The Flawless Consulting Fieldbook and Companion

too far. She wanted to create a professional atmosphere, and to do so she felt she must enforce policies with her staff, even though other managers did not always enforce the same rules. She concluded that if the advertising agency had universal enforcement of all of the rules, she would not have the problems she currently had with a number of her staff or the reputation for being so inflexible. She added that all of her staff had come to her from managers who were more relaxed about policies, so when she expected adherence, these people resisted because they did not believe it was fair to be the only group that had to obey all of the rules.

Furthermore, Pricilla's manager was a stickler for rules, and Pricilla worried about getting herself into trouble if she and her staff did not abide by them. So Pricilla's own fear of sanctions from her manager was a strong motivating force in abiding by policies. So was her need for order. She said, "Rules keep things in perspective, in control. They reduce chaos."

With these words, Pricilla revealed something very important about herself. Her need for order and control was linked to her personal way of surviving in what she perceived was a disorderly world. Had I not been so focused on an agenda, had I been more open to Pricilla's point of view from the start and more willing to let things happen, I might have learned this significant piece of information at the beginning of our journey rather than at the end. We all have our own ways of coping and surviving in organizational life. Perhaps this is where all of our stories should begin.

For More Depth

Cirlot, J. E. *A Dictionary of Symbols*. New York: Philosophical Library, 1962.

Gallwey, W. Timothy. *The Inner Game of Tennis* (rev. ed.). New York: Random House, 1997.

Jung, Carl G. *The Basic Writings of C.G. Jung*. New York: Modern Library, 1993.

Lamb, Wally. *I Know This Much Is True* (Reprint). New York: Regan Books, 1999.

Morgan, Gareth. *Images of Organization* (2nd ed.). Walnut Creek, CA: AltaMira Press, 1999.

Wolfe, Thomas. *You Can't Go Home Again.* New York: HarperPerennial, 1998.

Wouk, Herman. *Youngblood Hawke: A Novel.* Boston, MA: Little Brown, 1992.

About the Contributor

Andrea Markowitz is an independent consultant and assistant professor of industrial/organizational psychology at the University of Baltimore.

3

The Power of the Question

The alternative to basing service on advice is to put more faith in questions. We often serve our clients more through the questions we ask than by any advice we give. Questions have a life and power of their own; they carry a message independent of how they are answered. As we mentioned in the previous section of this book, the traditional stance of the consultant is to give answers. Too little attention is given to the impact of the questions we ask. In traditional social science we have separated the researcher from the subject. We act as if we can study something without changing it. This is an illusion, for when we are dealing with anything that is alive, it is always adapting to its environment. So the way we inquire affects what we are interested in.

Some questions carry a message of judgmental scrutiny. For example, have you ever asked juniors in college what they are going to do when they get out of school? Not nice. Another type of unfriendly question is to ask someone with a problem, "What are you going to do about it?" Ten percent of the time, this question might be useful, but most of the time it is subtly condescending. It pretends that the person never thought of that until we came along. It carries the message of our impatience with their confusion and our need for them to get on with it. It expresses our need for closure; it is a measure of our anxiety with an untidy world. Action questions serve to shut down the conversation and keep the understanding at the level at which it began.

The greatest value of questions is to deepen our mutual understanding of people and the world in which they live. Our goal is depth, not speed or quick resolution. Here are some categories of questions—all useful, some with more power than others.

DISCOVERY QUESTIONS

Some questions are purely diagnostic; they get people thinking about their work and their institution. These are the questions we are all trained to ask. They are the questions of science, social science in our case. They are asked from the perspective of the observer, as though the observer were independent of what is being watched.

Discovery questions are familiar to us. A long discussion of them is in *Flawless Consulting* and in every other book that deals with organizational assessment and diagnosis. Discovery questions are what the client expects of us. They are comforting to consultant and client alike, for they primarily focus on the external world, the supposed "objective" view of what exists outside ourselves. They are questions in pursuit of a picture. Although they have value to the person answering them, that is not their basic point. The message they carry is that the future will be created by better information and rational planning.

The particulars of these questions will vary with the nature of our expertise, and most surveys fall into this category. Their intent is data, their use is analysis, their risk is low. And this is their appeal.

CONSUMER QUESTIONS

Other questions are those a vendor or supplier would ask. Those being questioned are treated as consumers. The questions are: What do you want? What do you need? How do you feel about what you are getting? For consultants these questions are part of contracting: Tell me what your needs are, and I'll see if I can supply them. When we ask these questions our stance is one of marketing.

People love to answer these questions because they carry the implied promise that what they want can be satisfied. Questions of wants and desires are seductive because they affirm the desires of those answering and promise something that the person cannot quite achieve without your help.

CONTROL QUESTIONS

We are also familiar with questions designed to make a point. Leading questions are a way of withholding our intent and putting the

weight on the destination we have in mind. They are questions designed to persuade. They take us to a predictable end point. We know where we are headed and we use the interrogative to get there. Perry Mason was the master of these in the courtroom. He would time the questions so that the criminal would be exposed to the jury right at the end of the hour. His talent was as much in timing the question as it was in framing it.

Parenting relies on control questions for part of its lifeblood: "Why were you home late?" "Who didn't put their dishes away?" Trainers also use control questions with a certain finesse: "What are the six characteristics of a good leader?" "What were the times of peak performance and the conditions under which it occurred?"

Traditional sales training raised the use of control questions to an art form. It used to (perhaps still does) teach how to ask questions to lead people to the right answer. I sold encyclopedias one summer. When the prospect came to the door, we were instructed to show a picture of the books and ask, "If Colliers were to place these books in your home at no cost to you, would they be something you would value and appreciate having?" If they answered yes to this qualifying question, they were in for a forty-five minute sales pitch that was so clever that, for the first two weeks I was selling the books, I thought I was doing them a favor.

Control questions work. They have been a management tool through the ages. But the cost of using them is that they quietly alienate us from one another. They keep us in charge without risking the exposure of controlling directly.

DEEPENING QUESTIONS

There is a fourth type of question that raises the stakes higher and makes genuine change more likely. These are questions whose purpose is to engage the person. Not for the sake of analysis, not to persuade or control, but really to engage people with themselves. They are the questions of the therapist, coach, or philosopher.

The counterpoint to defining our value by the advice we give is to measure our value by the depth and compassion of the questions we ask. We increase our offer to the client as we develop our capacity to devise questions that confront them with themselves, which is really to confront them with their freedom. Joel Henning has a talent for using sentence completion as a way of taking people deeper. For example, some of the sentences he asks people to complete are:

- I lose power when I. . . .
- I acted confused when. . . .
- The refusal I have been avoiding is. . . .
- The loss I am reluctant to grieve is. . . .

This use of sentence completion gently forces us to face our defenses against moving forward. It supports us in our caution, yet exposes it at the same time. You can construct questions like this around any consulting project you are engaged in. Every change effort involves power, confusion, the ability to say no, the experience of loss and grief. There is no answer to these feelings, only acknowledgment and expression.

Whatever form they take, deepening questions acknowledge the paradoxical nature of life. They carry the message that choices in life are difficult, that anxiety is a natural condition. They are questions for which any answer, given honestly, is the right answer. Their message is that when we are stuck in work or life, an important element is our need to escape from our responsibility in creating the situation for which we seek help. Our rationalizations, blame, helplessness, confusion, and intellectualizing are forms of retreat, and they keep us from coming to terms with our own accountability.

What moves us toward more accountability and releases commitment and passion is to see the choice in front of us more clearly—and to know that the choice is between two valid paths, and that this is part of the human condition. This insight allows us to depersonalize the problem and thereby move beyond it. And it comes from questions that take us deeper into our own experience and connect the head, the heart, and the spirit. When this connection occurs, something shifts.

The skill of the philosopher, artist, or therapist is to construct questions that are difficult to defend against. Their questions gently request a hard inward look, without any implication that there is one right answer. The power of the deepening question is that whatever the answer, we are hooked, emotionally involved. Unable to escape. Guilty of being human, guilty only of one crime: Having been born. Guilt is the doorway to accountability. Guilt means I have made a choice and am faced with the prospect of saying no, running the risk of hurting or disappointing another, becoming vulnerable myself. These deeply personal concerns are at stake in each of our seemingly rational consulting projects. To not raise these questions is to proceed without emotional engagement.

As consultants, we may retreat from deepening questions, claiming that we have not been trained as philosophers or therapists. Well, we are in that role, training or not. And besides, it is life that trains us to care and have compassion, not higher education. The problem is that we find it hard to ask others a question that we are not willing to answer ourselves. Perhaps the real reluctance against going deeper with our clients is that we do not want to go there ourselves. Also we may doubt our ability to respond to the client's most personal concerns. What is needed at moments of personal questioning is a friend, and this is training we have all received, and given.

The point here is to treat all our questions as important, worthy of reflection, careful choice, and alignment between the question and the intent. There is a value to the question that transcends the answer. It also means that we help create the world that we try to understand, just by the effort to understand it and the way that we do it.

Chapter 13

Making the System Fully Known to Itself
Discovery As a Collaborative Process

Jill Janov

Jill Janov has a genius for working with the collective. Her eyes are always on the learning community, the system. Her fundamental question is "What will help people stay connected to each other?" She also expresses great faith in our capacity to see our own possibilities and to know our own solutions. In this article, she offers a whole series of questions that, when answered collectively, both create community and move people to a desired future.

Although much has been written about the field of organization development, little has been written about the change in nature of the OD consultant's role from directing change to partnering in change. In the beginning, the consulting role was conceived as one of change agent—a person who planned and implemented change. Today, however, many of us conceive of our work as scaffolding that supports a system in understanding and changing itself. But nowhere do our notions about our role have more impact than when it comes to how we support our client systems in becoming fully known to themselves. This process is one of discovery, and this essay focuses on discovery as a collaborative process.

125

SOME HISTORY

Given the industrial era paradigm of command and control, it is not surprising that OD consultants were conceived of as change agents, capable of "unfreezing" an organization's steady state, introducing something new, and then "refreezing" the organization into a new steady state. The skills that were required to perform this feat were ones of contracting, diagnosis, feedback, and implementation. If we have been paying attention to our work, we know that we do not have this much control. Organizations are living systems: They are not machines. There are no levers that we can push, no switches we can throw, no gears we can mesh when we engage human beings. Our work requires us to pay attention to what enlivens people, because without people there are no organizations. In particular, we need to pay attention to how we support these living systems in knowing and changing themselves.

THE CURRENT REALITY

In my mind, OD consultants are perturbers. In the best sense of that word, we disturb the status quo. If we are of value, it is because we are a presence that is otherwise absent in a system. We are challenged to be enough like the client system to not be rejected and enough unlike it to bring a different point of view to those with whom we work. We not so much plan and implement change as we perturb the systems that retain us. We do this by helping the system to convene and engage its constituents in ways that make the system fully known to itself—ways that support the unleashing of its full potential. Our work has lasting impact when our client systems develop these same skills of convening and engagement.

To be good at perturbing, we need to be skilled in four phases of consultation—developing the relationship, discovery, design, and deployment (which includes evaluation). We cannot consult without first developing a relationship, both with the client (the one who pays our fee) and the client system (those impacted by our work). Social contracting is critical to developing a good client relationship. It is a

skill that is too often omitted in graduate programs in OD and one that is not learned in the school of hard knocks. Yet it is at the heart of good consultation. So goes the contracting, so goes the relationship and, thereby, as a result, the engagement. Good contracting enables you and the client to know what your relationship will be.

DISCOVERY: THE HEART OF THE MATTER

Once consultation is agreed on, both the consultant and the client system need to uncover the organization's current reality (what is) and future aspirations (what is possible). This phase of consultation is all about *discovery*. Discovery differs in significant ways from diagnosis. Diagnosis is based on a medical model of finding what ails the system. More and more, consultation is focusing on finding what is healthy in the system and then using that health to achieve new goals. "Appreciative inquiry," which was developed by David Copperrider, is an example of a discovery process that engages people in dialogues about what is healthy in their current reality. My own goal in working with a client is to uncover both what is healthy about and what ails the organization. I first create greater awareness of what is—what works and what does not, what is difficult and why, what is possible, and what supports such possibilities. To do discovery well, I need to convene the system (or at least a microcosm of the system) and engage it in its own discovery process.

The Basis for Discovery

The basis for discovery is rooted in a consultant's view of her own expertise, her stance, and her practice theory. Every consultant lays claim to some expertise, whether it is about the competitive environment, the design of work processes, structures, strategies, or other knowledge that creates organizational capacity. How that expertise is used is what I call my "stance." It is how I enter the client system. My stance can be one of being a presence that is otherwise absent in the system or my stance can be one that exacerbates the conditions that prompted the client to call me in the first place. My stance impacts

every phase of consultation, and most particularly discovery. Most consultants, including those who engage the system in the design and deployment phases, conduct discovery in an expert mode. They act as if discovery is something done to a system, rather than being a collaborative process that is done with the system. Their mistake is in being the expert, versus using their expertise to engage the system in its own discovery.

My practice theory includes my beliefs about organizations and how they work. I believe the wisdom is in the system, not in the consultant. Further, I believe it is important to make visible what is invisible, which most often tends to be people's talents and potential. I also believe that progress is not a straight trajectory into the stratosphere: Rather, progress is made by building a mile of road, then driving a mile of road, then building another mile, and so on. My contribution to "what is possible" is made by helping my clients see themselves as a system—as a series of relationships in action. Therefore, I need to work in ways that help the system to know itself. I do this by engaging the system in gathering its own data, making meaning of that data, and then choosing what it wants to do.

No matter the intended intervention, be it training, redesign of work processes, development of a new vision or strategy, or whatever, the way in which a consultant handles discovery will reinforce what is either mechanistic or humanistic in the organization's culture. Mechanistic, command and control cultures tend to create conditions that reinforce passive, withholding, uncommitted, disengaged employees who work in silos, often compete for scarce resources, and do not see themselves as accountable for the whole of the enterprise. Humanistic cultures tend to create conditions that reinforce self-organized, interactive, participative, committed, accountable, and engaged employees who work interdependently in pursuit of a common cause.

When a consultant's stance is that of an expert or extra pair of hands, the discovery process tends to reinforce what is mechanistic in the organization. For example, in the expert mode, the consultant interviews individuals and groups, then analyzes the data and feeds it back, often only to the client and not the entire system from which the data

was gathered. In the extra pair of hands mode, the consultant works at the client's behest. Therefore, the process designated by the client will tend to reinforce cultural norms—often the ones the client seeks to change. Most often, clients are unaware that their dictates are reinforcing the very conditions they seek to change.

In contrast, when the consultant's stance is that of a collaborator, the discovery process tends to reinforce what is alive in the organization. In this stance, discovery involves engaging the system so that the system itself not only creates the data, but also connects the dots that form the picture that results from the data. It is important to emphasize that the consultant does not connect the dots—rather the consultant creates the conditions for the system to do this for itself.

SOME EXAMPLES OF COLLABORATIVE DISCOVERY

Some of my own work with discovery engaged fifty people in a 250-person office of a national law firm in uncovering why no one felt responsible for the paper generated by the firm. Partners, special counsel, associates, floor coordinators, legal assistants, secretaries, document production, and facilities management people discovered new options for changing the system from one designed around discreet job descriptions to one designed around shared accountability and real partnership among all work associates. Another discovery process involved sixty individuals in an 18,000-person health care system in a four-hour dialogue on the purpose of the system and ways in which current structures and norms thwarted or supported achieving that purpose. Yet another involved forty employees in a 180-person philanthropic foundation in discovering individual and collective learning and development needs and the means to support such needs. And yet another involved a microcosm of the staff functions in a newly merged national organization to determine which staff support systems needed to be combined, which needed to remain separate, ways in which each function could support the whole of the organization, and ways in which individuals in the newly combined staff functions could support one another as they pursued the greater mission of supporting the entire enterprise. In all of these examples, the design of the discovery process also was collaborative, involving eight to ten individuals who would participate in the actual discovery process. They worked with me on what questions needed to be asked, to whom they needed to be asked, and how to best create an environment in which it was safe to disclose the truth.

Whether we view it as diagnosis or discovery, at its core the process is one of finding out what the system knows about itself and whether there is energy to do anything about what is discovered. The way in which discovery is done will either make the system dependent on a consultant or interdependent within itself.

ENGAGING THE SYSTEM VERSUS CONNECTING THE DOTS

In an expert stance, the consultant is at the center of the discovery process, interviewing and gathering data, then analyzing that data—what I call connecting the dots to form a picture—and then feeding that data back to the system. It is the consultant who makes meaning of the data and it is the consultant's meaning that forms the picture that is fed back to the system. In a collaborative mode, the consultant partners with the system to create a container in which discovery occurs and then engages the system (or a microcosm of the system) in making its own meaning. Every person, in hearing every other person, is better able to distill his or her own experience and connect that experience with experiences of others. In so doing, the system comes to know itself—both as it is and as it can be.

What I do in the discovery phase sets up how the client system will engage itself in the other phases of consulting—design and deployment. How I work with the client system during discovery says everything about the alignment of my behavior with the behavioral norms desired by the client. A client system may be interested in work redesign, end-to-end business process re-engineering, total quality management (TQM), enterprise resource planning, future search, or any of a myriad of interventions aimed at creating greater organiza-

tional effectiveness and capacity. How these processes are introduced, and how the system is engaged in choosing whether or not such processes are relevant, timely, and fit the ways in which the system seeks to be, say everything about the kinds of outcomes that will be achieved. If we want to amplify what is alive rather than what is mechanistic in the systems in which we work, we need to focus on discovery as a collaborative process.

Example of a Discovery Process

To discover the learning and development needs of a foundation's staff, the following questions were developed and used.

Context Questions

- What do you need to know about the foundation to be an effective member of its staff?
- What are you certain about with respect to the foundation?
- What uncertainties face the foundation?

Purpose and Content Questions

- What learning needs to occur for you?
- Of what you need to learn, which are the core skills, knowledge, or competencies?
- What learning in others would be helpful to you in your work?
- What impact, if any, should training, development, and learning have on those the foundation serves?

Locus of Responsibility/Systemic Issues Questions

- Who should decide what to include in training, development, and learning, and why?
- Who should provide training, development, and learning, and why (e.g., program directors or officers, managers and supervisors, manager of training and development, outside consultants, peers)?
- Who should evaluate training, development, and learning, and why?

- What impact, if any, should training, development, and learning have on staffing (numbers and levels of people, retention), structure (silos), roles (generalist/specialist), rewards and recognition (performance management), or the foundation (culture and values)?

Policy, Timing, and Cost Questions

- What policies serve training, development, and learning (e.g., should these be mandatory core skills or technological skills, or voluntary)?
- What are the responsibilities of the learners for themselves and others (e.g., to support their own learning and that of others, to bring back learning to peers and others)?
- When you think of your role, do you think of your job, your function, or the work of the foundation, and what causes you to think this way?
- Should training, development, and learning be based on the work of a function, a skills matrix, or a job description?

How and When Questions

- How much time and cost per year should be devoted to training, development, and learning?
- What policies should guide payment of tuition?

Place Questions

- What combination of training, development, and learning should be supported—on-the-job, rotation, cross training, intranet, external websites, professional affiliations, conferences, college and university, on-site classroom—and how much of each (what percentage)?
- What organizational layout best supports a learning culture?
- What processes and technology best support learning?

Summarization Question

- What word, phrase, or one sentence describes what you discovered today?

For More Depth

Further Reading

Benne, K., W. Bennis, & R. Chin (Eds.). *Planned Change.* New York: Holt, Rinehart and Winston, 1961.

Cooperrider, David L., Peter F. Sorensen, Jr., Diana Whitney, and Therese F. Yaeger (Eds.). *Appreciative Inquiry: Rethinking Human Organization Toward a Positive Theory of Change.* Champaign, IL: Stipes Publishing, 1999.

Janov, Jill. *The Inventive Organization: Hope and Daring at Work.* San Francisco: Jossey-Bass, 1994.

Lippitt, Gordon L., & Ronald Lippitt. *The Consulting Process in Action* (2nd ed.). San Francisco: Jossey-Bass/Pfeiffer, 1986.

Nevis, Edwin C. *Organizational Consulting: A Gestalt Approach.* Hillsdale, NJ: Analytic Press, 1987.

Wheatley, Margaret J. *Leadership and the New Science: Discovering Order in a Chaotic World* (2nd ed.). San Francisco: Berrett-Koehler, 1999.

Whyte, David. *Fire in the Earth.* Langley, WA.: Many Rivers Press, 1992.

Whyte, David. *House of Belonging: Poems.* Langley, WA: Many Rivers Press, 1996.

Further Training

The Gestalt Institute in Cleveland's Organization and Systems Development Program. www.gestaltcleveland.org.

The Berkana Institute. www.berkana.org.

About the Contributor

Jill Janov consults internationally to public and privately held corporations, government agencies, educational institutions, and nonprofits and is the author of *The Inventive Organization: Hope and Daring at Work* (Jossey-Bass, 1994). Her firm, Jill Janov Associates, is in Denver, Colorado.

Chapter 14

Two Sides

Idries Shah

Part-colored dervish robes, since copied for teaching purposes and eventually imitated for sheer decoration, were introduced into Spain, in the Middle Ages, in this manner:

A Frankish king had a taste for pageantry, and he also prided himself on his grasp of philosophy. He asked a Sufi known as "The Agarin" to instruct him in the High Wisdom.

The Agarin said: "We offer you observation and reflection, but first you must learn their extension."

"We already know how to extend our attention, having studied well all the preliminary steps to wisdom from our own tradition," said the king.

"Very well," said the Agarin, "we shall give your Majesty a demonstration of our teaching at a pageant tomorrow."

Arrangements were duly made, and the next day the dervishes of the Agarin's teaching center filed through the narrow streets of that Andalusian town. The king and his courtiers were assembled on either side of the route: grandees on the right and men-at-arms on the left.

When the procession was over, the Agarin turned to the king and said: "Majesty, please ask your knights, from opposite, the colors of the dervish robes."

The knights all swore upon the scriptures and on their honor that the costumes had been blue.

Reprinted by permission from "Two Sides," in *Wisdom of the Idiots* (pp. 47–48) by Idries Shah.

The king and the rest of the Court were amazed and confused, for this was not what they had seen at all. "We all distinctly saw that they were dressed in *brown* habits," said the king, "and among us are men of great sanctity in faith and well respected."

He ordered all his knights to be prepared for punishment and degradation.

Those who saw the clothes as brown were sent to one side to be rewarded.

These proceedings lasted for some time. Afterwards the king said to the Agarin: "What bewitchment is this which can cause the most honorable knights in Christendom to defy truth, abandon their hope of redemption, and betray indications of unreliability which render them useless for battle?"

The Sufi said: "The half of each robe was blue. Without preparation, your expectancy causes you to deceive yourself about us. How can we teach anyone anything under such circumstances?"

The Flawless Consulting Fieldbook and Companion

Chapter 15

Resolving a New Paradox with Old Wisdom

Marvin Weisbord

There is a tendency among consultants to keep shifting their practice to what is new and fashionable. The price we pay for this is that we never really realize the potential of what we offer, nor do we take our clients deep enough to touch their fundamental beliefs. Marvin and his colleague, Sandra Janoff, have the patience and integrity to side-step fashion and persist with a few powerful ideas so as to understand how profound these are and how widely they can be applied. Their "future search" process is a good example of this.

Marvin, along with others involved in large group interventions, has also created a structure that puts the consultant in the background and makes the learning design dominant. This has two advantages: First, it makes the experience for the participants essentially self-governing. This reinforces self-sufficiency and the belief that the future can be created by those who are going to live it. Second, if the value is more in the learning design than in the personal presence and insight of the consultant, it makes the experience easy to teach and thereby easy to spread across the field.

The gifts of focusing on both the depth and the power of the experience are essential to the belief that each person has the capacity, with only a little guidance, to create a workplace and community they believe in. This belief, especially on the part of consultants, is an expression of faith in the human being, faith that we have the potential to transform how we think about learning, to improve performance, and ultimately to bring peace to the world.

For the better part of thirty years, I have passed most of my working hours in task-focused meetings. I say this with some astonishment because going to meetings was last on my needs list when I started consulting in 1969. My self-imposed mission in the 1970s and 1980s was helping people make their workplaces and lives more productive. To this end I met tirelessly in businesses, schools, hospitals, and communities. Rarely did I use the same format twice.

In the last decade, much to my surprise, I have made myself into a one-trick pony. I became immersed in "future search," a structured two- and one-half-day action meeting design that, varying hardly at all, enables culturally diverse groups of sixty to seventy or more persons the world over to do remarkable planning and implementing feats.

My early experiments with this practice began twenty years ago in business firms. The basis for organization development (OD) in those days was training in personal and group skills for communicating, making decisions, planning, managing conflict, and so on. OD practitioners, however, didn't just teach old dogs new tricks; they helped them apply what they learned and (bold claim) learn how to keep learning. Whether training or applying, I often heard a familiar litany: "The wrong people are in the room. Our boss needs this more than we do" or "This is too late. We should have done it last April" or "It's premature" or "I have more important things to do!" At some point, I stopped resisting and joined my clients. I too resolved not to attend meetings too soon or too late, with the wrong people in the room, for tasks few people cared about. I found that activities tended to go better built

The Flawless Consulting Fieldbook and Companion

around whole system tasks that the right people wanted to do right now. And I accepted that my job was to insist that they stay engaged long enough to do what they said they wanted to do.

I also found that most people already knew enough to improve their work lives and organizations. What they lacked was enough time and access to the right others. Such structural defects, unlike personality, "style," and skills, are easy to remedy. So future search became a set of simple principles. Start by getting "the whole system in the room." Explore the whole—personal, global, local, past, present and future— before trying to fix any part. Put problems and conflicts on hold. Establish common ground and see who wants to act. Invite people to take responsibility for the whole. No teaching, no experts. All interaction, all the time.

I first described these precepts in a book called *Productive Workplaces* (1987). I was astonished to receive letters and phone calls from dozens of people who had made up meeting designs based on a chapter in that book. They found that by thinking principles rather than techniques they could do things they had not done before. Stimulated by this, I set out to learn more. This led to *Discovering Common Ground* (1992) in which I and thirty-five others described a theory and practice for successful large group collaboration.

THE PARADOX

In 1993, prodded by local colleagues, Sandra Janoff and I, having run many future searches together, started a practitioner network dedicated to service, colleagueship, and learning. We began running future search learning workshops, giving away what we were doing as a small bit toward making the world a better place. To our surprise, people started adapting the principles and techniques in ways we never imagined. Whether trained or self-taught, they were taking future search into improbable situations in remote locales. The process seemed to help groups from diverse cultures bridge gaps of ethnicity, gender, race, age, occupation, class, and culture. And it also caught on in traditional societies beset by conflicts, technological change, and social problems.

My OD experience told me that what "works" in industry did not translate easily to schools, for example, or communities, and that methods invented in the first world didn't travel well to the third. Yet here was a way of doing things that seemed to have no boundaries of sector or culture. Future search was like a big empty bottle into which people could pour their hopes, fears, and intentions. It accommodated a wide range of languages, world views, and ways of being. This contradicted all my previous experience.

How to account for the successes of Mike Bell working with the Inuit of the Arctic? Or Katharine Esty and Gil Steil with UNICEF in Bangladesh, who with a few future searches started a ripple that has spread through South Asia and into Africa, opening the door to Kim Martens' work in Pakistan, Sri Lanka, Thailand, and South Africa and to the Bangladeshi consultant Anish Barua's work with Sharad Sapra, an Indian UNICEF project director in Iran? And Kees Jan Bender, who is Dutch, and his Australian colleague Colin Pidd in Zimbabwe with media people from across Southern Africa? And Tony Richardson, an expatriate Englishman, with Aborigines in Australia, and suburbanite Jan Williams with Native Americans, and city-dwellers Michelle Woods and Marilyn Sifford in both inner cities and rural areas in the United States?

Not only were our colleagues getting a charge from watching people grow their capacity for constructive action, but they got significant personal growth for themselves—greater patience, less anxiety, more openness. How could so much collective energy be mobilized with no strategic plan among a loose network of highly individualistic people? Why did such processes lead to unusual insights, new forms of cooperation, and extended action, when more elaborate, highly conceptualized planning systems often left people demoralized, mystified, and stuck? This was my paradox.

At one learning workshop I posed this question to an Indian friend, Bapu Deolalikar, who has consulted all over the world. "What you have here," said Bapu matter-of-factly, "is relatively culture-free." Neither Sandra nor I ever imagined we could transcend our own culture. Nor did we intend to. So we had a hard time digesting Bapu's comment. Nonetheless, encouraged by his puzzling observation, we issued a progress report on our learning, *Future Search: An Action Guide,* in the fall of 1995.

SITTING WITH THE PARADOX

A few weeks later I found myself sitting (unconsciously) with my question and Bapu's answer in an introductory seminar at the School of Philosophy and Healing in Action (SOPHIA), an integral program of the Traditional Acupuncture Institute (TAI) in Columbia, Maryland. I had had acupuncture regularly since the mid-80s. So I knew about needles and the flow of healing energy, sometimes fast and obvious, sometimes slow and subtle, that treatment could bring. My son Bob, later manager of TAI's clinical program, was then a student and enthusiastic about this evolving practice for lay people in which "words are needles." SOPHIA enables growth through awareness and responsibility for one's own and others' well-being. Its explicit goals include observing nature, confirming wholeness and the unity of life, and reducing suffering in the world.

Robert Duggan and Dianne Connelly founded the Traditional Acupuncture Institute in the early 1970s, the first such school in the United States to teach five-element acupuncture. They are also SOPHIA's godparents. Connelly and Duggan called their seminar "Redefining Health: Exploring an Ancient Approach to Personal Growth, Balance and Health," its purpose being to apply "the wisdom of Chinese philosophy to everyday life." Moreover, they had integrated Taoist teachings with such diverse disciplines as Jungian and Gestalt psychology, phenomenology, anthropology, linguistics, Ivan Illich's work, and a broad range of holistic health practices.

Although I knew some of their sources, many SOPHIA words and concepts were new to me, and at first a little strange, for example, a numerology of fives (elements, seasons, senses), sevens (domains), and twelves (officials, pathways). Although I struggled with the words, I found the music reassuring. Bob and Dianne attended to what was happening rather than to what they wished would happen, made no

judgments of individuals or group, accepted all statements as useful for learning, and sought to ground the conversation in first-hand experience. Oddly enough, their group leadership mirrored some of what Sandra and I had learned over many years constituted good future search facilitation. Now, sitting as a participant, I could enjoy the luxury of watching or jumping in as I chose, and I realized how freeing it was not to have to do any one thing or reach any particular place.

In one activity, volunteers "walk the seasons," using a large chart of circles on the floor displaying the five elements on which acupuncture is based. The chart is headed "Inquiry into a Concern." Each circle corresponds to a season in nature and can be imagined as energy moving within us in circular fashion from fall (metal) into winter (water), spring (wood), summer (fire), and late summer (earth). As many people know, each season puts us in touch with different sensory experiences and emotions. Within these are clues to what we need more of or less of to keep our lives in balance.

Walking the circles, people pause at each season and talk about a problem they have selected. (In the water place—winter—for example, the instruction is to "listen through like and dislike" and "don't try to fix it.") So doing, people teach themselves about every aspect of the problem and discover constructive things to do. I was moved to see a man work out a thorny relationship with his child. As he walked the seasons, speaking of denial, guilt, and anger, he came to a place of caring and resolve, replacing harsh judgments with acceptance and love. I found that an altogether extraordinary thirty minutes.

Listening to this man repair a long-buried part of himself, I happened to glance at another chart, summarizing other aspects of five-element theory. It was labeled "Conditions for Treating, Teaching, Learning, for Effective Actions for Life," reproduced below. Suddenly, I felt a shiver tickle my spine, tugging at my unanswered question. Future search—I was watching a future search by a group of one! Incredibly, if you start with the metal (fall) and proceed clockwise to earth (late summer), you have a journey that corresponds to an uncanny degree with the future search process.

The Flawless Consulting Fieldbook and Companion

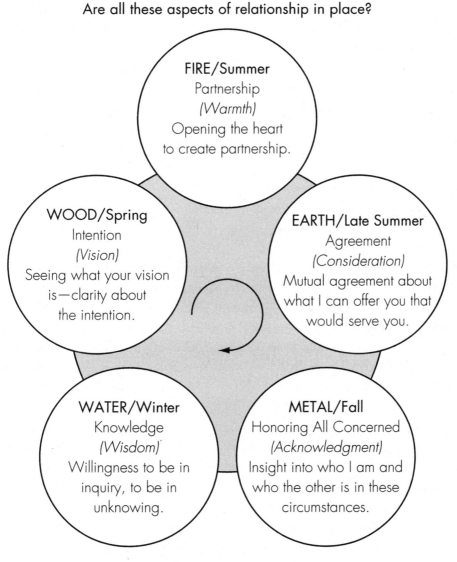

Are all these aspects of relationship in place?

FIRE/Summer
Partnership
(Warmth)
Opening the heart
to create partnership.

WOOD/Spring
Intention
(Vision)
Seeing what your vision
is—clarity about
the intention.

EARTH/Late Summer
Agreement
(Consideration)
Mutual agreement about
what I can offer you that
would serve you.

WATER/Winter
Knowledge
(Wisdom)
Willingness to be in
inquiry, to be in
unknowing.

METAL/Fall
Honoring All Concerned
(Acknowledgment)
Insight into who I am and
who the other is in these
circumstances.

Figure 15.1. Ongoing Conditions for Treating, Teaching, and Learning

Copyright © 1992 by The Traditional Acupuncture Institute.

There are five phases to a future search—the Past, Present, Future, Common Ground, and Action Planning. Each involves an inquiry into the experience of all participants. A future search starts by validating everyone's past ("honoring all concerned"), proceeds to the complexity and confusion of the present ("willingness to be in inquiry, to be in unknowing"), invites visions of an ideal future ("seeing what your vision is"), helps people discover common ground ("opening the heart to create partnership"), then moves to action planning ("mutual agreement about what I can offer"). That much I learned in the hour following my initial awareness.

SPEAKING WITH THE ANCIENTS

Now, it so happens that around the same time, Sandra Janoff and I were planning a future search with residents of Ko'olau Loa, a district of seven villages on the North Shore of Oahu, Hawaii. It would take place four months later in the islands' most heavily native-Hawaiian district, including also people from New Guinea, Togo, Tahiti, the Philippines, Guam, China, Japan, and the mainland United States. We already had witnessed how our steering group planned to ritualize their future search. They had embedded our work in ceremonies involving hand-made wreaths, Hawaiian-language chants, dancing, a "talk story" evening, and a conceptual framework to be included in workbooks. The latter explicitly reacquainted people with ancient beliefs in the oneness of mind, body, and spirit, and the inexorable links of person to family, neighborhood, community, and society that underlie many Pacific cultures (Janoff & Weisbord, 1997).

Back in Maryland, sitting with the circle of seasons, I caught my first glimmer of what the Hawaiians were teaching us that I would later come to appreciate. When Sandra asked, as we do in every planning meeting, how far back in time they needed to explore to understand their district, they had replied without hesitation: "Two thousand years!"

Following that future search, we watched with wonder as Ko'olau Loa residents took leadership in a host of projects—revamping school

curriculums, putting young people on community boards, integrating Western and traditional Hawaiian medicine, saving a local hospital, and reopening a day care center. What in the world was going on here?

IS THIS A PARADIGM?

For five years I have mulled over the connections between what I learned that weekend in Maryland and what happened in Hawaii. As I ponder my experience, I return always to the same place. What for twenty years I had labeled "new paradigm" social change processes are those that reconnect us with long-buried parts of our collective psyches, the natural rhythms of life. By stripping away management and OD language, removing the self-defeating demands of traditional facilitation, encouraging people to learn from one another, and enabling participants to use their diverse realities in service of vital tasks, my future search colleagues and I had stumbled our way back to an ancient place of mutual support and innate wisdom.

Dropping some of our once-revered categories such as diagnosis, resistance, personal styles, problem solving, conflict, and other stuff that needs fixing, we were helping people access latent parts of themselves that our society had put aside long ago to get on with the industrial revolution. As children of our own culture, so had we. People have known the oneness of mind, body, spirit, and community for thousands of years. No wonder modern Hawaiians called their future search a "Ho'o'pono," the ancient communal practice of conflict management meaning "to make things right."

Creating successful group processes based on archetypal patterns is not a matter of patching together techniques. Rather, it involves observing what actually happens when you take one step and follow it with another. The global success of future search and similar processes across diverse cultures cannot be explained by the techniques. To make things right, we have to do things right. That becomes possible when we go beyond a fixation on techniques and our need to look good and pay attention to our senses. Paradoxically, that is ancient wisdom. It involves no paradigm at all.

REDEFINING FUTURE SEARCH

I am confident that my comments, based on future search, apply equally to many processes informed by similar principles. Pondering what I learned about redefining health in SOPHIA and my work since 1996 in diverse cultures from Seattle to Singapore, Orange County to India, I have a new take on why paradigm may be beside the point. We come unstuck, move, grow, and develop one season at a time. Such is the common ground that binds every person who ever lived to every other. We are members of a single race, equally human. As we travel the whole cycle of the seasons in concert with others, we are more likely to live fulfilling lives and to do satisfying work.

Moreover, our collective unconscious may have given us another gift. Future search evolved as a set of very specific activities or tasks, by means of which we access the past, present, and future. In another time and place, these shared practices might have been an essential rite of passage defining a particular society. Every culture, every religion has rituals. They function to enable people to navigate significant life passages and mark them as special. Future search, I think now, serves as a kind of secular rite of passage, enabling people to do things tomorrow they could not do yesterday in order to get from here to there. This could not happen, I am convinced, if the impulse, the need, the capacity, and the deep desire for this experience were not already embedded in all of our psyches.

The making of time lines, the creation of a group mind map, the acting out of dreams as if they have come true, the placing of all aspirations on a "common ground wall" are repeated over and over again—in Africa, Asia, Australia, Europe, and North and South America, by people who have never met in service of tasks that are uniquely their own. In a world in which diversity has become the norm, few traditional rites and rituals survive intact, let alone cross the bridge from their indigenous roots to mainstream society. A diverse society needs rites of passage that bind us all. Future search, I believe, is one of them. The rituals of future search, largely culture free, belong to no one. Therefore they can be owned by all.

By supporting conferees in acknowledging one another and the world "as is" and trying out how they want to live together, we may inspire more partnership, clarity of vision, wise choices, and effective action than I, at least, with my vast inventory of "interventions," dreamed possible two decades ago. Now, having put away most of my tool kit, I find myself learning to do less so that others may discover they are ready, willing, and able to do more. Maybe now, as the awesome stresses of cyber-science overwhelm us, our strong primal urges for dignity, meaning, and community may help us relearn how, using simple meeting processes, we can live the Biblical injunction to make "a time for every purpose under heaven."

None of this, I fear, squares with the "shorter, faster, cheaper" frenzy by which we deprive ourselves of common sense and the evidence of our senses. So I understand my stubborn reluctance to shorten a future search. Or, indeed, to compromise many key aspects that hundreds of colleagues have validated with great courage among the world's cultures. Together we are rediscovering what our ancestors once knew. To have a bountiful fall harvest, we cannot cut corners. There is, regardless of the work we do, something deeply necessary about savoring all the possibilities of winter, summer, and spring.

For More Depth

Further Reading

Berman, Morris. *Coming to Our Senses: Body and Spirit in the Hidden History of the West.* Seattle, WA: Seattle Writers' Guild, 1998.

Connelly, Dianne M. *Traditional Acupuncture: The Law of the Five Elements.* Columbia, MD.: Traditional Acupuncture Institute, 1991.

Janoff, Sandra, & Marvin Weisbord. "Speaking with the Ancients," *Healthcare Forum Journal,* May-June, 1997, pp 26–34.

Sheldrake, Rupert. *The Presence of the Past: Morphic Resonance and the Habits of Nature.* New York: Vintage Books, 1989.

Sullivan, John Greenfelder. *To Come to Life More Fully: An East-West Journey.* Columbia, MD.: Traditional Acupuncture Institute, 1990.

Weimer, Joan Myers. *Back Talk: Teaching Lost Selves to Speak.* Chicago, IL: University of Chicago Press, 1996.

Weisbord, Marvin. *Productive Workplaces: Organizing and Managing for Dignity, Meaning and Community.* San Francisco: Jossey-Bass, 1987.

Weisbord, Marvin, & Sandra Janoff. *Future Search: An Action Guide to Finding Common Ground in Organizations and Communities* (2nd ed.). San Francisco: Berrett-Koehler, 2000.

Weisbord, Marvin, & 35 International Authors. *Discovering Common Ground.* San Francisco: Berrett-Koehler, 1992.

Further Training

Future Search Network sponsors two seminars, "The Future Search Learning Workshop," and "Facilitating the Whole System in the Room." For information call 800–951–6333 or go to *www.futuresearch.net.*

SOPHIA (The School of Philosophy and Healing in Action) runs many courses year round. Call the registrar at 410-997–4888. TAI is changing its name in 2000 to TAI SOPHIA and becoming a holistic university of many disciplines.

About the Contributor

Marvin Weisbord is co-director (with Sandra Janoff) of the Future Search Network. His most recent books, *Discovering Common Ground* (Berrett-Koehler, 1992) and *Future Search* (2nd ed.), with Sandra Janoff, (Berrett-Koehler, 2000) describe the Future Search process. His *Productive Workplaces: Organizing and Managing for Dignity, Meaning, and Community* (Jossey-Bass, 1987) is an organizational development classic.

The Flawless Consulting Fieldbook and Companion

Chapter 16
Change Is in the Details

Peter Block

Despite our infatuation with electronic substitutes, a lot of people still attend a lot of meetings. The ones I attend are usually intended to educate, align, enroll, and transform people. It continues to amaze me that most of these meetings are structured in a way that undermines these intentions.

THE ANGEL IN THE DETAILS

The meetings I attend are either public events, at which people from different companies come together to learn and network, or they take place within an organization that is trying to transform its culture or change its way of doing business.

What disturbs me about these meetings is that they are still designed with the same two questions in mind: Who is going to speak, and what are they going to say? Even if the avowed purpose of the meeting is to build community, empowerment, participation, and accountability into the world, the questions remain: "Who is going to speak?" and "What are they going to say?" As long as these remain the critical questions, we are still designing experiences for the sake of the teacher, the leader, and the trainer.

We hold on to the belief that change happens as a result of leaders' actions rather than as a result of engagement and grass roots accountability. In our efforts to transform our organizations, we tend to over-focus on the "larger" questions of strategy and scale.

An earlier version of this chapter appeared as "Large Ideas Expressed in Small Moments" in *News for a Change*, November 1999, published by the Association for Quality and Participation, Cincinnati, Ohio.

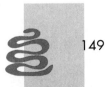

We want to know how to impact the greatest number of people in the smallest amount of time. We talk about large system change. We plot a sequence of events that builds the business case for change and involves top management in supporting the change.

We struggle with ways to enroll people in the change and achieve some alignment in goals and values. We revise the reward system to reinforce the change and design training to build the skills for change. And then we schedule events to launch, roll out, and sustain the effort.

The questions of how we are going to run the meeting, in what kind of room, and with what kind of evaluation are treated as the "smaller" questions. They become a later consideration, literally an afterthought.

I want to reverse what we call the "larger" and the "smaller" questions. The seemingly detailed concerns of how we engage the audience, in what kind of room, evaluated by what kind of questions may have more to do with transforming a culture than the best strategy, structure, or clear, compelling presentation. Transformation is as much a shift in consciousness, a shift in feeling, a change in relationship, as it is a shift in thinking and practices. When we meet for learning, who speaks and what they say make a difference. We do need to be open to new thinking, but it should not dominate our planning. Yet it does. Most learning events still string a list of speakers together and use question-and-answer periods as a way of involving participants.

People who plan the events at which I speak ask me only three questions: When will I arrive, what kind of microphone do I want, and will I be using flip charts, slides, overheads, or video?

I wish planning people would ask me three different questions:

1. How are you going to engage the audience?
2. What kind of room would be appropriate for your purpose? and
3. How are you going to assess how it is going?

These should be the "larger" questions of how we come together to learn and evoke change. Get these questions right, and who speaks and what they say might be brought back into perspective.

  The Flawless Consulting Fieldbook and Companion

KNOWING A GOOD QUESTION
WHEN YOU CREATE ONE

As the authors in this section of the book keep pointing out, we engage people more through the questions we ask than through the answers we offer. We bring people together, fundamentally, to be faced with important questions. What we need to understand is how the construction of a question makes a difference.

A good question has some of these properties:

It Is Ambiguous.
There is no single or clear answer. Each person has an answer, and each is right. The question highlights the complexity and paradoxical nature of change. It invites a diagnostic or inquiring stance rather than a problem-solving stance.

It Is Personal.
We ask people through the question to look at themselves, to disclose a part of themselves that is not part of normal workplace discourse. Learning quickens when we are vulnerable with one another, and the question should invite this.

It Carries the Implication of Individual Accountability.
The question communicates that we are each responsible for creating the situation we are in. We are each, consciously or not, actively sustaining the existing culture and acknowledging that whatever future happens will carry our fingerprints.

Here are some questions that have these engagement-enhancing qualities:

- What crossroads face you at this point in your work/life?
- What do you personally want from the people in your group and what do they want from you?
- What has been your contribution to creating the difficulties facing the unit or the organization?
- What are the payoffs for operating the way we currently do?
- What gifts exist around this circle and in what ways have people brought value to you this day?

Each of these is hard to answer. Each takes some courage to ask honestly and also is hard to defend against. Each carries the message that everyone is guilty (this is a good thing because it means you are living your life) and everyone is also an instrument of hope. Questions like these carry the belief that the struggle is the solution, that the dialogue—triggered by the questions we speak to—may be the point and the true means for shifting culture and our lives.

A friend and colleague, Cliff Bolster, wisely suggests that when we come together, we should call it a conversation instead of a meeting. This makes the detail of how we talk to each other important. Confronting difficult questions, and doing it openly with others that we work or learn with, brings us emotionally into the room far more directly than a good speaker with a strong message.

The search is for questions that are hard to defend against. The key is to invent some of your own questions that fit the intent of the meeting. Make the conversation the purpose of our gathering, and this makes our institutional intent of involvement and personal accountability enacted in the design of each event.

The Flawless Consulting Fieldbook and Companion

Chapter 17

Talk Is Walk
Language and Courage in Action

Peter Koestenbaum

Much of our current thinking about our behavior is influenced by the insights of psychology. Psychology, in its effort to be a legitimate healing science, tends to be focused on diagnosing and curing illness, weakness, and what is *not* working in a person's life. Management thinking and consulting have been heavily influenced by psychology and are filled with ideas of how to reinforce behavior that is valued and extinguish what is not. This has resulted in a body of organizational literature that is flooded with ways to control people and ultimately ways to control ourselves. Peter Koestenbaum brings a stunningly unique perspective to the world of leadership and the workplace. He has spent the last fifteen years of his life retrieving philosophy from its academic isolation and applying it to the unyielding reality of the marketplace.

The marriage between philosophy and business is not easy, although when he speaks, we all sense that there is something profound in what he offers. It was from Peter that I first began to realize that questions of purpose and courage and destiny might apply to my own life, rather than remain as ideals that applied only to those who had achieved some form of greatness. What is particularly important about these ideas is that they offer a way of understanding ourselves that is based on an optimism about our capacity to discover our freedom, face our anxiety, and choose our own future. And at the same time provide leadership to our organizations. Much of my work in the last twenty years is an outgrowth of Peter's insights, so it is a pleasure to include his voice within these pages.

"A man can be destroyed but not defeated."

Ernest Hemingway

This book is titled a fieldbook and companion and a "field book" means action. What might a philosopher mean by action? Action is words. Words can be words only, which means inaction, but there are also words that do things—action words. Consider a minister or a justice of the peace who says, "I now pronounce you husband and wife!" This is an example of doing things—and important ones at that—with words. A judge says, "I sentence you to the penitentiary!" and indeed the official is *acting* in a most pronounced way. During the Cuban Missile Crisis, President John F. Kennedy appeared on television and announced to the world that an attack from Cuba on any Latin American nation would be viewed as an attack by Russia on the United States. That pronouncement was words and words only—but words that changed the course of history.

When two CEOs sign a document activating a merger or a president signs legislation, you have mere words meaning real action—and powerful action at that. Treaties are words, constitutions are words, court opinions interpreting statutes are more words. Spending money is done with words. Selling is done with words, and so is buying. Some words are written, some words are signatures, and some words are merely spoken, perhaps accompanied by a firm handshake. In the modern information age, words mean action. Inaction is simply another set of words, words such as "I am calling in sick" or "I did not finish the report," that is, words about the fact that other words, in this case the report, have not been composed.

Words are ideas and ideas, according to Plato, are things. Not only things, but mental things. And beyond that, ideas are the ultimate real things. Being is a set of specific and concrete ideas. And it is only with the mind that we can grasp reality. Talking about anxiety refers to a set of ideas. William James, 2,500 years after Plato, coined the expression "the cash value of an idea." An idea has measurable value. What is the measurable value in helping people capture the nature of the idea of anxiety? Is it a million-dollar idea?

Action in the agricultural age meant tilling the soil. Action in the industrial age meant building machines. The modern executive means by action certain types of sentences or conversations. Behind the motto to "walk your talk," then, are deeper questions, conversation-starting questions: What kind of talk is walking your talk? and How do you distinguish walking talk from non-walking talk? Action in the information age means talking the leadership talk. Virtually all that goes on in the name of leadership is one form of words or another. And words make dialogue, and dialogues make conversations.

LEADERSHIP TALK

In the "new" economy, leadership consists in finding the kinds of conversations that will be perceived as constructive, as bringing bottom-line results. And because it is people who bring results, and it is people who measure them, it all comes down to how we design leadership conversations that are judged as bringing results. The choice of topics is therefore critical.

Examples of living topics would be strategy and finance, creativity and relationships. And probably no topic for intelligent leadership conversations is perceived as more helpful than conversations about *anxiety*. The new economy may have made some people wealthy and others envious, but it has made everyone anxious. The level of anxiety increases in direct proportion to the population's growing awareness of the stock market and its euphemistically called "volatility" (which really means "crazy-making"). Wealth is more fragile than those who are not affluent may think. Nor does wealth, for those who have it, solve the problems that ambitious strivers think it will. The fear of *death* and the need for *love* remain, and personal *meaning* and *significance* are as elusive as ever.

ANXIETY AND COURAGE

The reason we talk so much about anxiety is that anxiety is the key ingredient in talk about courage. And there can be no leadership without courage. And courage is commitment that involves risk. Commitments are a very special kind of talk. To learn to have intelligent conversations about courage, commitment, and risk, we must first have intelligent conversations about anxiety.

The "deep structure" of human existence that we usually call *courage* combines the elements of the soul that we have become accustomed to call by the names of, first, *freedom,* and, second, *anxiety.*

Courage is a free decision, an uncaused choice, for which I am fully responsible. I choose it. And that choice springs from the deepest recesses of my soul. What do these words of courage *do?* They redefine anxiety. How? In simplest terms, from bad to good. They tell us that anxiety is bearable and that people in fact can confront stunning levels of anxiety.

These words are language that redefines anxiety from bad to good. They tell us that anxiety is bearable, and that people in fact thrive even under extreme anxiety. If at all times we recognize that we have the capacity to bear these deep levels of anxiety, then that grounds us, secure and at home, no matter how severe the circumstances may be. We are a serene rainbow gracing a turbulent waterfall. The rainbow grows only more stately as the turbulence increases.

Human beings can in fact adapt to almost anything that life throws at them. This is the inspiration we get from heroism, which is

 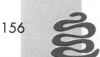 The Flawless Consulting Fieldbook and Companion

the noble free choice to continue to struggle even in the face of unceasing frustration and adversity. In fact, central to mental heath is to learn how to develop the inner strength required to see us through difficult times. Hemingway said it well, "The world breaks everyone and afterward many are strong at the broken places."

STRENGTH AT THE BROKEN PLACES

Authenticity in leadership is to learn how to develop this inner strength and to help others learn it. And we do this, at any age and at any time and at any place, when we understand the psychodynamics: Anxiety freely accepted translates into strength difficult to dislodge. Anxiety, far from being a sickness, is the actual experience of being strong, of growing, of building character, of achieving pride. And those are the final values of life, not shallow pleasure, but solid personality. How can we tell their different value? By comparing the two. But only people of courage are fair judges, for they have been on both sides.

Cyril Connolly said it well, "Melancholy and remorse form the deep leaden keel which enables us to sail into the wind of reality; we run aground sooner than the flat-bottomed pleasure-lovers, but we venture out in weather that would sink them."

If at all times we recognize that we have this capacity to bear a great deal of anxiety, then that gets us grounded, secure, and at home, no matter how severe our circumstances may be.

Historically, human beings in fact cope with almost anything that life throws at them. This inspiration we get from heroism, continuing the struggle in the face of endless frustration and adversity. Mental health is a code expression for the inner strength that we choose to build in order to survive harsh times.

It is more than just *bearing* anxiety. Nor is it merely becoming desensitized. It is choosing to make constructive use of anxiety. It is knowing that anxiety—which is a psychosomatic phenomenon, an event that occurs at the precise point of mind-body intersection—is *how it feels to grow authentically into the human being we were meant to be.* We work with the anxiety. We take charge of our own growth by how we address this anxiety, knead it into significance, and feel the greater strength suffuse our whole system.

We do this most effectively by promoting intelligent leadership conversations about anxiety, which include symbolic representations and guided daydreams.

THE CONSTRUCTIVE USES OF ANXIETY

When do we feel anxious? Taking on a new job, for example, creates concern and worry. It produces stresses that can lead to insomnia and family tensions, and even poor health. The root question is not what techniques and strategies to use to meet the requirements of my brand-new tasks, but how do I manage the stress that interferes with my doing what I know I must and can do?

Managing anxiety requires reframing it from being an illness to being an essential step toward health. The breakthrough point to remember is that *optimum* pain—the right amount of anxiety—is *exactly how growth feels.* Too much anxiety leads to either escape or collapse, and not enough anxiety yields no growth.

How does it feel to grow? Optimum anxiety becomes meaningful growth. Rather than disliking this anxiety and avoiding it, we can welcome it and feel good about where it leads us. This is a key "Aha!" for leadership development. The concepts of the "existential crisis" and of the distinction between *pathological* or neurotic anxiety and *authentic* or so-called ontological anxiety help us to consolidate this point of reframing the meaning of stress. It is the most successful way to cope with and to adapt to one of life's eternal truths: Be strong and secure inside in the midst of the maelstroms of chaos and crisis. Anxiety well managed is your key to security and inner strength.

LIFE AS A HEROIC JOURNEY

The Journey Diagram (Figure 17.1) traces the path of the everyday hero. The beginning (1) represents the start of the journey of life—either in reality, at birth, or symbolically, at a specific moment or a period of your existence. If you are a dreamer and if you are ambitious, you look forward (3) to a goal (2a)—a castle, a fantasy, some Camelot.

This hope may carry you through life, because life may in actual fact go downward instead in what we call the existential crisis or the crisis of the soul. But this dream can also become a dangerous deception, for the wall of reality (4) quashes the possibility of reaching your dream.

At the moment of the loss of innocence (5), you wake up realizing that life is not what you had hoped it would be or what you were promised it would be and that the fairy tales and myths, beautiful and inspiring as they may have been (especially when told to you under the loving circumstances of a presumed idyllic childhood), were also cruel deceptions. They did not prepare you for the disappointments about to come in life as it truly is: Full of potential, but brutal as well.

Matthew Scully, writing about Viktor Frankl's death in *The Wall Street Journal*, said:

> Throughout his life, Frankl spoke of the "tragic triage" of pain, guilt, and death. The door to happiness, he always said, "opens outward." We cannot pursue happiness—it "ensues" when we accept life on its own terms and understand that each person stands not as questioner but as the questioned.
>
> "Thus," he wrote, "life has meaning to the last breath." No matter what our circumstances there are always opportunities for courage, for "facing our fate without flinching."

THE CRISIS

The existential crisis—the "management of the stuck point," where it all starts, when we can't move forward or backward, yet move we must—is the transformation of anxiety into joy, depression into power, and despair into meaning (9). It is the chief angle of the journey of life. We are all in it, part of it. Those who accept going through this sequence in the involutionary-evolutionary curve come out of it mature, adult, and complete (11).

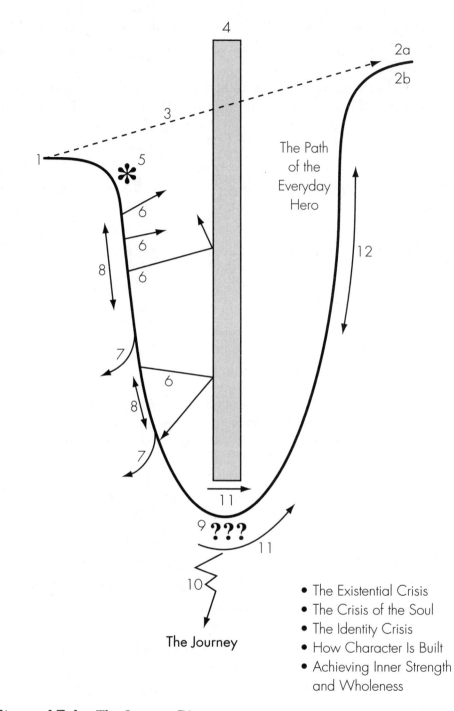

Figure 17.1. The Journey Diagram
Based on a diagram in Catford and Ray, *The Path of the Everyday Hero*

- The Existential Crisis
- The Crisis of the Soul
- The Identity Crisis
- How Character Is Built
- Achieving Inner Strength and Wholeness

The Flawless Consulting Fieldbook and Companion

This is the diagrammatic icon of the secret of courage, which is to translate anxiety into security, pain into peace—if we persist and go through it rather than turn around and avoid it.

Those who drop out along the way (7), or who fail to measure up to the moment of truth (9), give up their lives in any real sense (10). They live out the remainder of their days in "existential guilt," the inner recognition that one has thrown away one's most singular and unique life (10).

This despair manifests itself in seeking oversaturation of experiences, substance abuse, person abuse, sadomasochistic behavior, obsessive-compulsive lifestyles, and self-destructive and self-punitive actions, effectively destroying what little one may have left.

Many resort to psychosomatic illness as an excuse, as an anodyne, for assuaging the guilt. But if we instead choose to bear the anxiety of the guilt, we develop also the fortitude to turn our life around from despair to worthiness.

If we miss this turnaround, we may be given still additional chances. But the threat of those tests, given the subsequent continuing downward curve, become dimensionally steeper!

Sporadically we try, albeit pathetically, to reach once more for Camelot, only to learn once more how the wall stops us. It is not until we allow ourselves to reach the very bottom, as far down as the wall extends, that we see the tunnel that will allow us to reach the other side. That then becomes our moment of glory, of transformation, a true second birth.

A FRIEND

You need companionship: A friend, therapist, mentor, coach, support group, culture, society, books, "journaling," something or someone to stand by you in your great struggle (8,12).

Your life has now been transformed (2b). It is now different: You are strong and mature; you carry your own weight through your values, find comfort in solitude, are committed to serve and to make a difference (that is, give meaning), and therewith become the foremost supportive friend to your colleagues and the most benevolently selfless lover to your family.

This is how tragedy is transformed into meaning, emptiness into substance. And this is not a rationalization for the unfortunate but a deep structure truth about the human condition. We cannot go successfully through life without this knowledge, both conceptual and experiential. And the sooner we go through it, with clear understanding of what is occurring, the sooner we will have moved up from victim to hero. And you need a friend, even if *you* are that friend.

Here is a priest's poetic version of the existential crisis that informs the soul of every mature and growing person. The priest is not just any priest, but the archeologist who discovered Peking Man:

> We are impatient
> of being on the way to something new
> and yet it is the law of all progress
> that it is made
> by passing
> through some stages of instability
> and that may take a very long time.
> Our ideas mature gradually—
> let them flow—
> let them shape themselves
> without undue haste.
> Don't try to force them on
> as though you could be today
> what time will make you tomorrow.
> Only God could say
> what this new spirit
> gradually forming within you
> will be.
> Give Him the benefit of believing
> that his hand is leading you surely
> through the obscurity and the "becoming"
> and accept for love of Him
> the anxiety of feeling yourself
> in suspense and incomplete.

  The Flawless Consulting Fieldbook and Companion

Know that your activity has to be far-reaching.

It must emanate from a heart that has suffered.

We must offer our existence to God,

who makes use,

better than we could ever anticipate,

of the struggle in which we are enveloped.

Pierre Teilhard de Chardin

Knowing of this path, and recognizing it as a deep structure of human existence rather than as bad luck, can be a powerful solution to life's most intractable problems, transforming disaster, hopelessness, and being "stuck" into normalcy, faith, and moving forward.

KAIROS, THE MOMENT OF CHANGE

What happens at the base of the Journey Diagram (11) at the break-through point, at the moment of transition? This question is particularly important to someone who has just made a very difficult personal decision, such as changing a life-long career or relationship—something the person thought would never happen. The agony of the change itself is the discovery that it is all up to me, that I must live my life myself and in my own way, and that this is an insight of glory and not of despair. This discovery is true for every man and every woman, and not just for me. But not everyone is willing to go through the crisis. The Greeks called it *kairos*, the exact point of transformation.

Having done so, having reached the bottom of the downward curve, you have now changed. You will never be the same again. People will confirm this in how they now treat you differently from before, with more respect, deference, and recognition of your power.

There is an inner voice that knows what you must do before you die. That is your destiny, your inner strength, and if you violate your deepest and innermost integrity you suffer from existential guilt, the guilt that you are not living the life that your inner voice tells you that you must live.

It is a question of fundamental ethics, of knowing what is right and doing it, and the knowing is of the heart more than of the head. But it helps if the head understands what the heart sees. Pascal was right when he said the heart has its reasons that the mind will never know.

And when we heed this inner voice, we are then at our most honest, our most sincere, our most courageous as well at our most difficult point. We experience pain, even despair, and we are consumed with doubt, but there also is a compensating inner certainty that we must be honest and that we have no choice but to take a stand from the perspective of incontestable veracity. This is our existential crisis, our crisis of the soul, the very fulcrum of our transformation, the locus where we say, with God, "I AM"!

The soul at the moment of *kairos* is now open, revealing its true nature. The proof lies in the tears. Don't close the soul until you have fully absorbed what's there and what it wants to tell you. This is how it feels to have one's consciousness flooded with one's own unconscious. This is the moment of healing. This is the actual moment of true and real growth. Treasure it. Don't waste it. It may never return. You now have found your ground. Your soul stands on *terra firma*.

CHARACTER

Shakespeare made Hamlet say, as he lay dying in Horatio's arms, "If thou didst ever hold me in thy heart, Absent thee from felicity awhile, And in this harsh world draw thy breath in pain, To tell my story."

What is *your* untold story? What will telling it do for your "salvation"?

Think of this: Your life is constructed elaborately for the single purpose of avoiding the anxiety of being fully yourself. You think that how you live expresses your fundamental values. That may well be more true than you realize.

However, what happens if you say instead that the ultimate value is to *live the very anxiety of being free and choose for yourself* in a co-created and co-creating world? Your actual life is not much more than the web of resistances you have spun to protect yourself against this

The Flawless Consulting Fieldbook and Companion

anxiety. For you have allowed yourself to be brainwashed into thinking that being anxious is a disease and that being worry-free is both possible and even desirable. Have you forgotten about the Olympic feeling you can get from building character?

Going through this crisis is how leaders of character are made. Choosing to go through this crisis is how leaders choose to make themselves. Character is what happens when we talk intelligently about one key leadership topic: Anxiety.

For More Depth

Organization

Association for Quality and Participation

School for Managing and Leading Change

2368 Victory Parkway, Suite 200

Cincinnati, OH 45206

513-381–1959

Further Reading

Catford, Lorna, & Michael Ray. *Path of the Everyday Hero: Drawing on the Power of Myth to Meet Life's Challenges.* Los Angeles, CA: Tarcher, 1991.

Gardner, Howard. *Frames of Mind: The Theory of Multiple Intelligences.* (10th anniversary ed.) New York: Basic Books, 1993.

King, Ursula (Ed.). *Pierre Teilhard de Chardin: Writings.* Selected with an Introduction by Ursula King. Maryknoll, NY: Orbis Books, 1999.

Koestenbaum, Peter. *Leadership: The Inner Side of Greatness—A Philosophy for Leaders.* San Francisco: Jossey-Bass, 1991.

Koestenbaum, Peter. *The Heart of Business: Ethics, Power, and Philosophy.* Dallas, TX: Saybrook, 1987.

May, Rollo, Henri F. Ellenberger, & Ernest Angel (Eds). *Existence.* Northvale, NJ: Jason Aronson, 1995.

Scully, Matthew. Obituary: Viktor Frankl. *The Wall Street Journal,* September 4, 1997.

Yalom, Irwin. *Existential Psychotherapy.* New York: Basic Books, 1980.

About the Contributor

Business philosopher Peter Koestenbaum has been called a "behind-the-scenes sage to CEOs and other leaders" by *Fast Company*. His most recent books, *The Heart of Business: Ethics, Power, and Philosophy* (Saybrook, 1987) and *Leadership: The Inner Side of Greatness—A Philosophy for Leaders* (Jossey-Bass, 1991), are business classics.

Chapter 18

So, What's Working Here?
A Conversation with Elizabeth McGrath

These observations from an interview with Elizabeth McGrath could also have been entitled "Everything Counts." Elizabeth brings precision and order to her work. She is attentive to the detail of the moment and underlines the idea that the world is contained in the room you are in at the moment and that you, the consultant, are always part of the action, even if you may be participating in the illusion that you are an outsider. There are no outsiders in her view; everyone is a player. And Elizabeth gives you a sense of how she plays.

The two things that fascinate me most as a consultant are the strengths and value of "partnership," which I would contrast with the promise of "teamwork," and how powerful people become when they feel they are understood. I specialize in large-systems change and a lot of the work I do is with labor and management change "partnerships." Whether they care for each other or not, both realize that they cannot make significant progress unless they work together as partners. I think of partnership as the stepping stone to true teamwork. It takes a long time to become a team, and organizations tend to assume individuals can be a "team" long before they're really ready. I've found a good way to learn and practice how to be a team member is to first be a good partner.

I define partners as two individuals who are involved in something in which each has a stake. We can either contribute to one another's success or either one of us can keep the other from being successful. Our partnering presupposes something about sharing power. No matter where we sit in the hierarchy, partners move onto a level playing field when we realize that we are deeply interdependent. Even if you're three levels above me in the organization, something shifts for you when you realize that partnership with me would make sense. And something has shifted for me when I realize that, despite your position, I have the power to make you either more or less successful. We end up at some middle ground of responsibility and power sharing that bears no resemblance to the organization chart.

ENGAGEMENT BEGINS WITH DISCOVERY

A real shift in my thinking as a consultant occurred about fifteen years ago when it became very clear that the true beginning of my engagement with clients was during the diagnostic interview. I had always been disturbed by the impression that I was merely interviewing to gather data that would shape the intervention. At a gut level I knew I was involved in something more and that an actual intervention had already begun. I knew that whether I sat with one person or seven, their lives would be a little different for having spent time with me.

At the time I came to this realization, I had been reading Carl Rogers' *On Becoming a Person* and realized that the diagnostic interview could be a healing moment if the person speaking to me actually felt understood. Up to that point I was troubled by being an outsider, because there were things I knew that the people in the room did not know. I faced what I considered to be a moral dilemma: Should I speak up or dummy up when people raised a topic on which I had information? I saw myself on a teeter-totter of disclosure versus withholding. Then another visual occurred to me; instead of seeing myself on a teeter-totter, I saw that I was actually balancing on a fulcrum of understanding. When I made it my business to deeply understand their point of view, rather than alter or correct it, I felt more authentic. I also got

better information, and I made a better connection! The diagnostic interview became a deeply satisfying part of the consulting engagement.

I remember a consulting experience during which I was interviewing some administrative people—all women. They were angry because many of them considered themselves smarter than the men they reported to. And if truth be told, I agreed with them. But I also had a sense of how complex and demanding their bosses' jobs were, which they seemed not to realize. They just saw the bosses as screwing up, covering up, and acting childish. They said they often felt like babysitters! I was tempted to educate them about what it is like to be a boss, but I made a mental shift, realizing that my first order of business was to understand their situation rather than correct their perception. When they saw that I was truly interested in their points of view, the energy in the room changed. When they felt I understood their situation, they were eager to hear another perspective. The resulting conversation was charged with a combination of energy and peace.

Now whatever I share, I share as an equal because we are sitting together at a place of understanding. I know my diagnostic interview is a deep intervention because of the healing that comes from being understood.

This same series of conversations helped the managers of the administrative support staff gain appreciation for what many dismissed as "administrivia." They realized that administration should be included in the system-wide change efforts, as partners rather than as targets. The managers decided that having a member on a system-wide task force with an administrative point of view—not to take notes— would be a great addition.

SURFACING THE POSITIVE

When I lived in San Francisco in the early 1990s I heard about a process called "appreciative inquiry." Basically, I understood it to be an effort to find out about what's already working. I decided that it might be a good way to begin a diagnostic interview. One of the things I found depressing about diagnostic interviews was that people saw the

question, "What's it like to live and work here?" as an invitation to complain. Our conversation surfaced so much negative information that it was a huge downer for me and for them. I decided that I could still do a responsible job of information gathering if I started with the question, "What around here is working well?"

This question shifts the energy. Sometimes clients are startled by the question, but invariably a number of positive things occur to them. I often ask them to contrast those things that are going well with things that are not going well. They become very thoughtful as they discuss ways to bridge the gap between the two. So we move from an "Ain't it awful here with all the problems" conversation to a "Here come the beacons of hope" discussion. Although they pinpoint things that don't work and that get them down, they also generate ideas about how a positive difference might be made as well. I've never surfaced "a thousand points of light," but I have unearthed glimmers of hope that many have lost sight of. Before I shifted my interview technique, it seemed I only surfaced the negative. Now I surface both the positive and negative and begin to engage people in partnering around heart-head work that can build on what already exists. They identify the mechanisms that might make what doesn't work more like what does.

I've talked to some other consultants who discount appreciative inquiry as naive or Pollyanna-like. I see it as the beginning of a balanced process, with the positive as a starting point. A balanced approach results in people partnering with me in an exploration of the organization's positives and negatives. When I used my former approach, I was participating in an event in which people were merely information sources who felt victimized by the system.

I feel as though I'm doing a far better job for my clients. Even if a preponderance of the information is negative, people can focus on some reality-based positives that do already exist in the system.

I'm delighted that I've figured out the benefits of starting with the positives, and I'm distressed that so many good ideas, such as appreciative inquiry or dialogue, turn into three- and five-day workshops rather than a profound shift in one's thinking. I think sometimes we over-engineer our mental models. For example, the problem-solving

The Flawless Consulting Fieldbook and Companion

and decision-making models I've worked with over the years move people to finer and finer levels of precision. In order to cover all contingencies, I've split more and more hairs, ending up with pages and pages of three-hole punched paper. People lose sight of the key insights. We are all mired down in detail.

Here's an example of how details can detract from the key ideas. Let's say we're contemplating making a decision. As we discuss someone's proposal, a really thought-provoking question might be, "What could go wrong?" In the ensuing conversation, we could figure out what to do about that. But an analytical (rather than conversational) process wouldn't stop there. It would promote the analysis of the probability and seriousness of each thing going wrong. The analysis would address smaller and smaller levels of detail that are engaging intellectually, but that involve solving mathematical problems rather than staying with the key ideas.

I've ended up with folks discussing high probability and low seriousness, low probability and high seriousness, contrasting high-mediums to medium-highs. A thoughtful conversation with the right people, keying off two questions—"What could go wrong? and What makes you think so?"—is probably sufficient in most cases.

HOPE IN A HOLOGRAPHIC WORLD

It's fascinating that I can make such a strong human connection by wondering out loud, "Is anything working around here?" It engages people in a way that is surprisingly compelling. A lot of interviews I conduct are with three to seven people, and there's invariably someone in the room who offers something explicit and concrete that is working. So I end up being a little bit like Johnny Appleseed, sowing seeds of hope because something positive was described within earshot of people who did not have a positive response to the question.

For the past ten years, I've been intrigued by systems thinking. There are moments when I understand it and other moments when it eludes me. I've been told that, compared to economics, it's "the new dismal science." I find enormous hope in thinking of an organization

as a system that is holographic. If there can be a success in the accounting department with only seven people, in a holographic universe it can happen in every department and throughout the entire organization. Even if someone surfaces something that is "small potatoes," I now believe that if one little success exists in this system, other successes can exist as well. In my old mechanistic way of thinking, I'd think the problems were too numerous and overwhelming to hold out any hope for positive change. Now with my resurgence of hope through systems thinking, I can say to my clients with full integrity that this small example of success means: If it can exist here, it can exist all over the place. I am a more hope-bearing person than I used to be.

Systems thinking is also good for my own mental health, because sometimes I look at organizations that are so screwed up that I too lose hope. Now I rely on two things: (1) In a holographic universe if one positive exists others can as well; and (2) things change one conversation at a time and so let's begin those conversations.

For More Depth

Further Reading

Bohm, David, & Mark Edwards. *Changing Consciousness.* San Francisco: HarperCollins, 1991.

Faber, Adele, & Elaine Mazlish. *How to Talk so Kids Will Listen, and Listen so Kids Will Talk.* New York: Avon, 1999.

Faber, Adele, & Elaine Mazlish. *Siblings Without Rivalry: How to Help Your Children Live Together So You Can Live Too.* New York: Avon, 1998.

Macy, Joanna. *World As Lover, World As Self.* Berkeley, CA: Parallax Press, 1991.

Rogers, Carl. *On Becoming a Person* (Reprint). Boston, MA: Houghton Mifflin, 1995.

Workshops, Schools, and Websites

The Dannemiller-Tyson Associates Whole-Scale Change initiatives really opened my eyes about how powerful, informed, and wise large groups (in the thousands) can be.

I've found many of the health websites to be enormously helpful, and the search engines get better on a daily basis.

I learned a lot working with professionals from the National Education Association, lots of wonderful systems thinkers with several of us bearing sheepskins from NTL affiliated universities.

About the Contributor

Elizabeth McGrath is an affiliate consultant with The Symmetry Group in Wauconda, Illinois.

4 Emotions and the Personal

The moment you acknowledge that consulting is about building relationships and that change is as much about clients coming to terms
with who they are as it is about strategy and process, you have left dry

land and entered the wet world of emotions. At its core, change is dependent on the willingness to act with courage, to be vulnerable, and to choose optimism. These are all emotional concerns, and they are difficult to deal with in a world that worships the wedding of control and rationality and idolizes its favorite child, technology.

Most change efforts are a mind in search of its body. The mind knows what we need to create, but it is the body that provides the labor. It is vital to be strategic; there is no way to overstate its importance. But without action, which is the task of the body, strategy fails and we bounce from one vision to the next, looking for change in all the wrong places.

Successful consulting is dependent on channeling emotion to support the strategic. This is the difference between therapy and consulting. *Therapy* has the luxury of dealing with emotion and the personal for its own sake. *Consulting* operates in the context of a purposeful workplace, and the goal is to bring the emotional to work.

Unfortunately, the patriarchal workplaces we have inherited have taught us to leave the emotional outside the door, so opening that door and inviting feelings, doubt, anxiety into the office is a major challenge. We have become alienated from our "Self" at work. At some point touchy-feely became the problem and not the solution. How many times do we still hear the admonition to leave "that touchy-feely stuff" out of the conversation? This is a desire to leave our "Self" out of the discussion, to treat the personal as an unwelcome and somewhat dangerous stranger. Our work is to make a friend of it, as unpredictable and mysterious as the friend may be.

Most of art and literature and religion is designed to touch us, to enable us to feel again, to experience the joy and pain of life. Feelings and emotions, in fact, run rampant in the workplace, so to close this door to ourselves at work is to deny what already exists. One way to look at the wish to deny or control emotions is to see it as a logi-

cal outgrowth of patriarchy. Patriarchy is the belief that I can *own* other human beings—a kind of relational dictatorship. It is a contract between the feudal baron and the peasant. The baron provides protection, and the peasant in turn yields sovereignty: Sovereignty of the land, economic self-sufficiency, and, in extreme cases, sovereignty over the sexuality of young women.

Democracy was designed to renegotiate this contract, and while it succeeded at the ballot box and in the community, it has been slow to change much inside the walls of our institutions. The real cost of patriarchy is that as individuals we live with its internal effects long after the external world has loosened its hold on us. Ask many of us how we feel, and if we are honest, the answer is, "I don't know!" To avoid the emotional is the internal equivalent of denying our right to assemble. It compartmentalizes us and thereby steals our power. It is the power of emotion that we fear—the anarchy of our feelings.

We operate mostly in the masculine experience. To focus on emotions, which are the basis of passion and commitment, is to invite the feminine into the workplace. The emotional world, symbolized by the moon, is the home of passion, care, loyalty, willingness to endure pain. These are essential to the business of change and therefore consulting.

For change to occur, we need to be willing to step out of the sun. The learning organization depends on creativity and adaptability for change. What is paradoxical is that, for the person, change means becoming more of who we already are. It is an act of surrender more than an act of will or "drilling down." Embracing the moon, the dark side, the emotional side is needed to balance the brightness, optimism, and hunting determination of the sun at midday. This allows the day to complete its cycle, and the consultant's willingness to enter the moon world, the emotional world, is key.

Chapter 19

Balancing Competence with Consciousness
One Woman's Wisdom

Rosemarie Barbeau

When I started this book, I thought I wanted to have a whole section on women's issues in consulting. It became a forced fit. As the contributions from women came in, there was too much overlap between men and women in the roles and functions they serve and in their range of frustrations and satisfactions. There is something unique, though, about the way many women tend to see and experience the work of consulting. They more easily and naturally appreciate the importance of emotion, relationships, compassion, intuition, and care. I have come to think of that perspective as an expression of the feminine side of all of us, which is at the heart of real change and so the task of all who consult.

Rosi's story is about the shift within her of what we prejudicially call the "softer side." Her learning is common to us all. Where we began by betting on our minds, our rationality, and our capacity to be right, over time we discover that our heart and its capacity for surrender and its willingness to be true is where our most valuable offer resides.

After a number of years as an organization development practitioner, I have recently begun to attend to what I have learned as a woman in this field. I have become intrigued about what it is that I bring to my work as a result of these learnings and how this informs my practice. This essay is composed of a series of lessons that illuminate for me the path that I am traveling as a woman and as a professional.

I learned some of these lessons through the guidance of other women, and some with the help of men in my work and my life. Some of what I learned comes from the ways in which I am similar to many other women I know, while other lessons are born of the ways in which I experience myself as different. Whatever their origin, all of these lessons have become clear and meaningful for me as an OD practitioner who is a woman.

THE LABOR IS THE CLIENT'S

Some time ago I was working with a challenging client group, one in which I felt frustrated, confronted, and for some time at a loss as to how to intervene effectively. It seemed that the harder I worked to make things better, the worse things became. My learnings from this experience crystallized into the following poem:

> *The Midwife*
> Just wait, rest
> Now is not the time
> For pushing, straining, bearing
> Down
> This is not your labor
> This is not *your* labor
> You could be the midwife.

My great lesson from this experience was a reminder that whatever process I am working to support belongs first and foremost to the client, not to me. I also saw how central a sense of control has been for

  The Flawless Consulting Fieldbook and Companion

me in feeling comfortable in doing my work, and how illusory that sense of control actually is.

I love Angeles Arrien's definition of detachment: "A capacity to care deeply from an objective place." To me this means being able to stand beside the system with which I am working, to care about the people, the process, and the outcomes, without forgetting whose labor it actually is. This of course requires me to be able to tolerate, without "fixing," the messy, painful, and generally disorderly parts of organizational life that are some of the way stations to real and sustainable change. I am learning, at a whole new level, what it means to support clients when they are deep into those parts, without attempting to make everything neat, clean, and stress free.

THE IMPORTANCE OF BEING SEEN AND HEARD

One important learning occurred for me years ago after a colleague and I had just finished facilitating a meeting. He said to me, "You understood everything the participants said to you, but you didn't *get* their experience." These words have stayed with me over the years and remind me that often what is not said is as important as what is. They also remind me to listen for what is not yet ready to be said, so that we can begin to create the container in which people are supported in speaking their truth and being heard with compassion.

Clients, as do all of us, want to be seen, not just heard. In many client organizations, people will tell me, "We are different from other clients, other places you have worked." People want their organization, their culture, their work, and their experience to be seen and valued as distinct. This is true for those things they are proud of and for those things they feel much more vulnerable about. Clients want to be seen as unique, and I believe they are.

THE WISDOM OF THE NEXT SMALL STEP

Sometimes when I think I am going into an organization to help them do something really BIG, it turns out that my job is really to help them

take their next small step. This requires that I let go of any grandiose notions of making a difference and do the work in front of me.

Some time ago, I was asked to come into a school system to talk with them about facilitating a highly participative community planning process. I went into my first meeting with them all geared up to do a presentation on a particular kind of planning process in which I have expertise and in which they were interested. What I found when I met with them was that key players had not shown up for the meeting and, although there were some in this system who believed passionately that it was time to engage the community, at the highest levels there was little support for involving community members in planning for the next year.

The next small step in this case was to support those at this meeting to bring together a broader group of internal stakeholders in a second meeting, in which there was an opportunity for people to talk about how to best engage the community. By the end of this second meeting, there was not sufficient support for a community planning process, but what did emerge was a plan for a process in which this school system would get feedback and input from community members on initiatives and projects already in progress in the system.

My learning from this experience was that the wisdom of the next small step is found in a profound surrender to "what is," while at the same time solidly supporting those impulses in the system for change. What was required from me was a willingness to slow down, attend more closely, and let go of my expectations—about what they wanted, what they were actually ready to do, and what I was there for. I thought I was there to bring my expertise and "sell" a piece of work—something that did not actually happen. What I was there for, in hindsight, was to be a catalyst for a conversation that, given the political climate, most likely would not have happened otherwise. A small step.

RELATIONSHIPS MATTER— AND KNOW WHEN TO LET GO

Relationships—with colleagues, mentors, and clients—have always been central to how I have done my work. A while ago I had an experience that taught me something about working inside those relationships.

  The Flawless Consulting Fieldbook and Companion

I was partnering on a project with a colleague who is also a friend. In the course of the project, he and I came to a fundamental disagreement about how to proceed in the work. At a higher level, the decision was made to follow my recommendation rather than his. He felt angry and let down, and although he continued on the project, he chose not to work on the resulting issues in our working relationship. I, on the contrary, clearly came from a position that if there are incomplete issues in a working partnership, part of the work is to resolve them.

As he was unwilling to talk, I backed off and we continued to work together, with a decided frost settling on our relationship. Over time he came to see that there was some wisdom to the direction the project had taken, and eventually he softened a bit and we re-established some of the connection we had lost. The learning for me was that "drilling down" in processing a relationship is not the only way to go. There may be times I will need to live with the anxiety of remaining open to the possibility of reconnection, even when it seems as though there isn't much likelihood of it, so that the other person has something to come back to. I also need to accept the possibility that we may never circle back to each other.

WORK AND FAMILY INHABIT THE SAME LIFE

Recently I had an interesting experience at the intersection of my work life and my family life. I was invited to a social function one afternoon with a learning group that I would eventually serve as a faculty member for. Due to some logistical issues, for the first time in my professional life I arrived with both of my children in tow.

My four-year-old immediately took me to the name tag table and said, "Here, Mommy, let me make you a name tag!" So she did, slowly and painstakingly spelling out M-O-M. It was so beautiful, I couldn't not wear it, but it did leave me with a dilemma, since Mom is not the name I particularly wanted to be known by in the group. I solved the problem by wearing the Mom name tag on one side of my dress and the name big people call me on the other.

In reflecting about this later, I realized that in the eight years since my eldest child was born, at some level there hasn't been a waking

moment when I haven't been wearing both name tags. Yet it is a recent awareness for me that I have been holding my work life and my personal life as very distinct and separate. I had lost sight of the fact that I am the same person with the same strengths, issues, and challenges in both arenas.

The growing edge for me is to create more of a sense of wholeness out of my experience in these two roles. I have been experimenting with sharing more of my learnings from my personal life, as they seem relevant, with some of the clients I work with. I am also creating opportunities for people in the groups I work with to bring more of their broader life experiences into the meetings I facilitate. When I take these small steps, conversations seem deeper and richer. I am both more connected with my own experience and with those with whom I am working.

WOMEN TEACHING WOMEN

For most of my career, my teachers and mentors have generally been men, rather than women. There were simply more men around, and they were, frankly, more helpful. Now that I am in my early forties, I notice that suddenly most of the teachers in my life and in my work are women. The lesson I'm learning is how important it is to have these women lighting the way, personally and professionally.

They are women from a variety of walks of life: a well-known organization development consultant, a cultural anthropologist, an Aikido sensei, a German Buddhist. What all of these women have in common is that they provide a call to me to bring myself forward more, as a woman and a professional. They remind me that the dichotomy between "work" and "life" is a false one, that everything is truly connected.

It seems important that these women have emerged at this juncture—the beginning of the second half of my life. They remind me of the importance of bringing the feminine into the world of work and organizations. They show me what it means to be at the same time soft and strong.

The Flawless Consulting Fieldbook and Companion

"POWERFUL," "FEMALE," AND "PRESENCE" GO TOGETHER

As I grow older my presence in my work is becoming stronger, clearer, and more compelling. This is a good thing, particularly in a youth-oriented culture that often treats women, as they age, with less respect, as though they have less to offer.

I believe that *presence*, for women in particular, has something to do with how much of themselves they allow to be visible. For many years, out of a fear of not being taken seriously, I "managed" (or at least tried to manage) what I allowed to show. In particular, I hid the parts of myself that I felt to be unclear, not well thought out, and without an answer or solution. I also hid much of my feminine self and nearly anything sexual.

Some natural aspects of my presence have to do with clarity of thought, an ability to articulate, a sense of competence, and a certain physical presence. The task for me is to build on these, while allowing the emergence of the other parts as well.

It has become clearer to me that each of these parts of my self has something to offer, a richness to add. Also, the more fully I can bring myself, the more room and support there are for others to do the same.

IN CLOSING

A while back, a colleague and teacher of mine asked me, "So, what is it that you bring to the organizations you work with?" I answered, "Well, I bring clarity and order." By this I meant a cognitive bent, an ability to grasp and make order of complexity quickly, a strong task orientation, and a results focus. She looked at me for a moment and then suggested gently that it might be time to expand my repertoire. That is what these lessons represent to me—an expanding of my repertoire.

I believe that wisdom is born of lessons learned and integrated. My wisdom as a woman in this field continues to grow as I learn to build on that which comes most easily for me and at the same time to soften, deepen, and truly follow what has importance and meaning for me.

For More Depth

Further Reading

Arrien, Angeles. *The Four-Fold Way: Walking the Paths of the Warrior, Teacher, Healer, and Visionary.* San Francisco: Harper San Francisco, 1993.

Lao Tzu. *Tao Te Ching* (Stephen Mitchell, trans.). New York: HarperPerrennial, 1992.

Johnson, Barry. *Polarity Management: Identifying and Managing Unsolvable Problems.* Amherst, MA: Human Resource Development Press, 1997.

Remen, Rachel Naomi, & Dean Ornish. *Kitchen Table Wisdom: Stories That Heal.* Universal City, CA: Riverhead Books, 1997.

Weisbord, Marvin. *Productive Workplaces: Organizing and Managing for Dignity, Meaning and Community.* San Francisco: Jossey-Bass, 1987.

Further Training

The Organization and System Development Program at the Gestalt Institute of Cleveland. www.gestaltcleveland.org.

The 4-Fold Way Program with Angeles Arrien

Conscious Embodiment: A Training in Boundaries, Relationships, and Leadership with Wendy Palmer.

About the Contributor

Rosemarie Barbeau is an OD consultant based in northern California and a senior associate with the Chicago-based Axelrod Group.

Chapter 20

Nobody's Fool
Unconventional Guides for the Emotional Path

Andrea Markowitz

Consultants can do worse than to play the fool. It is the willingness to risk appearing absurd, even when we are the only ones who know there is method to our madness, that enables us to dive deep into uncomfortable waters and swim the difficult world of emotion. And yet, as Andrea observes in this piece, without a guide our faith may sometimes be too fragile. She brings us back to Shakespeare, Greek mythology, and clinical and Jungian psychology to offer us instruction by allusion and example, rather than by models and methods. What better companions to help us embrace the emotional side of our work?

> This fellow is wise enough to play the fool,
> And to do that well craves a kind of wit.
> He must observe their mood on whom he jests,
> The quality of persons, and the time,
> And, like the haggard, check at every feather
> That comes before his eye. This is a practice
> As full of labor as a wise man's art.
> For folly that he wisely shows is fit,
> But wise men, folly fall'n, quite taint their wit.
>
> Viola in Shakespeare's Twelfth Night: III.i.67

The wisdom of fools is a popular theme in Shakespeare's plays. He artfully used the fool's license to mock and provoke and be equivocal in order to expose truths that no one else dared. The jesting and expository roles of the fool long pre-dated Shakespeare, originating in ancient Europe when the nobility adopted people with physical deformities and mental disturbances and invited them to live in their households and act as diversions. Court fools were permitted to use inciting (and insightful) language that turned other people's worlds upside down and left it to them to set their worlds right again. They were allowed to get away with outrageous behaviors because, until the Middle Ages, people with physical deformities or mental disturbances were believed to have been touched by God. Their wit was praised as deep and sagacious because the ancients presumed that the indignities people suffered as a result of their abnormalities gave them greater wisdom and insight into themselves and human nature. Not surprisingly, some of the cleverest fools may not have been fools at all, but rather shrewd men who acted mentally disturbed in order to live the privileged life of a fool.

FOOLS RUSH IN

We may be at our best as consultants when we are fools. Playing the fool allows us to expose our clients' follies. According to Sallie Nichols, the traditional fool's mobility throughout royal circles placed him in a perfect position to gauge the disposition of the court and to shake up the establishment. Much the same way, consultants are in a position to gauge the temper of the organization and challenge prevailing notions about organization and management. Court fools could say things that, if said by anyone else, would result in their dismissal, even their beheading. We consultants can often get away with being outspoken, too.

In *Twelfth Night,* Viola noted that to be a fool requires a special wit that includes the ability to read others' moods and character and to time their barbs carefully. Without these aptitudes they might suffer unpleasant consequences because, while the royal fool's free speech was usually protected, it was not unheard of for him to be whipped for an especially well-targeted or poorly timed remark.

The Flawless Consulting Fieldbook and Companion

The fool in Shakespeare's *King Lear* summed up this occupational hazard when he said to Lear:

> I marvel what kin thou and thy daughters are. They'll have me whipped for speaking true, thou'lt have me whipped for lying, and sometimes I am whipped for holding my peace. [I.iv.199–202]

Similarly, consultants require tact and good timing. But even if the consultant's revelations please upper management, it is not always possible to please every faction in the organization. Paradoxically, the good news they tell management may be bad news for employees. And vice versa. Sometimes, following a particularly tough meeting in which others in the room do not like what we say, we leave the meeting feeling "whipped" by the group. Which brings us to another risk in being a fool: Becoming a scapegoat. When management or employees do not get the outcome they want, they can always blame the consultant.

Fools also served as alter egos, projecting the opposite quality of what their masters believed they were projecting to the world. Lear thought he was presenting himself as a wise and respected royal when he announced that he would divide his kingdom among his three daughters. He demanded that in return his daughters must eloquently declare their love for him. The two eldest daughters, Goneril and Regan, played his game and told him what he wanted to hear. Lear rewarded them by giving them their own kingdoms. Cordelia, his youngest daughter, said modestly and sincerely that she loved him as a daughter should love a father. Lear became enraged at Cordelia's lack of effusiveness and disowned her. The court fool chastised Lear for not having gained the wisdom that is supposed to come with old age:

> Fool. If thou wert my fool, Nuncle, I'd have thee beaten for being old before thy time.
>
> Lear. How's that?
>
> Fool. Thou shouldst not have been old till thou hadst been wise. [I.v.45–48]

After dividing his kingdom, Lear had no home of his own. He assumed that he would live part of the time with Goneril and part of the

time with Regan, but they became irritated with his uninvited meddling in their governing of their own kingdoms and kicked Lear out. Lear became more homeless than the daughter he banished, for she had found love and marriage with a nobleman in France. Lear wandered aimlessly through a furious storm, and with nowhere else to go, he went insane.

Ironically, Lear became more insightful in his madness than he had been when he was sane. Or perhaps he had been mad all along and his illusion of rationality was his veneer. Lear finally realized he no longer had control—over his kingdom, over his daughters, much less over nature. His daughters disobeyed him and the elements battered him. He was no better off than the suffering fools whom he had previously ridiculed and whom he now began to protect. His anguished cry as he staggered through the storm demonstrated that, in common with disfigured fools, his personal pain finally rendered him sensitive to the pain of unfortunate others:

> Poor naked wretches, wheresoe'er you are,
> That bide the pelting of this pitiless storm,
> How shall your houseless heads and unfed sides,
> Your looped and windowed raggedness, defend you
> From seasons such as these? O, I have ta'en
> Too little care of this! Take physic, pomp;
> Expose thyself to feel what wretches feel,
> That thou mayst shake the superflux to them,
> And show the heavens more just. [III.iv.28–36]

The fool is noticeably absent from the play after Lear's conversion. Although literary critics speculate that Shakespeare dropped him from the script because the fool had fulfilled his dramatic purpose of being Lear's foil, consultants might speculate that it is because Lear no longer had to depend on his fool for wisdom. The fool had consulted himself out of a job.

Toward the end of the play, Lear apologized to Cordelia and admitted his "folly":

> You must bear with me. Pray you now, forget and forgive. I am old and foolish. [IV.vii.84–86]

The Flawless Consulting Fieldbook and Companion

By acknowledging his foolishness, Lear demonstrated that he was finally wise.

Royal fools were not afraid to admit their ignorance. Their acknowledgment of ignorance was a sign of the highest knowledge, for without it, no learning would occur. In playing the fool, consultants serve the organization best by entering it as a blank slate, ready and willing for its members to imprint the organization's idiosyncrasies on the consultant's intuition and understanding. They seek to learn about and with the organization from the inside out, because they know that change works best that way.

Lear's relationship with his fool, who stayed by his side and supported him throughout his torturous descent into madness, parallels the plight of consultants in organizations that exhibit irrational behaviors. Before these organizations can heal, we must help leaders confront the manifestations of madness. As with Lear, the signs of madness will be more revealing of the organization's nature than any self-deluding displays of rationality. Consultants will guide their clients through the chaos and suffering, just as Lear's fool guided him through the storm, because they understand that chaos and suffering are the first steps toward healing. And like Lear's fool, consultants disappear after their clients' lessons have been learned.

THE HEALING ART

Shakespeare's fools practiced a paradoxical confrontational style by which they helped their sponsors identify their foibles by either exaggerating them or by suggesting that the problems were the opposite of what they really were. This technique is used today by therapists who practice *paradoxical intention*, which encourages patients to exaggerate their dysfunctions in order to learn that they control their symptoms—their symptoms do not control them. In essence, both fools and their therapist counterparts turn their benefactors' worlds inside-out and upside-down in order to create the conditions that allow them ultimately to set their worlds straight. J.E. Cirlot (1962), a historian and cataloguer of symbols, described how the behavior of fools could inspire others to "act out" to create new order by embracing disorder:

In their medicinal ceremonies and rites, doctor and patient "act mad," and, through frenzied dancing and "extravagances," they try to invert the prevailing evil order. The logic of the process is clear enough: When the normal or conscious appears to become infirm or perverted, in order to regain health and goodness it becomes necessary to turn to the dangerous, the unconscious and the abnormal. (p. 111)

Astronomer Carl Sagan (1996) reported a case in which a psychoanalyst unintentionally learned how the power of topsy-turvy thinking could summon rationality from a delusional patient (p. 176). After none of his other psychoanalytic strategies worked, the psychoanalyst entered the fantasy in which the patient recounted his alien abduction. The analyst included himself in the cosmic adventures that the patient described and, in the process, he began to believe in the fantasy. The patient eventually became worried about his therapist's state of mind and confessed that his abduction was a fabrication. After the confession, the psychotherapist recognized how easily an ordinarily stable person such as himself could penetrate the fine line between reality and imagination. Even more, he realized that for a while, he had become the patient, and his patient had become the therapist.

Consultants take on a role similar to that of therapist, comfortable or not. Patients in therapy carry the culture's ills, albeit in a more extreme fashion. Organizations do the same, and part of our work with them is to help them exhaust their symptoms. But we must be careful not to be seduced by organizational madness. In our zeal to fit in and be accepted, it is too easy to take on their symptoms. If they are a high-control, low-trust, very political system (which most of them are), it is seductive for us to become high-control, low-trust, and political. Sometimes we identify so strongly with the plight of the people in the organization that we become like them in the process of trying to help them.

SUPPORTING TRANSFORMATION AND INTEGRATION

Some definitions of schizophrenia mirror what we find in organizations. For example, David Rosenhan and Martin Seligman (1989) describe

the condition as "a disorder of thinking from which flows troubled behavior and troubled mood" (p. 364). Symptoms include difficulties in maintaining and focusing attention, in forming concepts, and in understanding reality, as well as false perceptions and expectations. These symptoms describe the problems in many organizations. In *The Politics of Experience*, R. D. Laing suggested that psychotherapists should help schizophrenics experience the full passage of their troubles before they journey to a saner place. Similarly, consultants can help their clients work through their pain before guiding them to a healthier place in the organization.

Laing's process for transformation is complicated, but it contains elements of every consulting project, or at least ones in which significant change is desired. Here are some of his steps, with parallels drawn for our work as consultants:

1. *A voyage from outer to inner.* Turning the attention of clients to their own experience, feelings, subjectivity.
2. *From life to a kind of death.* Accepting that something will be lost, something ended that has value.
3. *From going forward to going back.* Understanding what got us here, looking at the past in a more forgiving way.
4. *From temporal movement to temporal standstill.* Focusing on the present and seeing that learning from the moment plants the seed for a different future.
5. *From mundane time to eonic time.* Fancy words, but the intent is to stop being in such a hurry. Real change moves on its own schedule and is indifferent to the ticking of the clock.
6. *From the ego to the self.* A shift from arrogance, pride, and dominance to caring for the whole person, one's Self, as opposed to one's accomplishments.
7. *From outside (post-birth) back into the womb of all things (pre-birth).* Seeing the timeless quality of our experience. We are not the first ones to go through this.
8. *A return voyage from inner to outer.* Discovering ways for awareness to be brought into the world.
9. *From death to life.* An expression of our free will. The organization is there for us to create.

10. *From the movement back to a movement once more forward.* What we see is what we get. If we can cut the umbilical cord to the past, we can imagine a different future.

11. *From immortality back to mortality.* Bringing reality, limitations, the practical back into focus.

12. *From eternity back to time.* Caring again about the clock, schedule, moving ahead in the world.

13. *From Self to a new ego.* Being less concerned about control and career and keeping the valuable parts of our egos functioning.

14. *From a cosmic fetalization to an existential rebirth.* An affirmation of the spiritual side of life, to be reborn, approach the future with optimism and hope. (Laing, 1971, pp. 128–129)

AN EXAMPLE FROM MYTHOLOGY

The ancient Greek myth of Orpheus and Eurydice symbolically captures Laing's transformation steps:

Orpheus, a great musician and the son of Apollo and Calliope, fell in love with and married Eurydice. Soon after they wed, a poisonous snake bit Eurydice and she died. Orpheus voyaged from the outer world to the inner world of the land of the dead, where he begged Hades and Persephone, king and queen of this underworld, to return Eurydice to him. Orpheus' exceptional talent to melt hearts with his singing and lyre playing melted their resolve to keep Eurydice in the underworld, but they would not allow her to return without a test: Eurydice must follow behind Orpheus out of the underworld, and he could not look back at her until he set foot in the realm of the living.

During the long journey back to life, Orpheus began to doubt Hades. When he was almost at the entrance to the outer world, his doubts overcame him and he turned around to see who or what was truly following him. It was Eurydice, whom he glimpsed for only a moment before Hades' messenger whisked her back to the underworld. Because of Orpheus' lack of faith he lost his true love, and he did nothing but grieve for the remainder of his life. He sang continuously about his sorrowful fate, and his magic music aroused pity from all those who heard it.

The Flawless Consulting Fieldbook and Companion

He lost interest in all women except his Eurydice. Wild nymphs whose advances were rebuked by Orpheus finally became so infuriated that they attacked him. Their weapons and rocks did no damage because his music caused them to fall at his feet. Then the women screamed and made so much noise that his music affected neither them nor their weapons. They tore his limbs from his torso and threw his head and lyre into the river Hebrus, which carried them, still singing and playing, to distant shores.

The god Jupiter placed Orpheus' lyre in the heavens. The muses gathered the pieces of his body and buried them, and finally, in death, Orpheus was reunited with Eurydice.

Orpheus' story is a metaphor for Laing's journey of transformation—and our own work with the organizations we consult to. We all want our jobs to be simpler, quicker, less demanding, but they aren't. The story of Orpheus is about his struggle and initial failure to make the journey back to an integrated life after intentionally sinking himself into his deepest and darkest psychological depths. In the beginning of the tale, Orpheus' marriage to Eurydice symbolizes what Laing (1969) would call his need to integrate a "divided self"—a split in one's experience between his relationships with his world and with himself (p. 15). What this means is that he does not experience himself as a complete person, but rather as "split" in various ways, perhaps as a mind more or less tenuously linked to a body, or as two or more selves. Without this, he cannot experience himself "together with" others or "at home in" the world. Instead, he experiences hopelessness, aloneness, and isolation.

More than just needing to integrate himself, in Jungian terms Orpheus needed to integrate his male and female selves. He required his feminine Eurydice self in order to feel whole. To become whole he was willing to journey from life to death, to temporarily retreat rather than go on with his life. He chose to journey from the outer world, in which time moves on in an earthly fashion, to the underworld, in which time eternally stands still. He journeyed from his post-birth condition back to a world of pre-birth, where dead souls may be reincarnated.

On Orpheus' return voyage he moved from the inner world to the outer one, from death to life, forward from the dead world to the living one, from immortality back to mortality, from eternity back to time. However, he lost faith at the last moment and once again looked back, and so began the cycle again. The fact that he was alone is telling. Without a guide our faith is too fragile. We each need to make the journey in the company of those who have gone before us. Laing proposed that patients who have successfully survived the backward and forward journeys accompany others through their pilgrimages. He argued that therapists (consultants in our case) are not likely to have experienced the sense of being lost that a schizophrenic patient knows. But "people who have been there and back again" are better guides for this type of voyage because they can give full social encouragement and permission to embark and return.

Back in the world of the living, Orpheus isolated himself. His only universe was his misery. It took further disintegration (being torn from limb to limb) and finally death to give him back the life with Eurydice that he so desperately desired. For us, it is not a literal death, but a symbolic death, letting go, realizing that we are living out the dreams of whomever we were at an earlier time of our lives.

INTO THE UNKNOWN

Our work as individuals and consultants is to move into the future, mindful of but unburdened by the past. In every change project there needs to be some acknowledgment that something is dying. The acknowledgment may be elaborate, a ritual of some kind, or it may simply come in conversation. Too often when people are reluctant to move on we call it resistance, when it just may be a grieving process. To rush past the grieving and the sense of loss is to slow the process down.

In the story of Orpheus is our wish to change our fate, to become whole, to create our future rather than have it created for us. Orpheus was required to journey into the unknown, to cross the river from his familiar world, to find Eurydice, the lost part of himself, the part of himself he needed to find peace. He would not accept the death of his beloved Eurydice and felt compelled to bring her back to life. His initial attempt at reunion was purchased too cheaply; he tried to shortcut the process, looking back too soon and breaking his vow to trust that

The Flawless Consulting Fieldbook and Companion

she was behind him. It would take him longer than he imagined, and he would have to struggle more than he would have been willing, before he could fulfill his own possibility. Every effort at change faces the same crisis, and more than once.

If we are serious about changing organizations, we have to acknowledge that the process takes time, is often out of our control, and demands more of us and the client than we planned. Genuine change also entails suffering, the experience at times of being torn from limb to limb, and even then the outcome is in doubt—real doubt. What endures in the face of this is the spirit that gave rise to the effort in the first place. It floats on and survives through all the difficulty. What is common in all stories of transformation is the experience of dying and then beginning again. Only through Orpheus' own death did he successfully reunite with Eurydice—successfully integrate himself.

This is universal, this process of:

Death → hope of rebirth.
Risk, and death, give meaning to life. Nothing will change unless something dies. It's going to die no matter what you do.

Stories and myths like those of Lear and Orpheus teach us the real nature of our work. Their message is conveyed in language more vivid than we are used to. They require fundamentally an emotional and psychological investment, more than an intellectual or economic one. Plus they are a far cry from the project-management, get-it-done-yesterday thinking that pervades our culture. It is possible, under pressure, or as a measure of our own loss of faith, to drive change, to make it happen fast. But in the end, what we are left with is the experience of intense effort, coercive actions, a lot of money spent; and when we walk away, we leave behind a world much as we found it. This is not what we had in mind.

Like therapists, we follow the emotional path, which gives us the possibility of contributing what few others can offer. Like fools, our willingness to go against the culture, or even what the client is expecting, is what defines our value. The form in which we do it does not matter; the models or stories will vary. It is not even a question of how long it takes, for in the Sixties movie version of the myth, *Black Orpheus*, the whole journey takes place in one night of Carnaval in Rio. The emotional path is not about time; it is more about our willingness to become a student of this way of looking at change and to give it the respect it is due.

For More Depth

Cirlot, J. E. *A Dictionary of Symbols*. New York: Philosophical Library, 1962.

Laing, R. D. *The Divided Self*. New York: Pantheon Books, 1969.

Harrison, George B. (Ed.). T*he Complete Works by William Shakespeare*. New York: Harcourt Brace Jovanovich, 1952. Or consult any unabridged edition, edited by a Shakespearian scholar, such as *The Complete Works of Shakespeare* (4th ed.), edited by David Bevington, president of the Shakespeare Association of America (Reading, MA: Addison-Wesley, 1997).

Laing, R. D. *The Politics of Experience*. New York: Ballantine Books, 1971.

Nichols, Sallie. *Jung and Tarot: An Archetypal Journey*. York Beach, ME: Weiser, 1984.

Rosenhan, David L., & Martin E. P. Seligman. *Abnormal Psychology*. New York: W. W. Norton, 1989.

Sagan, Carl. *The Demon-Haunted World: Science As a Candle in the Dark*. New York: Ballantine Books, 1996.

About the Contributor

Andrea Markowitz is an independent consultant and assistant professor of industrial/organizational psychology at the University of Baltimore.

Chapter 21

In the Land of Fools

Idries Shah

Once upon a time there was a man who strayed from his own country into the world known as the Land of Fools.

He soon saw a number of people flying in terror from a field where they had been trying to reap wheat. "There is a monster in that field," they told him. He looked, and saw that it was a watermelon.

He offered to kill the "monster" for them. When he had cut the melon from its stalk, he took a slice and began to eat it. The people became even more terrified of him than they had been of the melon. They drove him away with the pitchforks, crying, "He will kill us next, unless we get rid of him."

It so happened that at another time another man also wandered into the Land of Fools, and the same thing started to happen to him. But instead of offering to help them with the "monster," he agreed with them that it must be dangerous, and by tiptoeing away from it with them he gained their confidence. He spent a long time with them, in their houses, until he could teach them, little by little, the basic facts which would enable them not only to lose their fears of melons, but even to cultivate the fruit themselves.

Reprinted by permission from "In the Land of Fools," in *The Dermis Probe* (p. 131) by Idries Shah.

Chapter 22

Up Front and Personal
A Conversation with Charlotte Roberts

You are about to encounter Charlotte Roberts. This interview captures her spirit well. She is an indomitable extrovert, and I think knows all of the earth's inhabitants. She speaks with a strong leadership voice and deals with the emotional and political aspects of the workplace in a practical, direct, personal, and at times fierce way. And she does this in a way that affirms the feminine. A powerful combination.

My life as a consultant began with my background in early childhood education. That was where I learned that to develop and advance the potential of a little person, you have to understand who and what you are dealing with. You need to identify the needs, the resources, and how to tap into the system. You need to find out how the child feels about himself or herself, about learning. Consulting is the same thing. Consulting is about helping design systems in which people can grow and flourish and achieve their desired future.

I would describe my consulting style as feminine, because for me consulting is all about relationships. When I meet a potential client, I ask myself right off the bat, "Is this someone I could be in a purposeful work relationship with? Is this someone I could care about, talk honestly and openly with—about the business, about each other's behavior?"

After I determine that I can have a relationship with the primary client, I ask myself, "Can I get the relationships working on the executive team or the other teams?"

Most often I'm called to help teams that are having problems. Just because I focus on the relationship doesn't mean I do only touchy-feely stuff. I believe the quality of relationships directly impacts productivity through several channels. I believe relationships get out of whack because they are caught in a poor structure, not because people are bad. So most of the time when there's a relationship that doesn't work, there's something about the job descriptions or information flows or structure that is causing it not to work. Most of the time, there are already hard feelings. When two people are having problems, they can at least get to neutral if we clean up the structure. I also try to work on self-awareness and truth telling with each person and, of course, learning.

I've always thought that my job is to help people have the conversations they are unable to have. I think you either hire a consultant to do the thinking for you or you hire a consultant to facilitate important conversations. I am not an expert, or "do-the-thinking-for-you" consultant, and I don't want to be an expert consultant. The responsibility for thinking and learning can shift to the outside; that's a disservice to the organization. I am a process consultant.

People say that I get away with a lot as a consultant, especially with being very direct. I tell clients that I chose to work with them not because I need the work but because I think we can do good work together and because I can be in a productive relationship with them. My clients and I become friends. I even have clients who come and stay at my home. I don't feel I have to be in touch with them all the time, but even when we're not working together, I call. And I always ask male clients if we can invite their wives to dinner, because I don't want wives to think I'm a threat in any way. I do think that's something I have to be concerned about because a spouse can undermine me by just not knowing who I am. If I'm going to be calling her husband at home, and I say, "Hi, this is Charlotte. I work with Jim and I'm a consultant," I think it's good to clarify roles and expectations within the

client's closest circle of relationships. My master's degree in human development with a minor in marriage counseling has served me well in considering family and team dynamics.

I have wondered whether the reason I get away with being so direct is because I'm a woman. Almost all the teams I work with are male. I've watched male clients engage with very personal or direct questions. They have said later that they wouldn't let a male colleague push them that way. (The exception is David Kanter, whom I aspire to emulate.)

Although I'm all for being direct, I'm not brutal. I say something like, "It sounds to me, because we have the same or less revenues coming in next year, we cannot increase base pay. No matter how much you care about these people, no matter how much you'd love to give them more money, no matter how insistent they are, the point is there's no money in the bank, and therefore you cannot increase base pay. Do I understand this right? Do you agree that you cannot increase base pay?" But my directness is not intended to make fun or embarrass others. It's about truth telling. I believe I once was fired for being direct and telling the truth. This experience still haunts me to this day. Here's what happened:

> A pharmaceutical company hired a colleague and me to work with a group of vice presidents and executive vice presidents. The job was strategy implementation. They had five strategic objectives, and they wanted us to help them map out the things to watch for during the next couple of years. The two executive vice presidents sat in the back of the room during the first day's work. The thirty vice presidents had been divided into groups and were working on elements of the strategy. We were mapping the reinforcing and balancing structures, time delays, resources, etc. The vice presidents were working earnestly, doing a lot of thinking, flip charting, etc. My colleague and I were going from table to table, interspersing different ways to think about things and work through the issues. With systems thinking, the first two competencies you go for are the ability to hear the story on different levels and the ability to ask questions to uncover more and take the story deeper. So I asked for the story and it sounded like the strategy was too aggressive, too fast. The vice presidents anxiously

agreed. I told them to be sure to mention it to the executive vice presidents, but the vice presidents said no way, because they would be fired. I discovered that my colleague had heard similar warnings about the strategy and the same reluctance to explain the strategy problems to the executive vice presidents.

At the end of the day, I said to the executive vice presidents, "When I listen to your vice presidents' scenarios, it sounds as though going in the direction that you have planned may be too fast, you'll be overinvested and set up the possibility of severe financial stress. Can you see that?" They glared at me and said, "Maybe." And I asked, "If some of the vice presidents wanted to develop a new scenario that focuses on a plan that doesn't go quite this fast or this far, could they?" One of the executive vice presidents crossed his arms and said, threateningly, "They could try." The tone suggested that they'd suffer consequences if they did try. I replied it was something we could think about.

At the end of the day, the executive vice presidents told my colleague that he could report back the next morning, but not me. I was fired.

No wonder the vice presidents were afraid to tell the truth. Three years later the vice presidents' prediction that they were over-investing came true and the company had to be sold. The vice presidents had felt like their hands were tied and there was nothing they could do to help the strategy be successful. All they could do was what the executive vice presidents told them to do. And in the end, the executive vice presidents didn't suffer financially from the company's financial stress; only the vice presidents and other employees did.

To me, this was a case of failure. And I thought, and thought, and wondered what could I have done differently? I believed it was my job to tell the "truth" as the vice presidents described it. Especially considering the warning. And all I did was prove to the vice presidents that they were right not to air their concerns—to tell the truth. The next day the vice presidents ended up working on the executive vice presidents' vision, and on accountability. But how meaningful is the vision when the people are scared to death, and when people believe the vision is great but the strategy to get there is too far and too fast? In cases like this, rather than accept accountability, they'll just salute the flag.

  The Flawless Consulting Fieldbook and Companion

I wondered why the executive vice presidents bothered to include consultants in their strategy meeting, when they were not open to alternate opinions. I think they wanted us to confirm the strategy and to make sure it was airtight. But no strategy can be airtight. If you're that rigid, you're setting yourself up to crash and burn. And when I pointed to a possible crack in their mental model, they would not tolerate any dialogue about that possibility.

It was from this experience that I learned that the first thing to do is to contract the relationship. My colleague had been the contact person for this consulting job. I did not have a relationship with the executive vice presidents. I was not clear about what the work was and why they had hired us. My colleague thought we were hired to really dig into the strategy. I don't even think the executive vice presidents were clear about the work. By the time that became clear to me, they ended the consulting. Because there was no relationship, there was no room to reframe the way we were doing it. And not only was I fired, but my colleague was not invited back after the following day.

Now I begin my consulting work with these four questions to be sure I can enter into a relationship with my clients:

1. What is the work you want me to do?
2. How do you want to receive feedback about your actions (written, verbal, real time, end of day)?
3. How do you typically gain unilateral control over a conversation that isn't going the way you want? (I ask whether the client uses humor, anger, or withdrawal when he or she wants to control, redirect, or stop the conversation. When I give those examples, a leader easily identifies a favorite method. I want to know the leader's typical strategy for unilateral control so that I can be aware when it's happening. From the previous question, I'll know how to intervene.)
4. What do you expect from me in our relationship?

I can't be sure that I'm always getting an honest response to all of these questions, but I think I get the client's best understanding of the questions at that time. In the first interview we are both checking out whether we can work together. I'm investing in the client's and organization's success. I'm investing my time, energy, and attention. We both have to make a decision to move forward. As a result of these initial meetings, I have said to some clients that I am not the right person to work in their consulting job.

Also, I never do "sales" calls. If I go see a potential client I will be paid a consulting fee and expenses because I will have added value by my visit there. Why bother wasting the client's time and mine on talking about what I *might* do? Let's start working together now so the client gets at least a day's worth of value and we both get experience of each other's work style. Whether the client wants to continue in that technique or process is a different story, but let's not play the show-and-tell game. This allows me to engage the system from the moment I begin. It has taken some people aback.

My first five years on my own I rarely did work under my company name. I was a subcontractor. That's how I started my business. I didn't care, as long as I was earning a living. I still do subcontracting. I'm not attached to whether or not it's my company's name that shows. If I do good work, they'll find me. I now do a lot of work through speakers' bureaus with their clients.

My rewards are those letters from people who met me and tried things I talked about and changed their lives. They keep me going and doing what I'm supposed to be doing.

For More Depth

Gardner, Howard. *Leading Minds: An Anatomy of Leadership.* New York: Basic Books, 1996.

Handy, Charles. *Waiting for the Mountain to Move: Reflections on Work and Life.* San Francisco: Jossey-Bass, 1999.

Handy, Charles. *The Hungry Spirit: Beyond Capitalism: A Quest for Purpose in the Modern World.* New York: Broadway Books, 1999.

Handy, Charles. *Age of Unreason.* Boston, MA: Harvard Business School Press, 1998.

Heifetz, Ronald A. *Leadership Without Easy Answers.* Cambridge, MA: Belknap Press, 1994.

The Flawless Consulting Fieldbook and Companion

Oshry, Barry. *Seeing Systems: Unlocking the Mysteries of Organizational Life.* San Francisco: Berrett-Koehler, 1996.

Senge, Peter M., Art Kleiner, Charlotte Roberts, George Roth, Rick Ross, & Bryan Smith. *The Dance of Change.* New York: Doubleday, 1999.

Senge, Peter M., Art Kleiner, Charlotte Roberts, Rick Ross, & Bryan Smith. *The Fifth Discipline Fieldbook: Strategies and Tools for Building a Learning Organization.* New York: Currency Doubleday, 1994.

Wells, Rebecca. *The Divine Secrets of the Ya-Ya Sisterhood.* New York: HarperCollins, 1996.

About the Contributor

Charlotte Roberts is an executive consultant, located in Sherrills Ford, North Carolina, and co-author of *The Fifth Discipline Fieldbook: Strategies and Tools for Building a Learning Organization* (Doubleday, 1994) and *The Dance of Change* (Doubleday, 1999).

Chapter 23

Women's Leadership Collaborative
Investing in Our Humanity

Nancy Voss

Becoming a good consultant requires a continuing investment in ourselves. Many consultants focus their learning on new techniques and developing new ways of thinking about the work. We sometimes talk about consulting as a series of "interventions," which connotes a certain professional detachment, as if there were a set of tools separate from ourselves that we bring to each project. We learn about new exercises, change strategies, and new models. We participate in the search for what is next. All of these are useful, but without a parallel investment in our own humanity, we forget that, in a service business, the person is the product. Who we are, our own consciousness, our own capacity to make contact, our own ability to see and work with compassion in the world as it is become the essence and foundation for our models and strategies.

The power of Nan's article is her deep understanding of the importance of the person, the personal, the emotional as they interact with the underlying and often unconscious societal assumptions and dynamics that shape our world view and interpersonal interactions. She shares with us a very personal, long-term investment she made, and what is compelling is the extent to which the women opened

209

themselves to whatever surfaced and whatever learnings emerged. It takes courage to be this open, to move toward dangerous waters, to value the pain as an essential part of our development. And it takes faith. Faith in ourselves and faith in the ultimate good will in the people on the trip with us. As you might guess, Nan not only writes about these qualities, but she brings them to the world.

Sixty women gathered in 1993 to explore the territory of all-female dynamics with each other. They hoped to create a map of that mysterious land that would help them better understand themselves, each other, and how, as women, they related to one another. Through those insights, they hoped to find ways to support all of their strengths and differences, encourage one another to stand individually and collectively as tall as they could, and in the long run help increase women's effectiveness in the world. Many of the women were consultants, artists, educators, or therapists with female clients. All were interested in women's processes.

The journey lasted five years. The women traveled through many different terrains. I was one of the explorers. My intent here is to describe some of the complex topography we entered as we attempted to cooperate and work together. The experiences and learnings have been incredibly broad, deep, and complex, and many are only now beginning to come into focus. I will share here some observations and thoughts that are emerging for me from this Five-Year Women's Leadership Collaborative, which I believe have relevance for women or men wherever they are working, consulting, or interacting with women.

This is not a practical list of how-to-manage-or-consult-to-women tips, but rather a perspective on some of the ways we found ourselves interacting with one another as women. I hope this view into our women's experience will provide an opportunity for continued reflection and dialogue, thereby increasing understanding and the ability to relate and work across and within gender boundaries.

The Flawless Consulting Fieldbook and Companion

We came together in response to a call from two women, our designated leaders, with our sameness and our differences. We intended to spend fifty days together over five years, exploring, interacting, and reflecting on our experience together. We ranged in age from our twenties to our eighties and represented various racial, ethnic, religious, sexual, and other identities and orientations. We gathered twice a year, in spring and fall, and collected and distributed a book of writings to each other in between each session. By creating an ongoing all-female community, we were able to go deeply into our selves and our relationships as women and to deal with and revisit issues as they occurred and recurred.

This article focuses on four major themes we encountered over and over again in our work together: connection/inclusion, sameness/difference, power/competition, and projection/scapegoating. Although none of these dynamics is unique to women only, I believe they happen differently when women engage with women. These aspects of our female-to-female interactions do not stand alone, but are connected and interdependent with each other.

CONNECTION/INCLUSION

As women, the beginning of our learning about relationships with other women is the mother-daughter dyad. In this very primary sense, we exist as women to be in relationships with one another, to nurture and be nurtured. Mother and daughter have been in intimate and intense relationship with each other since long before the daughter's birth. While in utero, the daughter has been a very real part of the mother. If the daughter dies, a part of the mother dies. If the mother dies, the daughter dies. Our choice is literally relationship or death. And as female child, daughter, potential mother, do we not each carry that primary primitive responsibility for relationship in our genes, in our bodies, and in our psyches/souls? As infants and young girls, we experience the world in families, whether biological or other. We first experience ourselves as daughter or sister and other females as mother or sister. Internalizing these archetypes of mother, daughter, and sister,

we develop our fundamental perceptions and our early coping skills with other females within this mother/daughter/sister triangle of relationships.

The group came to see that these ancient and archetypal patterns continue to play themselves out within or outside of our awareness. The way in which we coped in these early relationships is not forgotten. Female-to-female relationships bear the mark of this mother/daughter/sister triangle; this template becomes the overlay for all our subsequent female relationships.

Some of the patterns include:

- Nurturing mother, nurtured daughter;
- Nurturing daughter, needy mother;
- Over-responsible mother, irresponsible daughter;
- Crazy or irresponsible mother, over-responsible daughter;
- Dominant older sister, manipulative younger sister;
- Aloof mother or older sister, demanding daughter or younger sister;
- Competent mother or older sister, incompetent but powerful daughter or younger sister;
- Sisters vying for mother's love or favored-daughter position; and
- Mother/daughter alliance, excluding other sister.

Any of these positions may be occupied by any of the players, creating subtle differences and making the relationships infinitely complex. Questions to ask about female-to-female relationships are:

- Who is the mother?
- Who is the daughter?
- Who is the elder sister?
- Who is the younger sister?
- How are they/we interacting?

These patterns and roles are there—working with you, against you, regardless of you. For example, when a woman finds herself

The Flawless Consulting Fieldbook and Companion

intensely resenting a practical suggestion from another woman intending to help her, she might trace her response to a pattern of resisting a sister or mother who was always too ready with unwanted advice. With awareness of the pattern, instead of subconsciously resisting the sage advice of a peer, she can let go of her early need to differentiate herself from the overbearing mother or sister and take or reject the advice based on its merit, rather than on its impact on her unconscious.

As women, the intensity of relationships with one another established in the pre-birth symbiosis between mother and daughter and extended to the mother/daughter/sister triangle continues to be central to our identity as we grow up. Needing connection and nurturing for early survival, we continue to seek relationships with one another throughout our lives. As schoolgirls, we form intense friendships and tight cliques. In junior high and high school, most if not all of us know and passionately care who the popular girls are. It is critically important to us to belong somewhere. We are always aware of our connection or lack thereof to each other. We want to be included.

Inclusion is about our ongoing wish for connection to one another. In the collaborative, it was not an initial stage of group development to be resolved so that we could move on to do our work, as current group development theory indicates. It was an important part of our ongoing work together.

Over our five years together, we wanted to be included; we paid attention to whether or not others were including us and often were careful to invite one another to participate in official and unofficial activities. If some were invited and others not, we were careful to explain why.

Sometimes we were not careful to include one another. We did not always want to be connected. We often hurt one another's feelings deeply with our inclusion and exclusion. Who is in; who is not? Am I in; am I out? When we sat together as a large group, when we formed subgroups, when we gathered informally, inclusion and her sister, exclusion, were there with us.

We didn't always want to include one another because we also needed to differentiate. We had to stand apart, risk exclusion and dis-

connection, to achieve autonomy, leadership, intimate and honest connection. We had to try to find the balance. We had to rend and give ourselves the opportunity to mend. We did in fact disconnect many times. Sometimes those who tore themselves apart from one another came back together; sometimes they did not.

As we went along, various women removed themselves from the group. Whatever their reason for leaving, stated or unstated, those remaining were left to deal with the loss. Often the pain of disconnection was great. In our five years together, we again and again reaffirmed our desire and our struggle to be/stay in relationship with one another and our intense angst at failure to do so.

SAMENESS/DIFFERENCE

When people come together, some of their similarities and differences are more visible than others. At the first meeting of the collaborative, it was immediately obvious that we were a group of primarily white women. Our ages were more or less evident; when we spoke, our accents provided more information about who we were or where we were from. Some of our differences were not apparent until we declared or demonstrated them, such as values, biases, spiritual beliefs, sexual preferences, financial status, class issues, and personal history.

Our differences distinguish us from one another, make us unique and set us apart; our similarities join us. It is the combination of these two polarities that guides us to see ourselves as like one person, different from another, to include ourselves in a certain subgroup and exclude ourselves from another. Who we associate with influences who we are; who we are influences who we associate with. These images of who we are and who we are like become powerful parts of our identity as human beings.

As we go through life, each of us has unique experiences; based on these experiences, we each develop a lens through which we view the world. This lens is both influenced by who we have become and influences who we are becoming. These lenses invariably highlight some things and obscure others. If we are not aware that we are in fact

viewing the world through a particular lens, we assume that what we see is how it is. Even if we are aware that we have a certain lens, it is hard to know what we don't see. Therefore, sharing different lenses is a way to confirm and/or expand our knowledge of the world.

The very visible issue of our lack of racial diversity became a major issue in the initial gathering of the collaborative. We had to decide whether we had enough different lenses through which to see ourselves, or whether we needed a more racially diverse perspective to do the work of exploring women's processes together effectively. We had to share a number of our less visible identities and lenses, such as sexual orientation and preferences, to help us with this decision. This was the beginning of our work on more visible and less visible differences.

This was not a quiet and tidy deliberation, but a vital, heated, and passionate debate. The ultimate decision was to invite more women of color into the group in order to be a fuller mirror of female difference in which to see ourselves and each other. At our second meeting, a few of the women from the first session opted not to continue, a few women of color chose to join, and we closed our boundaries to ensure our ongoing viability with a slightly less skewed but still primarily white group of women.

Thus each of us had a lens that had some things in common with the group as a whole (we all had the female lens, for example), with parts of the group (subgroup lenses, such as straight, bisexual, or lesbian), and things that were unique to each person (individual lenses, such as a world view based on a meaningful encounter with a particular teacher). This combination of lenses created within the collaborative as a whole a kaleidoscopic view of the world. This is true for any group, and in the collaborative, dealing with these identities, lenses, similarities, and differences would prove to be some of our major work over our five years.

My particular lens is that of a white, anglo, middle class, heterosexual—the dominant cultural lens. It is the nature of the dominant lens to assume the rest of the world is the same, because it is so pervasive. I often don't even know I'm seeing the world through my dominant lens until someone with a different perspective shares another view.

Thus, for me as a white woman, I often am not aware of how women of color experience the world. As a heterosexual woman, I am sometimes blind to difficulties lesbians and bisexuals face. Within the comfort of my middle class status, I can be oblivious to issues of class. In my dominant entitlement, I can ignore these differences. They are felt keenly by those not of the dominant culture, however, who experience them constantly, must know and cope with the dominant lenses in order to survive.

As a member of the dominant group, I learned that I (and others) am often not only unaware of my own attitudes and assumptions, but that I also tend to overlook and deny my blindness. It is our dominant assumption that all people are basically the same, and we believe that we view and treat each person as an individual rather than as a member of a particular subgroup. We resist knowing that our behaviors have a different impact.

At one point in the collaborative, one of the women of color shared her perspective of how the dominant culture discounted her viewpoints and experience. All around were expressions of denial, rationalizations of behavior—the very embodiment of the point she was trying to make.

We saw that even when we are not part of the dominant culture, we are deeply influenced by those lenses, and often subconsciously incorporate aspects of them into our identity. We admitted that women of color have their own racism, lesbians their own homophobia, and we as females have our own sexism and misogyny. I think that for us as women, finding our own unrecognized cultural biases regarding women, the ways in which we have bought into the dominant patriarchy and our own subconscious, internalized sexism are a big part of our unfinished and ongoing work.

I believe that as women in a dominantly patriarchal culture, we often experience ourselves as a minority subgroup, with sensitivity to nuances and attitudes that are not obvious to and often denied by the dominant group. At the same time, we have incorporated many of those assumptions and biases about women and their roles into our own views and behaviors. I know that I am still sometimes surprised when my auto mechanic is a woman or the office receptionist is a man. And then I realize that I am stereotyping people and roles. More subtly, I am not surprised when the CEO is a man or the stay-at-home parent is a woman. And while I believe these things are changing, I do not always see the impact of my assumptions and expectations about myself or others.

In the collaborative, it was a continuous challenge for all of us to try to keep our eyes and ears open as best we could. We were all blinded by our lenses from time to time. Those of us who could see at any given moment had to keep reminding those who were not seeing and hearing to look and listen. It was hard work on all sides. It was important—and difficult—for us to keep trying to examine our lenses while looking through them. We have come a long way, and we have only just begun this part of our journey.

As we shared our experiences and our views of the world, ourselves, and one another, we began to learn more about other viewpoints. We disclosed stereotypes of each other and began to appreciate our sameness and our differences. Time and again the majority (whatever it was) had to learn what it is like to be the minority (whatever it was). We had to see the impact of our words, behaviors, and assumptions. We had to see that we daily inflict pain by our insensitivity and prejudice. As whites, for example, we often brush off the impact of our acts and words, such as a reference to the evil part of us as our dark side, claiming that we don't mean them racially or personally. It is difficult to understand and admit that our behavior has deep, often unconscious roots and a very different impact. Same-sex partners do not share the same legal rights and privileges as do heterosexual partners. It is our dominant privilege that allows us that insensitivity and audacity.

Those of us with certain viewpoints or awarenesses were continually overlooked or stepped on by those of us not seeing that reality. Certain individuals time and again raised concerns about sexism, wealth, class, homophobia, ethnic, religious, spiritual, and other issues. Time and again they told us we were not seeing. They wanted and needed to tell; they became weary of the telling. We wanted and needed to hear; we became weary of the hearing. We became frustrated with our going round and round certain issues. We became more than saturated with our stories and concerns, and at the same time needed more. We often frustrated ourselves with our women's process.

As we focused on one set of inequities, we often stumbled over others. While trying to focus on racial diversity, for example, we again glossed over the heterosexual/bisexual/lesbian issue, causing great pain in the process. The pain became so great in that instance that some women stormed from the room. We did not know whether they would return. I think they did not know whether they would return.

This was a time of great pain for all of us. We had torn ourselves apart while trying to pull together. We had to look at what we had done to ourselves and to one another. We had to open ourselves to one another and admit our part in the process. In our need for connection and understanding, we had disconnected and not understood at all. In our effort to lead and follow each other we had abandoned each other. All of our needs for connection, differentiation, recognition, leadership, collaboration, and support were intensely experienced in this exploration. As women, we found these events profoundly impacting our intense relationship needs and sensitivities and vice versa.

POWER/COMPETITION

In our five years as a women's leadership collaborative, we continually struggled to find ways to stand for ourselves and stand together in relationship. How could we differentiate ourselves, stay together, be powerful, lead, and also support and nurture one another? We had a difficult time finding this balance.

As women, we generally find open, straightforward competition difficult and uncomfortable. Those of us who were young girls in the 1930s, 1940s, 1950s, 1960s, and even 1970s did not get much instruction in the art of straightforward competition. There were few organized sports for women. We did not have that arena in which to learn how to be team players, how to be the stars of our teams, how to compete with our teammates for stardom, or how to support the stars of our teams

The Flawless Consulting Fieldbook and Companion

while maintaining our own identity and integrity, because for many of us there was no team.

We have learned how to compete, however. We often compete in covert ways. When competition goes underground and is unacknowledged, it is harder to see, harder to deal with. When we pretend we do not want a leadership position, for example, and then try to undermine the competition's ability to lead by talking behind her back about her competence, we are being competitive in a covert way.

In the collaborative, on a number of occasions, a woman would offer to lead a part of a session using her particular expertise, whether a form of body work, a conceptual framework, or some group activity. Often there were side conversations about her competence or lack thereof, her audacity, the people she chose to work with, or some aspect of her leadership. We knew we were talking about them when they were leading; we had to assume they were talking about us when we were leading.

When this happens, the leader or potential leader feels betrayed, may not know where her competition is or what is happening, and doesn't know how to fight back. For women, dealing with our competition is not an easy task; acknowledging it is not an easy conversation.

During our five years together, we competed in many ways. We competed for inclusion and connection. We competed for air time in the large group. We wanted our presence noted, our voices heard, our stories appreciated, our viewpoints acknowledged. We competed for identity and acceptance both in the large group and as members of subgroups. We competed for connection—to individuals we liked, to subgroups we identified with, to the designated leaders/mothers of the group.

We competed for position. We competed to be top dog, the fairest of them all, the recognized official or unofficial leader of something, or the one favored by the leaders/mothers. We got ourselves noticed in many ways—by being bold, nice, creative, friendly, brilliant, sensitive, confrontational, charming, whatever.

We competed to be underdog: the most oppressed of all. In this inherently paradoxical competition, the winner is the biggest loser. In this contest, the winner/loser/most-oppressed gains recognition and thereby honor and support for her oppression. We competed again and again for this dubious honor. Which of us is the most oppressed sub-group—whether by race, religion, sexual orientation, age, or other differentiation? We wanted our oppression noted, recognized, understood, and appreciated.

Because we live in a male-dominated society, we often experience ourselves as being oppressed and sometimes feel forced to use our feminine power in subtle or devious ways. In this all-female community, we found ourselves quite capable of oppressing each other! Not only could we enjoy the martyrdom of the oppressed, but we enjoyed the dominance of the oppressor and the righteous fervor of the liberator as well. We found in ourselves the capability of taking on all three of these roles. We didn't need the men.

Struggling to find our balance in our power, we also found ourselves in a continual dilemma between the polarities of too much/not enough. Am I applying too much force, or not enough? Am I too bold, not bold enough?

Am I:

- Too polite?
- Too loud?
- Too needy?
- Too bossy?
- Too wild?
- Too sexy?
- Too aggressive?
- Too nice?
- Taking up too much time?
- Occupying too much space?

Am I, on the other hand:

- Not visible enough?
- Not forceful enough?
- Not kind enough?

The Flawless Consulting Fieldbook and Companion

- Not wild enough?
- Not sexy enough?
- Not assertive enough?
- Not inclusive enough?
- Not decisive enough?
- Not tolerant enough?
- Not taking up enough time or space?

Because we are so relationship focused, we are continually looking to the group to let us know whether/when we have gone too far. We struggle to differentiate, but not to venture out so far as to lose the relationship. We want to stay connected, but not at the cost of our identity and integrity. We want to lead, but in doing so risk the loss of identification and connection with our peers.

Although we were competent leaders in our back-home communities, successful entrepreneurs or managers in our businesses, respected professionals in our careers, we had lots of difficulty trying to lead and be led by one another. Often, as someone would stand up tall in her particular way of leading, the system would take her down. It was as if the appearance of a particular strength or a particular team's style was intolerable to the whole. The timing was off, the style was wrong, the subject matter unacceptable, or the makeup of the leadership team not right. She was too much of this, or not enough of that. We had trouble allowing a peer to lead us.

Here was an unconscious pattern of sexism, sneaking in to pull down a strong woman at her moment of testing her strength. Much wounding took place during these times. Many women who tested their leadership subsequently left the group. Although I don't really know why most of them left, my belief is that the pain of working through the competition and relationship issues was too great. We found that old adage "Men kill their weak and women kill their strong" haunting us. We had to see that we could not blame the men.

We often connected through our pain. When a woman shared her pain about something, we could understand, support her, nurture her. When she shared her strength, we often fought her. It is perhaps the fine line between nurturing and dominance, between feeding and forcing, and the ancient mother/daughter/sister triangle that contribute to our power issues and dilemmas as women with women. In our five years together, we found it hard to stand in our power, our female authority, maintain connection at a deep and supportive level, and not victimize or oppress ourselves in some way.

PROJECTION/SCAPEGOATING

Intimately related to understanding connection, difference, and power is the idea of projection. Projection is the convenient mechanism by which we see aspects of ourselves that we like, wish we had more of, or dislike and reject "out there" instead of "in here," thereby releasing us from the burden of owning and coping with these parts of ourselves directly.

When we attract ourselves to another person, it is often through our connection to the attributes we see in them that we also value in ourselves or would like to develop in ourselves. We like their style, admire their capability, respect their candor, value their practicality, appreciate their sensitivity, and so forth. We also tend to place on them an expectation about their behavior, based on our values, our wants, and our needs.

When we are put off by someone's appearance, demeanor, or behavior, it is often attributes of ourselves we see in them that we do not appreciate and would rather not acknowledge. It is far easier to malign the competitiveness in another than to acknowledge our own— far safer to criticize the exhibitionism we see "out there" in another than to own the desire "in here" to prance about and be seen.

We frightened ourselves with our attractions as well as with our repulsions. Learning to cope with a positive transference can be as burdensome as dealing with a negative one. Attraction between women carries with it the possibility and often the unspoken fear of sexual intimacy between women. If I approach her, will she misinterpret my motives? If I acknowledge her admiration of me, will she demand more of me than I want to give? What if I really like her body? If you are working with women, you can assume that attraction and homophobia are alive and well, often deeply buried and vehemently denied.

The Flawless Consulting Fieldbook and Companion

We projected and transferred desired or undesired attributes out onto any woman who, by her behavior at the moment, was available to carry the projection and, often, onto the identified leaders/mothers of any given moment. I believe the intensity of these projections is related to the intensity of the connection/inclusion and power/competition dynamics among women.

Thus, a real issue to be dealt with for women accepting or assuming a leadership role with other women is that all sorts of projections with their accompanying expectations and evaluations will be directed toward her. Women who assume leadership roles with women need to be prepared for this likelihood. With women's high sensitivity to connection and relationship, this dynamic can be difficult to manage.

When groups project onto individuals, the process becomes that of scapegoating. In scapegoating, the group disowns some part of itself, some aspect it would rather not see and deal with. A group cannot scapegoat, however, unless someone is willing to be the goat. In the collaborative, someone would unwittingly volunteer to serve as the goat from an unconscious and hence unacknowledged place in her psyche by violating some unspoken, unspecified rule or expectation in a way that the group would find offensive and would rather not own—too much of this or that. Always too much of something is put onto the scapegoat. The group deals with its turmoil and terror by seeing the attribute as attached only to the individual currently personifying the issue and not embodied in the group as a whole. This process proceeds relentlessly as the pain in the system intensifies until someone calls a halt and resolution can begin.

In our collaborative, the group selected a different woman for each of its most difficult aspects. Whatever was the "too much-ness" of the moment needed a demonstration. We saw too much intelligence, too much sexuality, too much spirituality, too much wildness, and too much domestication.

As we competed endlessly for connection and projected our undesirable attributes onto one another, we feared being ousted from the group and simultaneously wanted to oust any threat to our security. We wanted connection with and acceptance by the group; we wanted to disown any parts of us that threatened that connection and acceptance. At the same time we unconsciously longed for the disowned parts of ourselves that we heaped onto our scapegoats, even as we scorned those designated carriers of our hated/feared attributes. Longing and loathing merged and fused in obscure and painful ways. As long as we had the goats, we could deny the real issues within us. After the goats, we had ourselves to deal with.

Over time, we became better in our ability to own our own feelings and perceptions and to see and acknowledge our desire to annihilate some part of ourselves that we saw out there and then pretended that we did not. We became better at reeling in the projections we had flung at one another. Each issue that requested a scapegoat also required a deepening of understanding of self and one another. These were big, painful, important, and ultimately rewarding learnings.

It takes a great deal of self-awareness, maturity, and trust for a group to move beyond this dynamic. With awareness of our own propensity to collude in scapegoating certain difficult issues, we can perhaps see more clearly the ongoing dynamics and support a group's ability to confront the reality it is avoiding and deal with its real issues.

THE ONGOING HOPE

The Women's Leadership Collaborative. We spent five years together trying desperately not to become an oxymoron by putting these three words together. We were learning to understand our uniquely female dynamics and to enhance our ability to co-exist with one another and with other women.

Hope for our success resided in our capacity to become more intimate, more honest with ourselves and with one another. As we became less and less "nice," we became more and more authentic in our communications. We became more able to speak directly to one another; we experienced deep woundings and developed deep relationships. We have learned a lot and opened ourselves to more learnings.

We were—and still are—an action research project. Although we brought the five-year project to a close in 1998, nearly half of the original women have re-formed into an ongoing collaborative to continue the exploration. We have generated many more questions than answers. We have raised our awareness of the all-female dynamic; we continue to go deeper, to explore old patterns, and to experiment with new ways of being together.

As women, we live within and reach beyond the dynamics of the mother/daughter/sister triangle. We continually struggle to find our balance between too much and not enough. We strive for connection, differentiation, and leadership.

For me, putting together this account brings up all of these issues. Am I too much or not enough? Have I been too bold? Have I not been sensitive enough? Am I occupying too much space? Will I hear my mother's voice saying, "You did what!?! How could you do this to me?!?" What will they say behind my back? How will I deal with reactions to this act of leadership? Can I stay connected as I find my voice?

As mature women, we can learn to know and love ourselves in these powerful and inherently skewed ways of relating to one another so that we can incorporate them in productive ways and/or move beyond them. I believe we can find our voices as women, stand in our own authority with integrity, and lead and support one other. The reward is enhanced individuality and deepened connection. The risk is, of course, to lose the self or the relationship by being too much, or by not being enough.

And how might these experiences and resulting learnings help a consultant or manager in the workplace? All of the workplaces I know have important objectives to accomplish, heavy schedules to manage, real work to do. They have neither the time nor the inclination to analyze women's interactions with each other in depth. How could these insights be useful?

I have no doubt that these female dynamics are present in all of the groups and organizations I consult with in which women are present. I believe they are there with intensity, with or without awareness. Whether coaching a female manager, facilitating a strategy meeting, conducting a consulting skills workshop, or planning a large-scale redesign, these learnings have helped me interact and intervene with more awareness and authenticity. As a result of the collaborative, I now enter a relationship, group, or consultation with a growing sensitivity to the way the dynamics of connection/inclusion, sameness/difference

power/competition, and projection/scapegoating may be impacting and influencing the women (myself included).

With increasing self-awareness of my own need for connection, for example, I can see how that wish sometimes gets in the way of my risking rejection by saying to the client what I think is going on in the organization or between us. I know more about where the fear in me is coming from, and I can decide what to do about it. Conversely, I can be more reassuring that I will stay connected with a client when asking her for feedback. I have more compassion for the struggle of other women coping in organizations in which relationship is tenuous and often not overtly acknowledged or valued.

When I find myself feeling always reassured or easily irritated by a particular woman, I ask myself, "Is my mother in the room? Am I being a needy or rebellious daughter?" When I recognize the mother/daughter/sister triangle in me, I can let go and deal with the issues at hand.

When I feel myself stuck in a disagreement with a co-consultant or client about how a certain issue or intervention should be handled, I can examine my own power and leadership struggles and ask myself what is really going on here. Then I can address the real issues, whether they be power or content related.

I can recognize my own inclination to project my unacknowledged issues onto another woman. I remember one woman on a team I consulted to whose propensity to say whatever popped into her head was driving me crazy. I wanted to strangle her. How could she be so indiscreet, so oblivious to the impact of her words? I would never say those things. My reaction was intense. Not until I examined my own careful and usually-but-not-always-successful attempts to control that part of me, could I let go of my acute irritation and deal with her as a competent manager, one of whose strengths was that people counted on her for information about anything and everything because she would tell all and, in the long run, trusted her honesty because she always said exactly what she was thinking.

As women, the challenge we face is to know ourselves deeply, to recognize our ancient patterns as they manifest themselves in our daily interactions, and to confront our own yearnings, biases, and fears honestly. As consultants, the challenge we face in working with women is

The Flawless Consulting Fieldbook and Companion

to recognize these issues and dynamics as they appear in their unique manifestations and to help women to know them, honor them, and work through them.

The reward for meeting these challenges is transformation of our relationships, in the workplace and elsewhere. The opportunity, now, is to ask, "How might these insights apply to me, my life, and my work? What might be better in my world as a result of this Five-Year Women's Leadership Collaborative?"

For More Depth

Further Reading

Arrien, Angeles. *The Fourfold Way*. New York: Harper, 1993.

Duerk, Judith. *Circle of Stones*. San Diego, CA: Lura Media, 1990.

Eisler, Riane. *The Chalice and the Blade*. San Francisco: Harper & Row, 1987.

Perkins, John. *Shape Shifting*. Rochester, VT: Destiny Books, 1997.

Quinn, Daniel. *Ishmael*. New York: Bantam, 1995.

Quinn, Daniel. *The Story of B*. New York: Bantam, 1997

Further Training

The Body Lab by Jerry Perlmutter, which has now evolved into the Soul Workshop by Jerry and his partner Murry Perlmutter.

The Self-Differentiation Lab, originated by Joyce and John Weir and continued by Alexandra Merrill and others.

A Shamanic Journey to Ecuador, led by John Perkins.

The School for Managing and Leading Change, sponsored by AQP and Peter Block.

The Women's Leadership Collaborative, continued by several of the original five-year members and open to new members.

About the Contributor

Nancy Voss is president of Voss Consulting, in Arlington Heights, Illinois, and a senior associate of The Axelrod Group in Chicago.

Chapter 24

Sneaking the Spirit In
A Conversation with John Schuster

The challenge of consulting is to bring the spiritual and the practical together as one whole, within one person—our self. The reminiscences John shares in this interview are an expression of this task. He is immensely practical, believes deeply in the value of economic success for the well-being of the soul, and yet is clear that he does the work for something more. He also comes to his work as a businessman, which means he is applying his beliefs to his own life. It gives his voice a ring of reality, revealing a tenacity to see things through and to do this with his full humanity.

The biggest challenge for me as a consultant is how to create some kind of forum within which you can do your best work. You spend a couple of years developing a product—a set of services and processes that people might buy and that answers a real need. Sometimes the perceived need is different from the real need, so you have to act like a virus and infiltrate the organizational immune system. Once you get in, you start doing your real work.

The marketplace is tough because it pulls you in the direction of your past—whatever you get known for. I've seen so many consultants die psychologically because they become good at something and people buy what these consultants used to be good at,

over and over again. They can't break into new ground. So you have to be very careful of success, because it will keep you in your past. Also, it's extremely hard to be unique because everybody seems to do the same thing.

Another challenge is that most clients don't want to hire a firm. They want the individual. So you try to team up with people but can't, because the marketplace tends to atomize you into units of one. And if you're on the creative edge, you usually don't have anybody buying your product because it is too creative and ahead of the marketplace. Consulting takes a capacity to separate the fads from the trends. Too many consultants jump on fads.

Other challenges include working with CEOs, because their jobs are so hard, making your changes permanent, managing your own anxiety, and taking on the organization's stress.

When we do our best work we are usually inside a business helping people engage in some significant way, and if we do our work well we align the interests of shareholders with interests of customers, managers, and employees. One of my specialties is business literacy—open-book management, trying to put a human face on capitalism, trying to generate wealth that works for everybody. That's what capitalism is all about. So let's not have performance compensation systems just for top managers. Let's have variable pay for everybody; let's teach everybody how to make a difference, read financial statements, and understand their cost structure. Then people have a reason to generate wealth because they get some of it back.

DOING THE REAL WORK

Everyone's now a consultant. There's an oversupply compared to the 1980s. I coined the term "consultant abuse." There are so many consultants around now that there are some clients who treat us like the commodity we've become. They don't answer our calls, and they're rude. Even clients with whom we've had close relationships act this way.

What has not changed for me since I began consulting is that relationships are everything. The presenting problem is usually a time when

The Flawless Consulting Fieldbook and Companion

the clients are quite anxious, and one of the things they hire a consultant for is to lower their anxiety. They're trying to relieve a symptom. It became apparent to me that any consultant who relieves symptoms will be busy all the time. Good consultants will only relieve symptoms that need to be relieved and then push the client to do the work.

I like to say about myself that both feet used to be planted in midair. When I started consulting I was a theory in need of an application, but not anymore. Now I'm impatient with my colleagues who are still only theory-based. They conduct one or two workshops and go on to their next client. In our consulting firm we try to hang in with clients as long as they need us, to help them implement theories into practice. There are also a lot of people who call themselves consultants who are really hired hands—for example, IT (information technology) implementers. Although they work for "consulting firms," they are not the kind of consultants we're talking about in this fieldbook.

So there are people who implement at nitty-gritty levels, those in midair, and those in between. I like thought leaders. I like Deming's approach: "Here are the principles, you figure out how to use them. I'm not going to give you a cookbook."

Another thing that has not changed since I began consulting is the human tendency to create hierarchy and dominance systems. I think this tendency is in our brains and in our consciousness. I'm convinced that this is the way the human brain is structured. We can't break ourselves free of hierarchy systems. So I disagree with consultants who go against biology and champion alternative models for how organizations work.

WITNESS TO THE SPIRIT

Something that *has* changed over the years is that "spirit" in work is finally being recognized. It was not there when I started and I had to sneak it into conversations.

My best work is when I help teams to bond deeply to each other around their values. That's a wonderful sense of accomplishment, to facilitate and be a part of that. I like to watch a community of meaning

emerge, where before it was a community of tasks and efficiency and getting work done. But when higher meanings and purposes start to evolve and people pour themselves more deeply into their work, that's always a joy to me. You never know when it's going to happen. It's exciting seeing individuals and teams and whole companies find new mental models, paradigms, and thinking shifts. The scary part about consulting is that you enter these engagements never knowing whether any of that is going to happen. Sometimes the people who talk the best have the hardest time delivering, and the skeptics end up learning the most.

My approach after all these years has been to assume that objectivity, observing and diagnosing from the outside as an expert, is not the way to go. My philosophy is based on the notion of a participatory universe. The act of observing changes what is being observed. If I just try to put my best foot forward for my clients from the beginning, if I really love my clients and engage with them heart and soul, then I will change the process. Maybe they will as well. By far the best thing I can do is offer all the expertise I have and love the best I can, and that will be my most authentic act as a consultant. But creating such deep relationships can make you feel lonely when you leave a job.

For instance, when I was working as a consultant for a coal mine company in Wyoming, I enjoyed working with the guys because there were no pretenses. When it was over I missed them so I called them once in awhile to see how they were doing. I probably put my heart out there too much. But I'm also good at using my head, providing people with good tools, and assessing managers. Most managers I work with undersell people's capacity for change. But some have too much heart and are overly optimistic.

EVOCATEUR

I'm an evocateur. Evoke means to call forth. For me, consulting is inviting clients to work at a deeper level and to work from a deeper dimension. When I do my best work I evoke. The best thing managers can do is to be evocateurs for their employees and customers.

I believe life is ultimately sacramental. Being raised Catholic, I was taught that sacraments were outward signs instituted by God to give grace. So I've always thought about the outward signs or outward symbols of this deep, deep inner reality that we have. And for me, evocatuers look at the sacramental, deepest levels of people. That's what you try to tap. I used to call it "working the veil." Without too much trouble you "work the veil," you tell a couple of stories and before too long they will be in that deep place in their hearts. You have to be afraid of that because it can be pretty manipulative, but now I do it at more authentic levels. Stories about children and personal stories are good for starters. I often tell the story of what my high school basketball coach did for me. When telling stories, you have to engage people's senses, you make a few facial expressions, change your voice a little bit, and evoke the physical reality, and soon the audience's imagination takes off. The skeptical, left-brain, data-driven part of that disappears and suddenly they're in the story with you. Tell stories about caring, triumph, growth, growing past your limitations, and people are with you.

FREEDOM IS MORE THAN JUST ANOTHER WORD

The satisfying part of consulting is the freedom. I'm addicted to my freedom. Feedback is great when it happens so you learn what difference you make. I like the intensity of marketing, and of the work itself. I enjoy the money, but it's never been great. The money's great for a few people, but just good for a whole bunch more. The work is suitable for overachievers and workaholics who are not afraid of long hours. I enjoy the people, the travel, and the variety. Consulting teaches you a lot about the world, whole segments that you don't know about. You learn how different sectors of society work.

The hard part of consulting is building the business. Consultants need to ask themselves, do they want a practice or a business? A practice is just selling your professional time. A business could be selling your professional time, others' professional time, having overhead, a bunch of people working together, generating some wealth and profits,

and selling a product. They are two very different things. It's all about how hard you want to work. Consulting takes tenacity. You have to be sales-driven, patient about the sales process, with clients, and with yourself, and more energetic than the average person. A lot of people who are great consultants are terrible in business because business is all about implementing, and a lot of consultants want to be artists, and they should be.

Diagnostic skills are important, but partnering is better. Partnering to me is deepening the relationship to anticipate client needs. Partners have to know one another better than hired guns. I try to partner with clients for the long term, learning who they are, what they need. I try to hear what they say and hear what they are not saying, and to be a good resource. Clients try to get to know you and what you are capable of.

I've often said that the most fun times in consulting are when a client uses you well. Some clients are terrible at using you. Yet you still take the work and you say maybe I'll get a chance to be used better, but it doesn't happen often. You become discouraged, but then you find a client who knows how to use you brilliantly. They call you to ask for things. You're not in a sales mode. You're in a renewing-the-contract mode for the next set of needs. Clients will accept the financial part with ease and negotiate with fairness. It feels good. They want you to share in the fun, too. They take you places with them. They want you there. You've become part of the team.

For More Depth

Further Reading

Schuster, John, with Jill Carpenter and M. Patricia Kane. *The Power of Open-Book Management: Releasing the True Potential of People's Minds, Hearts, and Hands.* New York: John Wiley, 1996.

Schuster, John, with Jill Carpenter and M. Patricia Kane. *The Open-Book Management Field Book.* New York: John Wiley, 1997.

Schuster, John, with Jill Carpenter and M. Patricia Kane. *Hum-Drum to Hot-Diggity: Creating Everyday Greatness at Work.* Kansas City, KS: Steadfast, 2000.

Further Training

The Association for Quality and Participation, School for Managing and Leading Change. www.aqp.org.

The Hudson Institute of Santa Barbara, Frederic Hudson. www.hudsoninstitute.com.

About the Contributor

John Schuster is co-founder of The Schuster Kane Alliance/Capitol Connections in Kansas City, Missouri. His publications include *The Power of Open-Book Management: Releasing the True Potential of People's Minds, Hearts, and Hands,* with Jill Carpenter and M. Patricia Kane (Wiley, 1996) and *The Open-Book Management Field Book,* with Jill Carpenter and M. Patricia Kane (Wiley, 1997).

5

Valuing Capacities

We have a deep-seated and institutionalized habit of focusing on needs and deficiencies as a means of improvement, as if we or our organizations were broken and needed to be fixed. While this may, at times, be helpful, we have gone way overboard—to the point where we have become immunized to "constructive criticism" (another oxymoron) and realize very little change from hearing about what is wrong with us. The untapped potential for change and building strong community comes from shifting our attention to gifts and capacities.

Change and learning are more likely to occur when we begin speaking about our capacities and gifts to each other. Most of us are rather blind to our strengths—we sense they exist, but cannot see them clearly on our own. We need to hear from others how we contribute. At the simplest level, we need to talk about what we have received from one another as a part of every conversation and every meeting. We need to do this for reasons deeper than simply feeling good or to better understand our strengths. Something more is at stake, especially when we engage in public expression of valuing and appreciation and do it as a main agenda point, not as a parting afterthought.

Talking to one another about our capacities gives expression to the possibilities, the mystery, and the miracle of life. If we wish our workplaces to be places in which our spirituality is affirmed, then we must bring that belief into our everyday practices. Our spirits are enlarged through what we do well. Our work as consultants is to bring communal rituals of affirmation into our clients' lives, and into our own. John McKnight, author of *The Careless Society: Community and Its Counterfeits,* defines community as the act of bringing, or inviting into the center, the gifts of those who are not in the center, those who are on the outskirts, on the periphery. Community becomes that place where all experience themselves as being in the center of things.

This needs to happen publicly. In the meetings we conduct, it can be done by inviting those on the edge of the room to come and sit for a while in the center and having those who have been in the center move toward the edge, staying as close to the center as possible. It is a form of acknowledgment that the whole is not complete until all have the experience of being in the center. This is an essential part of being a catalyst for change. We build a container for caring about the whole, and we use our position as catalyst to design experiences through which all members feel connected.

The Flawless Consulting Fieldbook and Companion

THE COMMUNAL IMPORTANCE OF NAMING

We need to see that people's gifts and strengths are named out loud, especially at the end of the sessions we conduct. Acknowledging gifts can become a ritual of parting. We always think there will be a better opportunity later, but that is not true. This meeting will not occur again, even if the same people with the same agenda come together in the same place and do it soon. Later the same day, the next day, that gathering will be of a different nature. The end of a meeting signifies the end of a phase of our development—and the beginning of a transition to a future that we can wish for but not predict. Every moment of transition is a fragment of our transformation. So it needs special attention, recognition that we offered all that we were able and that the offer was seen by others. We were visible, which we do not know until we have heard it from one another.

You could say that consultants are holders of the collective possibility. This is one way to look at culture. Culture becomes known by the experiences we have when we are all in the same room. When we talk about individual strengths publicly, our capacities are affirmed by witnessing the meaning particular people have for one another. If this is not acknowledged publicly, it will remain private, forever hidden and collectively unknown.

Having small groups, seated or standing in a circle, state what they have received from each other changes the whole room and in that moment the whole culture changes.

We do not need to know all that has transpired between people, only that something important has taken place. The act of public appreciation heals the wounds of the broken and fragmented collective. This is what is forgotten and abandoned by our individualism. Our institutions are dominated by fear of the dangers of public dialogue, public speaking. The most popular fear-based myth is that if you speak up you will get shot. In most places this is not true, but the myth is strong and reinforces the belief that the community is dangerous, even though its members may be our close friends. Our job is to challenge this myth, and to do it in public ways. And to do it by naming what has been of value.

  The Flawless Consulting Fieldbook and Companion

Chapter 25

Leading from Behind
Talking with Sled Dogs

Sam Magill

It might not be immediately apparent to you, but consultants are high-control people. I know we all sell models of teamwork and participation, but we are not too good at it. We like control, we would rather be the teacher than the student, and we think we have an answer, or at least a process, for everything. All the more appropriate this article by Sam Magill is about surrender. We all know the definition of surrender, and we mouth the rhetoric of consultant as learner—but we are just waiting for the experience. Sam had the experience. Lucky Sam.

Imagine being charged with consulting to a group of highly committed individuals who have worked together for a long time. They know the territory better than you do and are more at home in the particular business environment than you are. What's more, they are so skilled at their craft that they work from an instinct that is not immediately obvious. They are alert to changes in the situation that you miss entirely. If that isn't enough, they know whom the real movers and shakers are in the organization and don't pay much attention to people who wave their arms a lot without earning respect.

Although I've experienced this both as a manager and as a consultant, the scene I've just described did not occur with other people. It happened to me in Calgary, Alberta, while visiting Will Black, who teaches leadership to people by having them work with

sled dogs. The experience exposed me to a culture rich in relationships, purpose, invitation, and faith. And it exposed me to my own needs for control.

There's an old saying, perhaps from China, that if you want to be a leader, find a parade and get in front. Part of the difficulty of working with sled dogs is that there's a fast-moving parade, but the human is at the back of it, being dragged through the snow. It was certainly the most challenging "consulting" engagement I've had, and it brought new meaning to the term "flawless."

Like most engagements, this one had several phases: the test ride, the plan, relationships, the jump to action, and review. The test ride was like riding in a flight simulator—it's safe and gives you a taste of the real thing. The plan was just that—what we expected to do. Relationships had to be formed in advance because there would be no time once we jumped to action. The jump to action separated talk from the real thing. The review anchored what I had learned so that I could use it again.

TEST RIDE

Before going solo with a team of dogs, I needed to get a feel for the team and the medium, so Will took me out with nine dogs. He was the driver and I was freight. Each dog, he said, produced a force of three hundred pounds. Nine dogs deliver 2,700 pounds of thrust—enough so that the "driver" cannot physically control the team.

My first lesson was to be quiet and watch. How many times do we think as leaders and consultants that we have to say a lot to show we're in charge? In this case, too much talking confuses the team and leads to their ignoring what the leader says—a phenomenon that also happens in our human teams. After a quiet ride, Will offered me the chance to ride on the sled's runners. I was to continue to stay silent and let him do the talking because the team knew his voice. I was a stranger. An experience I had in a large manufacturing company came to mind, where managers were reassigned regularly as if they were interchangeable parts. Then management wondered why no one listened.

The Flawless Consulting Fieldbook and Companion

The next part of practice was a sport called skijoring. Whoever invented it is fortunately not available to me. It involved my body being hitched to two dogs while my feet were locked into cross-country skis. I am not a novice at cross country, but after spending the first hour being dragged on my face, I wanted a change. This lesson taught me to balance between saying the word "stay" and keeping the team interested in the project and my voice. They looked frequently for Will and the other dogs (who were off having fun) until I demanded that they stop.

What was the consulting lesson? Go out on a practice run to see what the team does when it's working well—before intervening. Get into their medium *and* insist on a few ground rules. Say what you mean—and then be quiet. When I was tired of being on my face, I first worked only on the rules of stopping and staying stopped. I put my skis across the trail and held them there until all was quiet. I practiced getting up without being pulled forward. Then, and only then, I said "hike"—quietly was enough. I'm not advocating for consultants to run the rule-making show, only that we must come to some agreements about language and ground rules.

THE PLAN

To add to the next phase of adventure, Will arranged a midnight outing with light snowfall thrown in for extra fun. The first thing I noticed was that all the preparation and planning had only a vague correspondence to really doing it; planning was safe, a concept, an ideal, easy, no strain on anybody—a very low level of commitment.

In our fast-paced organizations, I sometimes see enormous attention to planning as if it were the real thing. That's not to say that it isn't important, just that it's not the same thing as reality. Furthermore, with an eager team who knows what they are doing, long planning becomes distracting. It's as though the team says, "Get on with it or let us go home. Being in this harness is fine as long as we're doing something!" The more fun the better; and, in this case, better means running. Besides, if we're going into unknown territory, planning simply can't be done.

RELATIONSHIPS

Before this whole system was to go into action, there were a few more details. Because the dogs were more skilled than I, it was important to take time to get to know them before expecting cooperation. In this case getting to know each other simply meant spending time together doing the simple tasks of living. Literally, it meant cleaning the yard where they're kept, feeding them, and clipping their toenails. For dogs, the latter is a very intimate act and, if they allowed me to do it, a clear sign I was making progress. It was their choice!

The simple relationship created by simple acts of service and time spent hanging out together skijoring provided a crucial foundation. In an organization in which I managed a group of consultants, I once helped with a simple task of opening hundreds of envelopes from 360-degree feedback forms. While I was doing it, my boss walked in and chastised me for wasting my time. The task was beneath my position, she said. Well, so was scooping up dog litter, but when push came to shove the relationship I built made all the difference in the world.

THE JUMP TO ACTION

There comes a moment when it's time to move from planning to action. During the harnessing phase, a stout rope holds the sled and dogs to a full-size pickup. To move out, one stands on the sled's runners and pulls a trigger release. The dogs know what's coming and bark, howl, and jump in a frenzy of anticipation.

I stepped on the runners, grabbed the release trigger, and . . . stepped off. My body seemed to know that once I released the sled, I was no longer in charge. So, I went unconsciously to Will to ask a question. Any question would do; I didn't even have one.

This is the edge of faith: Faith in my teacher, faith in the dogs, faith in the snow on the ground and the weather, faith in myself, and ultimately faith in the relationship I had with the dogs. This is the edge of action—a different domain in which I'm really along for the ride into their territory. My leadership was not solely of my own doing; it would

The Flawless Consulting Fieldbook and Companion

have to be more like a dance with a partner who knows the steps better than I. I've also experienced this as the edge of consulting, when the client takes over. Perhaps our job is merely to release the team. If we don't let go, the team is ever dependent on our wisdom, which is inadequate for them to live on.

Will advised me to either get on and go or put the dogs in the truck. The greatest number of dog fights occurs when the dogs are hooked up and anchored. They are committed to work, that is, running. And when they don't get to do it, they turn to their next commitment, settling who's in charge among them—and the cost to the loser *and* to the winner is high. How often do we create teams of capable people, only to let them sit idle with vague purposes and tasks, or, worse yet, occupy their time in areas to which they are not committed? (I think of a parallel here of people who attend staff meetings in which nothing important happens—no tooth and claw but lots of whining.)

At last, I pulled the release, said my Hail Mary's, and flew down the dark trail. It was exhilarating! Snow flying, dogs barking briefly, then silence except for my quiet epithets.

Our plan had been for me to turn at the first trail junction and stop until I saw Will's headlamp. So, I turned, called to the lead dog, Sakani, and collected on the relationship she and I had built skijoring: She stopped quickly. I planted the snow anchor and, keeping one hand on the sled (never, never let go of the sled) looked for Will.

I saw his light and stepped back on the runners, then leaned over to pull the anchor and called to the lead. Silence. Nothing happened. I stared in disbelief. The dogs were gone. Gone! My mind raced. Then, recalling Will's advice to say as little as possible and never get excited, I called twice to Sakani to stop. My headlamp illuminated four pairs of red eyes looking back at me. Stay, Sakani. Stay.

Will came around the corner expecting me to be moving and nearly ran me down. He stopped. I said in a quiet sort of way, "We have a problem." He, too, stared in disbelief.

Now here is where plans don't count. Relationship and communication and staying connected and inventing are the way out. Will asked me to stand in front of his team: They are so loyal to him that they were likely to follow him forward. He approached my team because they knew him better than they did me. When he got to them (Sakani had stayed as I asked), he first straightened them out, to separate the antagonists on the team, then called me.

Quietly, slowly, I walked on the trail until I got to Sakani. Then I stepped off the trail up to my knees in unpacked snow and led Sakani back to the sled. Again, invention mattered. If the team started to run, we were dead. The four of them were much stronger than Will and I. I picked Sakani's front feet up so that she hopped her way back to the sled. It neutralized her strength and is the method for getting the dogs from kennel to truck, but it's not generally used on the trail. The others followed her as I made a wide circle to avoid fights.

Once back at the sled, we made the same circle again to get pointed back down the trail and found out what had happened—an old rope with a broken knot.

REVIEW OF THE EVENT

The sequence in this breakdown is important.

1. I saw and acknowledged that something unexpected had happened.
2. I called on my relationship with the lead.
3. I stayed calm and quiet so not to introduce more trouble. No arm waving allowed.
4. I called on the available expertise.
5. As a team, we invented a solution one step at a time. We did not sit down and plan it abstractly. All of it was in action. If the action worked, we kept going; if not, we made up a new step.
6. There was no blame anywhere.
7. Once the problem was resolved, we went back to the primary commitment—running.

The rest of the trip consisted of checking turns on the route, building Sakani's and my ability to communicate about turns, and enjoying the

The Flawless Consulting Fieldbook and Companion

ride. Back at the truck, my job again became the steward: Water, praise, and a warm box on the truck for each dog.

LEARNINGS

So, what does this adventure have to do with consulting and leading based on stewardship, relationships, and faith in human organizations? If *stewardship* is choosing service over self-interest, then the simple acts of tending the needs of the team must be the beginning and the end. No fancy program or set of principles or strategies can replace them. Some of the acts are spoken; some are in silence. Many would be called menial.

Relationships begin before the adventure and are the basis for success. They are all there is to call on when plans come unknotted. They are strengthened by making requests and not by pushing it. (When I was cutting the dogs' toenails, I let them walk away when they wanted to, then called them back. When they'd had enough of my clumsiness, we stopped for the time being.) Unless a relationship is built on choice for all the parties, it is a dictatorship.

Faith in each other and in our ability to figure out what to do next provides a foundation for venturing into the unknown. Each time we make a change, take on a new project, or have a meeting it is a venture into unknown territory. Because there is no guarantee, it is an act of faith.

When we call to the team we are making an *invitation*. If they don't accept it, we must start once again by doing the simple tending. I'm very clear that humans and dogs aren't the same, and business is not exactly the same as going for a sled ride, but don't we sometimes make assumptions about our relationships with people that even a dog wouldn't accept?

As for "flawless," in my experience planning for perfection is a formula for falling short. Strong relationships between skilled partners and exercising faith in each other over and over during action are as close to flawlessness as we're going to get—or need to be.

For More Depth

Further Reading

Axelrod, Richard H. *Terms of Engagement: Changing the Way We Change Organizations.* San Francisco: Berrett-Koehler, 2000.

Bellman, Geoffrey M. *The Consultant's Calling: Bringing Who You Are to What You Do.* San Francisco: Jossey-Bass, 1990.

De Hartog, Jan. *The Peaceable Kingdom.* New York: Atheneum, 1972.

Hudson, Frederick, & Pamela D. Mclean. *Life Launch: A Passionate Guide to the Rest of Your Life.* Santa Barbara, CA: Hudson Institute Press, 1995.

O'Reilly, Mary Rose. *Radical Presence: Teaching As a Contemplative Practice.* Portsmouth, NH: Boynton/Cook, 1998.

Palmer, Parker J., & Martin E. Marty. *The Company of Strangers.* New York: Crossroad Publishing Company, 1981.

Rogers, Everett. *Diffuson of Innovations* (4th ed.). New York: Free Press, 1995.

Sardello, Robert. *Facing the World with Soul: The Reimagination of Modern Life.* Hudson, NY: Lindisfarne Books, 1991.

Schuster, John P., & M. Patricia Kane. *The Power of Open-Book Management: Releasing the True Potential of People's Minds, Hearts, and Hands.* New York: Wiley, 1997.

Stone, Richard. *The Healing Art of Storytelling: A Sacred Journey of Personal Discovery.* New York: Hyperion, 1996.

Tannen, Deborah. *The Argument Culture: Stopping America's War of Words.* New York: Ballantine, 1999.

Further Training

The Hudson Institute. www.hudsoninstitute.com.

Powers of Leadership, The Whidbey Institute, a workshop on leadership to sustain our common interests, from The Whidbey Institute. www.whidbeyinstitute.org.

Weir Lab's workshop on self-differentiation.

About the Contributor

Sam Magill is an independent consultant in Edmonds, Washington.

The Flawless Consulting Fieldbook and Companion

Chapter 26

Homeopathic Consulting
Learning Is Free, Teaching Is Not

Cliff Bolster

The willingness to focus on capacities is an expression of our faith. Organizations do pretty well in acknowledging faith in God, but fall short in acknowledging faith in their own people. Cliff's article on self-managed learning and change is about developing this faith. Consultants as a group tend to be rather cynical about the capacities of their clients. When we build a client's dependency on us, when we act in ways that lead them to believe they do better when we are around, we reinforce our lack of confidence in client capacity. Cliff's approach to consulting is based on the wonderful observation that "learning is free, teaching is not." The highest cost of teaching is that we reinforce the belief that the teacher is needed for learning. In everyday language, which Cliff is good at, his being and his thinking are a fine expression of modesty and humility. Rare among consultants, all the more precious in our work.

One year I conducted several repeat sessions of a workshop based on the systems thinking work of Peter Senge. I noticed one person coming to all of them. I became curious about this person and wondered why he didn't get bored. He said that even when the material was the same, he experienced it anew and got something deeper from that experience. At the last workshop I asked him how he was applying the concepts and ideas he had been exposed to over the year. He described a study group composed of four other executives and himself in this large city. They were all intrigued by the ideas of learning organizations and wanted to deepen their understanding of those ideas. So they began meeting together for two hours every month at lunch to discuss learning organization concepts. They circulated readings to one another and listened to the person who was attending the workshops describe what he had learned as well. After six months they noticed that they were meeting for six hours at a time, and wanted more. In addition they took it on themselves to implement one or more of the ideas in their own organization and report back on their experience. They all reported that they had stimulated important and positive changes in their organizations and that they were personally invigorated by the experience.

THE NATURAL POWER OF LEARNING

How simple. One person took some courses, read some material, gathered together some kindred spirits who took the ideas seriously, and five change processes were begun. There was no fanfare nor announcements from the top. No consultants nor project plans with deadlines and consequences. They were bringing about something they cared about, beginning with one person at a time. They were practicing homeopathic change.

Homeopathic consultation is an approach to change rooted in the natural power of learning. The idea of homeopathic consulting was inspired by homeopathic medicine, in which administering minute doses of an agent results in the system taking on full-blown symptoms of the agent. In homeopathic consulting, the consultant administers learning in small doses (to individuals), who administer learning to more individuals, resulting in full-blown organizational learning. It works because it is a system intervention that stimulates individuals' intrinsic desire for growth, which has a positive effect and consequently leads to productive change. In contrast, today's

The Flawless Consulting Fieldbook and Companion

conventional wisdom is that to bring about system change effectively, an intervention must be large and comprehensive in scope and backed by the reinforcing power of top leadership. But the implementation of massive change initiatives for other than true survival situations can do serious harm to the longer term health of the system because they may trigger substantial resistance. In most cases this resistance is driven underground, giving the impression that it has been overcome.

Learning and Results

The relationship between learning and results is virtually axiomatic. If one is continuously learning on the job, performance will automatically improve and results will flow. This is true in all aspects of our lives. Those who engage seriously in a "hobby," such as golf or gardening or art or chess or music, know that learning is interwoven so deeply in the experience as to make it inseparable from the doing. Learning is growth, and growth is one of the deepest sources of human joy. Sometimes my clients will ask me to justify a recommendation designed to create learning at the work site. Over the years I have learned to be patient and understanding with them, because deep down I know that if this is a question in clients' minds, they are unaware that what they are missing is growth in their own lives.

Learning, Enjoyment, and Motivation

Mihaly Csikszentmihalyi, the author of *Flow: The Optimal Psychological Experience*, contends that learning is a continuous source of joy in every culture around the world. Reframing our work from being a burden or necessary evil to a source of learning and joy is a difficult yet worthwhile task. Tapping into the bottomless reservoir of curiosity that exists in everyone is a real challenge. Later in this article I will describe a case of using after-action reviews (a learning structure) to improve results and ignite the joy and energies of workers in a manufacturing plant.

Learning and Cost

Learning is free. Teaching is not. Our education system is an extension of the parent-child relationship. We needed the protection of our parents when we were very young or we would not have survived. When we left home for school, we looked to teachers to tell us what we needed to learn and what was right and wrong. They obliged by giving us answers to even the most impossible questions and motivated us by placing letter grades and gold stars on our work. In the earliest years of school, when we arrived home, we were greeted with the question, "What did you learn today in school?" We responded enthusiastically with stories of the day and the wonders we had been exposed to. At some point, however, our parents began to ask a different question: "What did you get on your report card?" This change represented a fundamental shift away from learning the material and set our focus on what we had to do to get good grades. Some of us quickly caught on and learned to get good grades. Learning became a means to get good marks.

We then moved into the workplace, where supervisors became the teachers and parents. They graded our work and gave us the answers. We learned to do what they expected and were deemed successful as we ascended the ladder. Along the way we would attend "training programs" that were cleverly designed and often thought-provoking and well-presented. But many found it hard to transfer the learning to the workplace. We wanted relevant, practical, useful tools that could be immediately applied and were guaranteed to work. These training events were expensive and, quite frankly, yielded little, not because they weren't well designed and delivered, but because we were learning disabled.

If we change our assumptions about learning—that is, as fully functioning adults, we aren't as dependent on others for answers—we can be "learners" and our work can be our teacher. The cost of learning will drop significantly. Occasionally, we will seek outside help, but we will be clear as to what we want from them and can collaborate with them as equals in our quest for learning. The feedback we perceive from our experiences at work will teach us what we need to know. We will become perfectly capable of discovering our own answers.

The Flawless Consulting Fieldbook and Companion

HOMEOPATHIC CONSULTING FLAWLESSLY

Homeopathic consulting is aligned with the principles of flawless consulting. It requires both the consultant and client to agree that the consultant is to play a collaborative role. They must also agree that one of the major objectives of the project is to build the capacity of the client and his/her people. Finally, and above all, it requires the consultant's and client's capabilities to express themselves authentically. There is no idea that has been more useful in my consulting experience than the "authentic statement"—putting what one is experiencing into words at the moment they are being experienced.

Homeopathic consulting is designed to achieve great results, tap the bottomless reservoir of intrinsic motivation, and do it with little out-of-pocket cost. For the process to fulfill its potential, there are a few necessary prerequisites, which I have detailed below and illustrated with a case example. I am not advocating the superiority of homeopathic consultation, but offer it as a viable and powerful role when the conditions are appropriate. Consultants serve many roles and provide a wide variety of services. The homeopathic consultant focuses on development of capacity, using real problems and situations as the field for learning.

Requirements for Homeopathic Consulting

I have worked with many consultants over twenty-five years of practice. I have also served as an executive of large companies and played the client role with consultants I hired. During that period I have asked myself, "What distinguishes the quality of consultants?" Leaving technical expertise aside (a big request, as most consultants are hired for their technical expertise), I want to narrow the focus to aspects of the consultation process and the client-consultant relationship. What follows are descriptions of four capabilities that I believe are necessary to practice homeopathic consultation: (1) A deep reverence for learning and personal humility; (2) the personal capacity to care for the client; (3) the willingness to speak the "truth"; and (4) the ability to uncover the power of choice.

At its heart, consultation is a form of facilitated learning. Therefore, one distinguishing characteristic of homeopathic consulting is that the client learns something worthwhile when in the presence of or as a result of working with the consultant. Two clients recently told me they value my visits because whenever we work together, they (and I) learn something useful, valuable, and important. This is the most gratifying feedback I have ever received.

I do not have the perseverance or inclination to lead long, complex change projects. Many of my colleagues do that quite capably. My contribution is to spend time with one, five, thirty, or more people and help them reflect on three learning capabilities:

1. How they perceive their current reality (perception skills);
2. How they interpret those perceptions, that is, how they are thinking about their reality (thinking skills); and
3. How they see themselves acting as a result (behavioral skills).

Most clients have found this work helpful and high-leverage. Those who have a different opinion choose not to engage me in the first place or don't continue very long as a client. Being and remaining a client in homeopathic consulting is a clear and voluntary choice on the part of both the client and consultant.

The focus of the homeopathic consultant is the capacity or capabilities of the client to deal more effectively with the harsh reality he/she faces. Many consultants promise that they will "teach their clients how to fish," not just "feed them fish." Few clients and consultants take the proverb seriously. Their tacit agreement is to feed the client and leave, only to be called back when the client is hungry again. Intense focus on results overwhelms attention to the other matter of developing client capability. Homeopathic consulting puts learning first, assuming that the presence of a current problem is at least partially caused by the lack of capacity of the client to prevent or resolve it.

The underlying core belief of homeopathic consulting is that the client has the latent or manifest capacity to solve his/her own problem. When I draw the conclusion that my client is incapable of solving his/her own problem, I become judgmental and ineffective. My experience in executive and managerial roles in large organizations has taught me to appreciate what it takes to lead change, particularly if it necessitates facing issues like leadership, culture, attitude, and motivation, all of which play an important part in every complex change effort, regardless of its business or operational nature. I recently witnessed a large-scale change project being driven mostly by the consulting team that promised the client measurable results in a specified period of time. In their zeal to achieve, the consultants often erroneously concluded that client personnel who did not immediately accept their solutions were deficient in some important capability or irrationally resistant or had a devious political motive. As I wandered throughout the client's organization, I heard many comments that led me to believe that nothing would substantially change in this project. The results would be realized by legitimate or questionable scorekeeping, and they would move on to the next crisis.

A reverence for learning requires a distinction between levels of knowing, none of which match certainty. The stance of a "learner" supersedes the orientation of the "knower" in the practice of homeopathic consultation. Otherwise, as Meg Wheatley, a renowned scholar in systems change theory, has observed, "If you think you have the answer, the only rational action for you to take is to try to impose your answer on others."

Some consultants believe they have the answer to even the most complex problems. The homeopathic consultant assumes the client is in the best position to know what he/she needs from the consultant. I do not want to impose myself or my solutions on others, but if invited, I will offer my views based on my experiences. This is a difficult position to adopt with many clients and potential clients. After all, they want answers from the consultant and have consciously or unconsciously concluded that they do not have the answer and are incapable of discovering one. The presence of the consultant is often testimony to

the lack of confidence clients have in themselves and their people. This is quite understandable, because we all learned to look outside ourselves for answers from the time we were born. We were given answers by our parents, our teachers, then our supervisors, and now consultants. The restoration of that confidence is at the heart of homeopathic consultation.

My consulting role model is the character Yoda from the *Star Wars* Trilogy. Yoda was the quintessential homeopathic consultant. He slowly worked with Luke Skywalker to bring out of him what lay dormant. Yoda is a humble role model: He lived in a swamp, he had only one client, and the client couldn't pay any fee. Homeopathic consultation is humble, too. It is not a recipe for wealth and recognition. Most of the work I do is embedded in the "white spaces" between milestones and results. It is virtually impossible to see, let alone measure. At the same time it is deeply satisfying and gratefully received.

Caring for the Client

Homeopathic consulting is very personal and intentionally so. It requires the capacity to connect with the client in a relationship before going too far into the content of the situation or the tasks required to deal with it. I have noticed that I have done my best work with clients I truly like and respect. We develop a relationship based on trust, support, and mutual learning. My best work has seen me in the role of partner and collaborator, not ahead or behind, but *beside* the client. When I am honest with myself, I can recall situations when I felt at best ambivalent toward a client. I assess my performance in those conditions as professional and competent, but hardly superior. When I harbor negative opinions of the client that remain unresolved, the work is difficult and rarely achieves the desired results.

Early in my consulting career, I had the opportunity to work with a client who was a former colleague. During our first day he noticed that I was "all business," continuously making suggestions and attending to the task at hand, the deliverables, the project plan, and on and on. After lunch he drew me aside and said, "Stop trying to earn your fee! I know who you are; you have nothing to prove to me!" Ever since that day I have been attuned to those occasions when I'm "trying to earn my fee," and with that awareness I can relax and connect with the client before getting to the task.

If the core focus of homeopathic consulting is learning, we must attend to the conditions that generate and inhibit learning. The research is clear that a supportive, "safe" environment is necessary (albeit not sufficient) to create learning. We also know that fear prevents learning. The development of an open atmosphere between client and consultant is a first step in the practice of homeopathic consultation.

Speaking the Truth

No learning can occur without feedback. So the homeopathic consultant must be willing to deliver, receive, and develop the client's capacity to seek whatever relevant feedback is contained in the situation. This principle applies whether the feedback is about the personal effectiveness of the client, the quality of teamwork in a work group, or the presentation of difficult diagnostic information about the system. Such feedback is the primary source of instruction and learning, not the consultant.

I was fortunate to be born with the ability to deal with people as equals regardless of differences in status and power. I am not particularly intimidated by hierarchy. I am not wired to be submissive or nonassertive to those in more powerful organizational roles. This capacity allows me to give direct and timely feedback to clients at any organizational level. They don't always appreciate what I have to say and are occasionally put off by my frankness, interpreting it as disrespectful. However, when we are able to work through the process of giving one another feedback, our relationship takes a measurable leap forward.

I never claim to have the "truth" with regard to another, but I have observations and reactions to which they are entitled. Truth and caring are mutually reinforcing, much the same as levels of performance and job satisfaction; as one variable increases or decreases, it causes a similar change in the other variable, which in turn causes further change in the originating variable.

I am doing my best work when I can influence my client to re-examine his/her thinking or actions based on some feedback that was important to the problem and difficult to communicate and hear. In the same way, when my client gives me direct feedback about something he/she considers important in our working relationship we are working well together. My experience has taught me that even the most critical feedback can be well-received if delivered with a caring intention. The slightest criticism is blocked by defensiveness if the giver's intention is perceived as hurtful.

Uncovering Freedom of Choice

The homeopathic consultant continuously encourages clients to see alternatives and opportunities for choice. The underlying assumption is that learning occurs best for those who choose or commit to learn. It is also founded on the belief that Tim Gallwey has articulated so well in his *Inner Game* books: "The only thing we control in our lives is where we place our attention." Our environment bombards us with stimuli to attend to, but when we purposefully focus our attention on something we want to focus on, the perception can become conscious thought and accessible to analysis and choice. Viktor Frankl, even in the horrific confines of a concentration camp, found a deep source of life energy when he focused on things he could affect and let go of those he could not.

The power of choice is something that I encourage in all my engagements and interactions with clients. I want them to choose and commit to courses of action, rather than simply do something because they are deferring to my consultant expertise. The choice also applies to the continuity of our relationship. One of the most difficult consulting-client situations is when the client does not believe he/she has any choice but to do a project or work with you, the consultant. Corporate, or higher ups, have decided to do this, and the client perceives there to be no discretion whether to participate or not.

The Flawless Consulting Fieldbook and Companion

I have found it helpful to uncover genuine choices within the domain over which the client may feel no choice. He/she may have to do the project, but how it is implemented and managed leaves a large area for discretion and choice. Helping the client to shift focus to these areas, rather than lamenting the fact that he/she had no choice to start, can be helpful and healthy for establishing a productive relationship. I was faced with just such a situation in a recent consultation with a manufacturing client, described below.

THE MANUFACTURING CASE: JUST SHOWING UP

For the past three years I have been working with a client in such a way that both of us are getting what we want from the working relationship. I wanted interesting work and some compensation for my services, and my client wanted to change the organization in a particular way and develop some particular personal abilities as we went along.

The client organization is a global manufacturing company. The project began as a worldwide corporate initiative to improve the quality of factory performance in all their major plants around the globe. A corporate-level manufacturing team had concluded that breakthrough operating performance would come from changes in the way people were thinking and interacting. Most of the manufacturing operations had been through a number of "people" initiatives over the previous ten years, so we decided to adopt a radical approach: Let each plant decide for itself whether it wanted to engage in the initiative or not.

In order to help each plant make an informed decision, we asked one thing of the refinery senior leadership: To convene a meeting of key formal and informal leaders (approximately thirty-five people, including union leadership) during which we would introduce the group to the services we had to offer and discuss how we might move forward if they chose to. In his introduction to the meeting, the plant manager communicated his skepticism with regard to the plant's autonomy when he stated, "Corporate says we have a choice, but I really don't think we have any choice." He went on to say that, nevertheless, he wanted to see

what we had to offer and to let this group decide whether or not to proceed any further. If the response was favorable, this group would then play an influential role in designing the process of moving forward.

As we were in the early stages, it became readily apparent that the vast majority of key leaders in the refinery were simply tolerating the project. There were frequent references to previous attempts to change the plant's culture and, with some pride, statements regarding their failure. This was the classic consultant situation in which you are in the bowels of the client organization and realize that they don't want you there, while at the same time you fully believe you have something valuable to offer. It was at this instant that I decided to begin the practice of homeopathic consulting. I simply asked whether I could attend a number of their regular meetings over the next few weeks in order to meet people and have them become more comfortable with me. I sat quietly for over a month, simply attending production planning meetings, maintenance meetings, capital project planning meetings, staff meetings, and the like.

It wasn't very long before some people would ask me privately, "What did you think of the meeting?" And I would offer an observation such as, "Keeping track of all the information must be difficult." Eventually, one person said, "I don't understand most of what we discuss in the meeting. I just want to make sure I know what I'm supposed to do." From that conversation came some work with those attending the meeting on making their communication and deliberations *in that meeting* more effective.

As a result of that and similar experiences of small, timely interventions, I began to see my role as someone who was at the plant to help people become learners in any way I could. I was no longer the "teacher" of the five disciplines, but Cliff Bolster, learning consultant and "coach," working alongside the client while he/she did his/her work.

SEEDS OF CHANGE

The work of the project team continues and has achieved moderate success. However, a number of small initiatives have been planted, seeds that are beginning to grow and bear fruit. The project team chartered a subgroup with different members to focus on "performance education." This group has taken it on themselves to develop a high level of business and operating literacy throughout the plant, covering all employees. Borrowing from "open-book management" principles and practices, they have implemented communications and learning sessions for the plant community so that everyone is fully aware of what the plant must achieve, how measurements are calculated, and how each person impacts the measures.

I have become very interested in "after-action reviews," a learning structure designed to develop the reflective capacity of individuals and teams. After-action reviews, in my opinion, are the most effective learning structures I have yet seen. They require one to perceive the feedback directly from the experience, and they acknowledge that no one person has a corner on the "truth," the idea being that the more diverse the perspectives the higher the quality of the reflection. The after-action review requires a lowering of fear in order to be effective. Finally, after-action reviews are easy to learn and adopt with powerful results. They are elegant interventions.

At the plant we began after-action reviews in the maintenance department. When there was a breakdown of equipment, we would gather a small group of operators, maintenance technicians, and sometimes an engineer and ask four simple questions:

1. What result did we want in this situation?
2. What result did we achieve?
3. What caused the gap?
4. What have we learned?

After a short while we noticed that the quality of the interaction between operations and maintenance had improved, and those who were participating in the reviews were enjoying their work more. Our plans are to expand the after-action reviews to the end of each shift so that a crew would meet for fifteen minutes before the end of their shift to ask the four questions as they related to the shift they had just worked: "What results did we want on the last shift?" "What results did we achieve on the shift?" "What caused the gap(s)?" "What did we learn?" This simple intervention has opened the entire plant in ways that we could not have imagined. The after-action review we expect will become a routine way of doing things at the plant.

And what was my role in this change? I brought the idea of after-action review to the plant organization development person. He became interested and searched his company for additional information. He learned how to conduct the sessions and started with a couple of crews during a maintenance shutdown. Meanwhile, I led two after-action reviews that involved larger numbers of people and two particularly volatile situations. Both were extremely effective and well-received. There are several people now conducting after-action reviews in the plant, and they are stimulating change at a steady and manageable pace.

I had a small and consequential role in this change. Was it an identifiable program with a name? No! And I firmly believe that was a major reason for its success.

For More Depth

Further Reading

Csikszentmihalyi, Mihaly. *Flow: The Optimal Psychological Experience.* New York: HarperCollins, 1991.

Gallwey, W. Timothy. *Inner Skiing* (rev. ed.). New York: Random House, 1997.

Gallwey, W. Timothy. *The Inner Game of Golf* (rev. ed.). New York: Random House, 1998.

Gallwey, W. Timothy. *The Inner Game of Tennis* (rev. ed.). New York: Random House, 1997.

Gallwey, W. Timothy. *The Inner Game of Work.* New York: Random House, 1999.

Palmer, Parker J. *The Courage to Teach: Exploring the Inner Landscape of a Teacher's Life.* San Francisco: Jossey-Bass, 1998.

Vaill, Peter B. *Learning As a Way of Being: Strategies for Survival in a World of Permanent White Water.* San Francisco: Jossey-Bass, 1996.

Further Training

Gestalt Workshop and Dimensions of Learning Using Golf as the Medium.

About the Contributor

Cliff Bolster is an independent consultant based in Brunswick, Maine, with more than twenty-five years of experience as both an HR executive and consultant.

Chapter 27

Milk and Buttermilk

Idries Shah

Murid Laki Humayun put this question to the Maulana Bahaudin:

In the town of Gulafshan there is a circle of followers. Some of them are in the condition of exercises, but the majority are those who collect weekly to learn from the daily transactions and teachings of the *murshid* (guide).

Many of the *murids* (disciples) understand the meaning of the tales and the events, and use these to correct their outward and inward behavior.

Many of the outside followers, however, do not appear to benefit from the events and the transactions, seeking instead books and teachings which will give them precise promises of progress.

How is it that disciples are in pain when ordinary followers fail to understand the meaning of the stories and events, especially since many of the latter are their close friends and each desires that there should be a unification between disciples and followers even of the outward sort?

Bahaudin replied:

Discipleship was instituted in order to concentrate those who can learn without raw objectives. Disciples who grieve because their followers are not learning in the same

Reprinted by permission from "Milk and Buttermilk," in *Wisdom of the Idiots* (pp. 31–32) by Idries Shah.

manner and at the same rate are grieving because they have imagined that affection must produce capacity. Capacity, however, is earned: affection is given and taken.

Accidental collections of people centering around a teaching will always endure a separating-out, like the separating of butter from milk, in the presence of the agitating factor, which is manifest or concealed but none the less present, whenever a renewal of teaching starts to work. This is the shaking of the vessel containing the milk. People imagine that, like buttermilk, when there is a movement, they will all be affected in the same way. But both butter and skimmed milk have their functions, although these may be in different fields.

  The Flawless Consulting Fieldbook and Companion

Chapter 28
Consulting As Capability Building

Lou Ann Daly

Lou Ann is a poster child for the belief that the future is ours to create and whatever we can imagine we can bring into the world. Rather than focus on the skills or practice of consulting, she speaks more to the consciousness and presence of the consultant. When the person is the product, who we are when we are with our clients is a significant concern. Lou Ann gives voice to the importance of our capacity to know ourselves and our capacity to know who we are at every moment.

"Well, if you're not going to give us the answer, you can at least make yourself useful and get us some popcorn," the client railed as she handed me a bowl to fill. So, I left the room and returned in a few minutes with a bowl full of popcorn.

In the past several years I have been working with individuals and teams to tap into and enhance their innate learning capability, most specifically their capability to learn how to learn. Although we learn all the time, much of what people learn in organizations may actually inhibit their ability to create effective learning environments. Effective learning environments are places in which the collective can be clear and open about what they want to create, honest and forthright about what's going on in the current environment

267

to inhibit or support those desired results, and able to work together in productive ways to achieve those results. When a team or organization wants to develop a collective understanding of what they are learning and how their learning is either working for them or against their potential to get what they want, they focus on developing their learning capability. They literally develop the ability to know what helps them learn so that they can accelerate their ability to adapt, change, and generate new ways of creating results. In a world in which immediate action and bottom-line results matter most, such work is rarely understood or appreciated in its initial phases because it requires slowing down to notice what is happening when it happens.

The type of consulting I do is called "capability development." It consists of services performed in a way that leaves the clients with new skills, new awareness, and abilities to do the work themselves. The intention is to create less dependency, and over time no dependency, on the consultant to do the work.

Capability development is an organizational necessity in terms of its investment in the people of the organization and its core systems and processes. It is a requisite for the organization's agility in competitive markets, sustainability, and repeatability of results. In capability development, the consultant must understand principles of individual and collective learning. The consultant also has to be aware of how his or her own ways of learning will either accelerate the client's capability development or reinforce dependency on the consultant. Organizations must be aware that one of their goals is to learn how to build capability without the assistance of a consultant.

THE CONSULTANT'S ROLE

In the popcorn scenario described above, I was in the position of coaching an internal consulting team to develop their ability to learn how to learn together so that they could help their respective clients learn as a team to accelerate business results. My approach to this and all of my consulting projects is based on my deeply held beliefs about the consultant's role in teaching people how to build capability. I believe consultants must:

- Be completely present and aware of their own intentions.
- Understand and recognize what structures inhibit and what structures support personal learning. (Structures include patterns of thought, ways of interacting, meeting designs, and physical environments.)
- Be learners. (The focus is on "being," not on "doing," meaning that the consultant is actively involved in the learning. This is both fundamental and critical when building capability.)

This last point requires a bit of explanation. It is fairly subtle and often foreign to consultants whose focus is on getting results by "doing." When working with clients to develop capability, the consultant's ways of working become paramount. The focus is on helping the clients become more aware of their thinking and decision-making processes as they occur. The consultant must be a learner rather than an expert. Being a learner puts the consultant in the frame of mind to notice what might be inhibiting clients from getting results and to create a context in which clients can discover for themselves what is happening. Being a learner creates opportunities for the consultant to do a variety of things in the moment to help the client develop necessary skills and awareness.

LESSONS FROM THE FIELD

The following is a list of some of the lessons I have learned and conclusions I have drawn regarding what it takes for consultants to be successful in helping teams and organizations learn to develop desired capabilities.

First, I believe it is the consultant's job to be consciously aware of which structures (meaning patterns of thought, ways of interacting, meeting designs, and physical environments) cause clients to confront themselves and their own assumptions and beliefs. At the same time the consultant must be aware that clients will not confront themselves until they are ready. Such awareness means that the consultant does not "fix" discomfort or frustration, but will instead ask questions that encourage the client to choose consciously to either lean into the dis-

comfort and frustration or flee. The bottom line is that clients become aware of their choices. Thus begins the journey of capability building for those who choose to develop their capabilities.

Second, I believe people have different ways of approaching what is new and potentially threatening to their views of themselves and their world. Therefore, it is the consultant's job to really listen and pay attention to how individual clients and teams learn and how they avoid learning.

Third, consultants have to be honest with themselves and their clients about where they are stuck and about how they personally embrace or flee learning opportunities.

Fourth, the consultant needs to enter any assignment or meeting fully centered, clear about outcomes, and clear about how his or her design and facilitation choices affect client learning. In my experience, to facilitate learning a consultant must recognize and suspend his or her own needs to be right and to believe there is a right answer, because those needs and beliefs will inhibit the client's ability to feel free to discover and learn.

Fifth, the consultant must explicitly design for, or at least keep in conscious awareness, the need to work at the "heart" level and not the intellectual "head" level. Building capabilities often requires unlearning current ways of operating, and unlearning current ways of operating means letting go of emotional ties to what has worked in the past. It is critical to engage at the heart level to personally connect with emotions. Staying at the head level feels safer because clients can detach, but that detachment will slow the capability building process.

Capability building requires that the consultant know which of his or her behaviors and choices reinforce learning disabilities. Learning disabilities can be thought of as whatever blocks the client's openness to seeing new opportunities and considering new ways of thinking. For example, a consultant who wants people to be comfortable will be more likely to rescue clients who begin to experience and express conflict and dissatisfaction with how the process is going. Intervening at this point to make everyone feel good will usually block the clients' opportunity to wrestle with and discover why they are stuck and what

  The Flawless Consulting Fieldbook and Companion

they need to do to move forward. Another example occurs when a consultant who needs to be in control encounters the chaos that typically occurs when a team really begins to confront what has been keeping it from being effective. If the consultant has never been a part of a high-performance team, the likelihood of intervening too early and proposing a path for the team is high. Such behavior actually makes it more difficult for the team to learn how to help itself operate effectively in the future.

LEARNING TO LEARN TOGETHER

In the popcorn example, both the client and the team were working on understanding a particular learning tool that could be used to help their organization improve the quality of their thinking, creativity, and communication. My job was to help everyone on the team thoroughly understand the underlying design and intended use of the tool. My clients expected that I would both help the group to learn how to learn together and make sure that the individuals in the group learned what they needed to know to help their respective clients. They assumed that I had the answers, and they desired that I arrange them in a clear and highly structured way that would be easy for them to duplicate with their clients.

However, my view is that the world is not so structured, and that when consultants structure the learning process to make everything explicit for clients, it actually takes clients longer to discover the gaps in their thinking or deeply held beliefs that limit them from obtaining the results they want. They don't actually learn how to take an amorphous or ambiguous area and approach it from a learning orientation to discover what works and why. And that, in turn, slows down the speed at which they can build learning capability.

The good news in this case is that the client was committed to developing learning capability. We continued to meet and to make explicit what was frustrating about the process and what we were learning as we went. By having clarity of purpose and shared intent to build learning capability, and by being willing to name what was going on in

meetings, they progressed in both individual and collective capability. We surfaced thinking that was helping, discovered gaps, and continually adjusted course. And while there were many points of conflict and frustration, there is also ample evidence of personal "ahas" and successes with their clients. Evidence that the changes have been sustainable is that the group has continuously changed membership since this work began and that core purpose, quality of work, and results have not varied significantly.

P.S. This client today is both effective and successful in building learning capability.

For More Depth

Hutchens, David. *The Lemming Dilemma: Living with Purpose, Leading with Vision.* Waltham, MA: Pegasus Communications, 2000.

Lindbergh, Anne Morrow. *Gift from the Sea.* (Reissue) New York: Pantheon, 1991.

Myss, Caroline. *Anatomy of the Spirit: The Seven Stages of Power and Healing.* New York: Random House, 1997.

Wheatley, Margaret. *Leadership and the New Science: Discovering Order in a Chaotic World* (2nd ed.). San Francisco: Berrett-Koehler, 1999.

About the Contributor

Lou Ann Daly's consulting organization, O! LAD (Organization for Life Architecture and Design), is based in Massachusetts.

The Flawless Consulting Fieldbook and Companion

Chapter 29

Getting Real

John O'Connell

We are all guilty of making change and learning seem more predictable and straightforward than they are. After years of consulting and training, John took an internal organization development job. This is the story of his struggle to live out the ideas he had held dearly for a long time. His struggle is our struggle, for it is so much easier to talk about our lives than to live them. It is also a story of how much harder it is to be an internal staff person than to stand outside, at a distance, and look wise.

It is hard to "get real" in our communication, to openly share our perspectives and opinions creating genuine "dialogue." The pressures on us to perform in groups, and—particularly in management teams—to achieve results, "keep the peace," maintain fragile relationships and a sense of team are truly challenging. The often insidious inducements of "being in" as a member or "being on the same page" as a group all work against the honesty that will make the team most productive.

Think about how much is not said in any marriage or relationship for fear of hurting the other person or disturbing the harmony of the relationship. Nearly all the "left-hand column" material that is edited out of each one-to-one relationship is complicated by multiple factors in the group—the number of individuals, the different sub-interest groups, past history, how people outside the group might react or be affected, and myriad assumptions, particularly about what will work or not work. Maybe it is more remarkable that we have any effective communication at all than it is that our communication isn't better.

On top of the above mentioned problems, there is the difficulty of even a good team maintaining its effectiveness in the face of new and more difficult challenges. After twenty years in the martial art of Aikido, I know I can still be "thrown" by certain circumstances. Just so, a team can be thrown by circumstances and lose its "center," its sense of wholeness, and its members' ability to be authentic. This is a cautionary tale of just such an incident, a glimpse at some of what got in the way of the team "getting real" and a few of the lessons learned, which may help us avoid being thrown in quite the same way in the future.

ONCE UPON A TIME

Once upon a time, I did a wild and crazy thing. I accepted an offer from one of my clients to become their senior vice president for organization development. Because most of my career has been as an outside consultant and I had never even been a junior vice president of anything, this was quite a leap. But, because I had worked for almost a year with the management team of which I would be a part, and I respected, liked, and trusted the other members of the team, particularly the COO and the soon-to-be-my-boss CEO, I decided to take the leap.

We had been through numerous sessions together from team "vision" retreats to large-scale management meetings with hundreds of the organization's managers. We had worked with "dialogue" and "team performance." We had models and "working agreements" and a good track record.

Still, every day is a new game and, well, marriage changes everything.

As one of my colleagues, also a relatively new hire from the consulting ranks, remarked to me, "You used to be a special event who helped everybody. Now you are just another mouth at the table." Lesson one: Even if you think you have not changed, you have. Perception is reality. Lesson two: You used to play the neutral facilitator; now you are a player, with a mission from your boss, a position to present and defend, and a whole new set of biases. It is hard to be a good facilitator when you have a position. Notice that every once in a while a team will have a player-coach, but they never have a player-referee!

So here is the short form of the story, with apologies to everyone, including myself, for simplifying our roles, besmirching our characters, and making rash assumptions about our motivations. Take it all with a gram of salt. It is a good story nonetheless, and the lessons are worth learning, especially if you can do it on our tuition.

THE MERGER

We were a merger of two regional superpowers facing an increasingly tough marketplace. It seemed we had a better chance to exploit our niche more successfully by doing it together than by competing against each other. There was even the "vision" that by combining the best of two very talented organizations, we could create a new entity that would serve as a shining example to the world of what could be done. And we were doing great things for people every day. We had great people, so it was not unrealistic to think that we could be responsible for breakthroughs that could make for a better world at the same time that we set a national—even a world—model for collaborative venturing.

There were, of course, a few hundred significant hurdles. Among them, we faced a very tough marketplace and we were a "merger of equals," perhaps the toughest game in town, with a long history of rivalry between the two main organizations and a concomitant share of suspicion and distrust. In addition, each organization brought to the table a smaller business unit that had been recently although not completely incorporated.

Still, after the first year of the merger, through heroic efforts and amidst difficulties and complaints from all sides, the new enterprise managed to realize modest savings from the merger. The grueling part was that in many ways the enterprise was acting like a holding company,

with a huge amount of "back room" work going on to allow the different business units, now rearranged to be three, to continue to function as if not much had changed. The stress on newly combined central services to operate in three different languages was tremendous and their level of service to the units still received more complaints than kudos. And where was our common culture?

Following significant meetings and what seemed to us to be real "dialogue," the senior management team chose to pursue a strategy of "enterprise integration" to develop common systems, standards, and culture across the organization. It seemed like a good idea at the time.

It also seemed to be one we were all committed to. Shortly after the management team formed this strategy, we successfully rolled it out to about three hundred top managers through a successful large-scale meeting. Over 90 percent of feedback respondents supported the strategy and were willing to work to make it happen. Meeting with a group of the top technical professionals within the system, we all recognized the value of integration, although clearly there also was trepidation over the possibilities of departments being consolidated and the potential for numerous positions being threatened. Still, we were on a roll. There was a path to the vision, even if it was long and precarious.

AN UNHOLY ALLIANCE

Then, as it will, the environment changed. As a result, we anticipated a major financial crunch in the following year. At the initiation of the finance department, our new organization development department worked with finance to develop a plan for rebudgeting the entire enterprise. The goal was to cut expenses by 10 percent. Using the rebudgeting process to move toward the goal of enterprise integration, this unholy alliance of finance and OD developed a grand plan: Instead of budgeting vertically within the business units, perhaps we could budget by function across units, thus creating an "action forcing" process that would cause managers to work with their counterparts in the other units and promote "enterprise integration." By having functional managers, with down-to-earth experience, work together across sites, we

hoped to bring the business units closer together by understanding each other's approaches and standardizing their systems and procedures through sharing best practices. But with sites fifty miles apart, the logistics of scheduling hundreds of department manager meetings to exchange information, hammer out ideas for new, shared approaches, and cut costs were monumental.

No problem. We would organize a series of ten large-scale meetings to carry out the seven phases of the budgeting process. Functional groups would work in parallel, so no one would be more than a few minutes' walk away from anyone he or she needed to talk to in order to work out a deal. For added value, while we had everyone together, we planned to incorporate some badly needed management education in teamwork, planning, decision making, and meeting process. Creating common language tools and frameworks, we believed, would help the budget teams do their work and build a matrix for the natural growth of a new enterprise culture. Thus, from a late-night brainstorm, a project between finance and organization development was formed, without sufficient concern for how such a radical, sweeping agenda might be perceived.

Over a series of two months the "budgeting process" became a regular agenda item at our senior management team meetings. Although there seemed to be acceptance of the plan as it evolved, from that first meeting my Aikido sense was tingling. It seemed as if people were listening but not hearing. There was acceptance of the underlying financial issue, which was actually progress, but the agreement on the action plan for dealing with it seemed to be more compliance than commitment. The functional budgeting approach had to be discussed in endless detail, and the large-scale process went completely over people's heads. Listening but not hearing.

Some non-specific defensive action also was going on, but it was too vague to name. I talked with the CFO to say, "We don't have it. People are going along, but it isn't commitment." We chalked it up to team members' anxiety about how this process might have unforeseen effects on them downstream. Instead of stating our concerns to the whole group directly, we managed to have the COO, our team leader,

explicitly call the question as to whether the team was committed to the process. Although everyone said yes, the voices of two of the three business unit chiefs were decidedly faint. My gut level told me we weren't there; we weren't together; and we definitely were not getting real with each other. In the pressure of the moment though, with deadlines upon us, compliance seemed good enough. With the wisdom of hindsight, it wasn't.

LOSING OUR CENTER

At the moment at which we seemed to confirm our agreement, we lost our center. It had started a long way back, but it was at that point—saying "yes" when many of us knew we really meant "no"—that we gave up a level of integrity. We gave up a certain honesty with each other and we sacrificed the wholeness of the team and our ability to tell the whole truth about what was going on. As we were attesting to our unity on an operational plan level, we were belying it on a deeper level of trust and authenticity. The center of who we were to each other and to ourselves was off balance.

The next month was hell on earth. The task forces that were organized to implement the plan—which were made up of direct reports to our team—became the battleground for a host of unresolved organizational issues. A few participants became the surrogate champions of their bosses' complaints. Word would leak back of comments from the unit chiefs that not so subtly undermined the process. Meetings were very difficult to organize, and once people arrived there were always complaints about things being organized at the last minute. Every meeting seemed like slogging through knee-deep mud. To avoid meetings we would engage in endless e-mails, which ended up in an enormous waste of time and energy to correct the misunderstandings endemic to that high-tech form of miscommunication. As we trudged forward, we could feel the fracture lines snaking into the organization; the forerunners of fragmentation had started at the center and were working their way outward. The sense of "us" and "them" that developed only served to motivate the "us" side to push harder to make the process work, and it probably raised the resentment of the "them" being dragged along.

  The Flawless Consulting Fieldbook and Companion

Still, we made progress. The majority of task-force members and senior executives worked hard to launch the project in spite of the turmoil around them. Grueling as it was, we made it through the first large-scale meeting with a fairly high degree of success. Some of the most contentious task-force members began to give grudging support and even showed occasional bursts of enthusiasm. The personal and professional connections across the enterprise were forming, and good work was being done at the grass-roots level, bringing managers closer together than ever. The process was up and rolling, but it was definitely *work* and the underlying tensions were still apparent.

BENEATH THE SURFACE

It took till the third session, as the project began to function smoothly, for me to catch enough of my own center to realize that, although we were winning on the surface, we weren't addressing the deeper game. By organizing a meeting of key players from the "us" and "them" factions of our management team, we began to formulate a new way to work together to advance the project. It was a cautious meeting, with acknowledgments all around and tacit acceptance that we had all let things get out of hand; there was perhaps even a glimmer of recognition that something more fundamental had been violated. This was the beginning of a great deal of work to rebuild the relational quality of the team to match our operational expertise.

So, what was going on? Again, with the wisdom of hindsight, we can use the Drexler-Sibbet "Team Performance Model" to understand part of what was going on (figure 29.1). Like many such incidents, a book could probably be written to cover all the subtleties. That's for the next lifetime.

Stage 1. Orientation

Some fundamental differences in the orientation and direction of team members surfaced around this project. Money issues have a way of doing that. The "budget process" was one flow within the greater flow of "enterprise integration," within the greater flow of the merger itself.

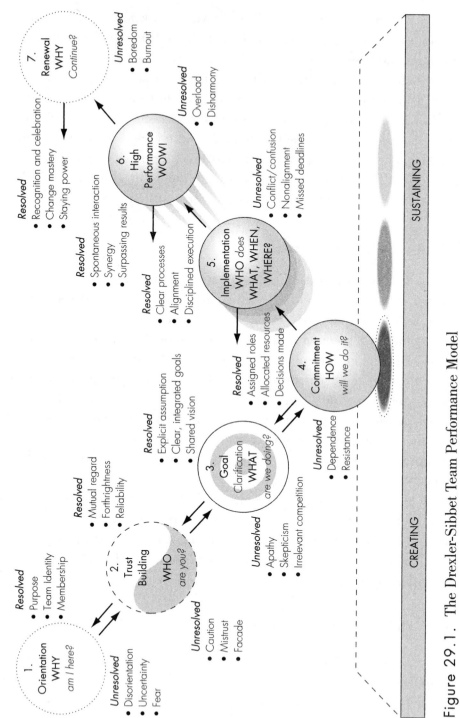

Figure 29.1. The Drexler-Sibbet Team Performance Model

The Drexler-Sibbet Team Performance Model™ is used with the permission of The Grove Consultants International, San Francisco.

The resistance of the business unit heads and the differences between them and the central service heads probably reflected unresolved concerns and lack of alignment about the overall integration effort. A slight discrepancy in orientation, which had been manageable in earlier situations, became a gap with the pressure of budget formulation and cost cutting.

Stage 2. Trust Building

Despite previous successes as a team, and perhaps because of reservations about integration, the trust level within the team was not sufficient for team members to directly express their concerns about the budget process, especially early on. Members weren't able to express who they were and began to develop doubts about who the other team members were. Everyone became cautious about fully revealing beliefs about what was positive and what was negative or caused them concern. The lack of trust diminished the individual and collective authenticity, which limited the "dialogue," making it difficult to achieve clarity and agreement.

The litmus test of the group's trust was that none of us felt safe enough to pull the plug on our own process and say, "We aren't being real with each other."

Stage 3. Goal Clarification

The difficulties with trust and communication experienced by the management team made it difficult to achieve clarity throughout our planning meetings. Our inability to reach shared understanding on a host of issues, including goals and methods, was both a product of the trust problems and served to exacerbate them. A good example was clarifying the role that the business unit heads would play. In spite of numerous conversations, which some of us thought made their role very clear, they never felt that they had one. What wasn't clear, until later, was an implicit assumption they had that, because they were ultimately responsible for implementing the budget, they should have a greater role than others in creating it, as they had in the past.

Stage 4. Commitment

Not surprisingly, with all that went before, the depth of commitment was shallow. Although we had verbal agreement, the actual behavior ran the range from enthusiasm to compliance to resistance—and even to inadvertent sabotage.

Stage 5. Implementation

Within the management team, planning and preparation became tedious. Deadlines for task-force assignments were missed because key players failed to produce the lists of proposed members as promised. Resolution of operational details became the escape from confronting more fundamental issues. As the implementation of the program moved to the task-force level, it became even more of a struggle to make progress. It felt like driving with the parking brake on, which of course is exactly what we were doing.

Stage 6. High Performance

Although we ultimately produced results, the cost in time and emotional energy was far greater than expected. Many of us were stretched to the breaking point, which made implementation of every task more of an effort. It also added another dimension to the trust/relationship issues of Stage 2. On the good side, success in the first session had a salient effect on the unresolved issues from the earlier stages. We began to get more done with less effort once we began manifesting positive performance.

Stage 7. Renewal

In many ways the essence of our difficulties was our failure as a team to be able to step out of "production" mode and do the reflection necessary to the renewal stage. As an outside consultant, I had a mandate to push the team toward self-evaluation and learning. As a team member, that mandate disappeared. I was as accountable as anyone for let-

The Flawless Consulting Fieldbook and Companion

ting the team default on its responsibility for learning and recognition. Typically, even after the team agreed to take time to focus on team issues, our first session became largely consumed with "urgent" operational items, and subsequent sessions were postponed or canceled for the same reason. We let the tyranny of the present subsume the future well-being of the team.

THREE LESSONS TO BE LEARNED

An important aspect of the renewal stage is learning and mastery. For our management team, it took too long for us to begin to learn the lessons that our experience was offering us. Following are the top three of many lessons we had to confront. Each seems to me to be a lesson that is not "learned" in a final sense, but one to be worked on continually, like practicing martial arts, religion, or the discipline of teamwork.

1. Be Aware!

We have to learn to recognize that "felt sense" when something is right or not right. Call it a gut feeling or whatever, there is a tangible physical sensation that identifies those moments when, as an individual or as a group, we are not being real with ourselves. The feeling is there; we just have to notice it. Sadly, once we start denying it, we begin not to notice and finally we don't even notice that we don't notice anymore.

2. Get Real!

When we do notice, we have to have the courage to "call it off" to the rest of the group, especially if no one else does: "You know, I'm not sure what's going on, but something isn't right. It just doesn't feel like we're being real here." These aren't the kinds of conversations executives usually have in management team meetings, but they should be.

The courage to tell the gut truth comes from having a level of trust, like an energy field, built up within the group. Telling and supporting the truth strengthens the field, and this makes it easier to tell

the truth the next time; failing to tell the truth weakens the field. We all lose courage in a field of mistrust and facade, or even in a field that only recognizes "hard" business realities. So we have to learn to build the trust within the group to foster courage and wholeness.

3. Learn or Else!

We have to invest the time to do the Stage 7 (see Figure 29.1) work of learning and renewal. We have to notice the group's patterns and our own; then we have to be willing to talk about them and make choices about how we are going to manage them in the future.

Our team failed to recognize its counterproductive pattern of having to get things done: "Make progress, hit the milestones, make the targets, whatever it takes." We failed to notice how operational we all became under pressure and how typical it was for us to succumb to "the opiate of action." Operations are "safe"; they are definite, "hard," and manageable. And they produce visible results.

We all want that, but no one wants to go back and do the really hard work of answering the really difficult, "soft," squishy questions of "Why?"—as in, "Why are we doing this?" "Are we doing it for the same reason?" And who wants to confront the questions of "Who?"—as in, "Who are you and what is your motivation in promoting or opposing this project?" let alone, "Who am I and why am I really taking the position I'm taking?"

Doing the work to learn as a team, especially about how our team really works, is like a fitness program and just as hard to maintain. Being in good shape won't guarantee immunity from sickness or injury, but probably will make us more resilient. As we learn our group patterns, we can start to avoid falling into them or at least catch them more quickly when we do. Investing our time in getting fit and learning as a team will help us become better at recognizing and talking about the issues we need to talk about.

The overarching issue will be getting and staying real with each other. If we can achieve that authenticity and wholeness in our work, then we have a better chance to make work a greater contributor to wholeness and happiness in our lives.

For More Depth

Further Reading

Young, Arthur M. *The Reflexive Universe: Evolution of Consciousness.* Novato, CA: Anodos Foundation, 1999.

Further Training

Any good Aikido class at a local Aikido Dojo.

About the Contributor

John O'Connell is director of Interplay Network, a San Francisco-based organization development firm, and a faculty partner with the Center for Executive Development in Cambridge, Massachusetts, a partner with the Paragon Consulting Group in Vail, Colorado, and a faculty member of the Boston University Leadership Institute.

6

Integrating Strategy and Experience

287

The clarity or wisdom of a strategy does not mean it will be acted on. Many a brilliant strategy has died because no one was personally committed to its success except those who created it. Most consulting practices are quite sophisticated in devising new business strategies, but surprisingly limited and naïve about building support for them. School reform is a good example. We know a lot about curriculum and teaching methods that will improve classroom performance, but we have had a universally difficult time in making them work.

Our traditional thinking about implementation, especially when we want to change the culture, suffers from an engineering—and even coercive—bias. We have believed that implementation will occur if we can put five elements in place:

- A detailed blueprint of the desired change,
- Top management support,
- Clear communication,
- Legislation and rewards, and
- Precise measurement.

These are basically political tactics and are designed to create compliance. They fall short in gaining commitment and accountability. Methods of implementation that embody commitment and passion and a willingness to take a chance are needed. If we want to create a culture of more accountability and concern for the customer, the implementation itself has to manifest this spirit. For example, you cannot measure and legislate teamwork and participation into existence. You cannot get people to care for a customer if they do not feel cared for themselves. You cannot move a traditional organization into the entrepreneurial ethos of the new economy if your own people have no choice or freedom of expression.

Implementation approaches that are based on engagement

and build strong accountability are introduced in three new chapters in the Second Edition of *Flawless Consulting* (Chapters 15, 16, and 17). The chapters in this section of the *The Flawless Consulting Fieldbook and Companion* go even further into new ideas and proven methods for putting various kinds of engagement strategies to work. The thread running through all of them is this: If we want to create a culture of accountability, the actual dialogue about the strategy must involve real conversations between people and their leaders plus, more importantly, dialogue between and among peers.

This sounds simple, but most change projects do not take engagement seriously enough. We are too prone to sell changes; we talk of burning platforms, shifts in the environment, and promises of new leadership. Our selling strategies carry their own resistance, for they are subtly coercive and imply that the change agent and management know and the workers or citizens do not. The alternative to selling is to create experiences in which employees and citizens struggle with the same questions that face the strategists. Accountability is created from a struggle with purpose, choice, and difficult conversations. We now know how to do this fairly quickly with hundreds of people at a time.

None of this is an argument against strong support from the top or changes in reward and measurement systems. But it does promote the idea that, as a change initiative passes through the organization, every level needs experiences that signal that this strategy cares as much about dialogue as it does directive. There has to be a recognition that any change demands courage and a willingness to act in the face of an unpredictable tomorrow. Courage and the will to face unpredictability are elements of choosing our freedom. As consultants, it is our task to design experiences that move away from selling events toward ones that foster connection, freedom, and their ultimate effect—accountability.

Chapter 30

The Engagement Paradigm
Changing the Way We Change Organizations

Dick and Emily Axelrod

This article is a reflection of Dick and Emily's work over the last ten years. It gets to the heart of the question of how strategy becomes action. Based on their groundbreaking work with the Conference Model©, it offers the specifics of how engagement strategies can change the world. Dick and Emily have a symphony conductor's sensibility for the elements of how to bring people emotionally into a project. They contrast selling versus engagement and provide a set of principles for bringing deeper engagement into all aspects of our work lives.

You bolt upright, heart pounding, drenched in sweat. After fumbling for your glasses, you look at the clock radio. It's three a.m. What began a few weeks ago as a nagging anxiety now takes the form of full-blown terror. You are now absolutely certain that the organizational change initiative that you have been trying to implement is on the verge of collapse. The minutes seem like hours as you try to figure out what to do. You have few—if any—answers.

If you've ever found yourself in this situation, you were probably following the conventional wisdom for creating organizational change. As a consultant you formed steering committees and design groups representing all levels and departments of the organization. Participants in these groups were committed to the task and were genuinely excited about the challenge of bringing about this important change. Yet the rest of the organization began to view those working on the change process with distrust, wondering what "they" were going to do to "us." This prevailing attitude of suspicion and resistance brought the change process to a grinding halt.

Who is to blame in such a situation? Are you? Are the leaders? The team members who put in so many long hours? Actually, no one is at fault. You and your clients were all following current best practice. The change management paradigm that guided your actions has been widely accepted as the best way to bring about organizational change. The problem is that this paradigm—once considered revolutionary—no longer works in today's business climate. Rather than creating acceptance for the needed change, it often alienates the very people whose support is essential to success. In the name of participation, the change management paradigm actually increases bureaucracy, reinforces top-down management, and increases cynicism and resistance. We'll explain how this happens shortly, but first let's examine the paradigm itself.

THE OLD CHANGE MANAGEMENT PARADIGM

Beginning in the late 1970s and continuing into the 1980s, employee-involvement change processes became popular. These processes, which eventually became a model known as the "change management paradigm," relied heavily on the construction of a parallel organization, a temporary organization that operates alongside the regular organization to create, manage, and implement change.

Fundamental to the concept of the parallel organization is the belief that the change process is best managed by a select few—typically, the members of a sponsor team, steering committee, and one or more design groups. The sponsor team is a cross-functional group composed of senior leaders whose role is to lend their support to the needed changes. Thus, they initiate the process, cheer lead the effort, and provide funding. They are not involved in the day-to-day developments, but their approval is usually required for key results. The steering committee is composed of people from all levels and functions of

the organization. Their role is the day-to-day management of the change process. Design groups are also cross-functional and multi-level. Their role is to work out the details of the needed change, such as new organizational hierarchies or new steps and substeps for core processes. In organizations with labor unions, union leadership participates in all these structures.

What It Claims to Do

The change management paradigm claims to break down organizational silos while creating high-quality solutions. The cross-functional nature of the three teams is designed to allow for a systemic, rather than a unit or functional, perspective. Thus, solutions should favor the total organization rather than a single department.

Reducing organizational red tape is another purported benefit of change management. The three levels of sponsors, steering committee, and designers collapse the regular organization's multiple levels and allow for the participation of all key decision makers. Instead of wending their way through the hierarchy of the regular organization, new proposals can be adopted quickly within the parallel organization.

The parallel organization also encourages cooperation across levels and functions. Committee members learn participatory behaviors and group decision-making skills that are not dependent on authority or position. The belief is that members then transfer their new knowledge and skills into the day-to-day workings of the regular organization.

Most important, the change management paradigm claims to ensure support for needed changes. The thinking goes like this: First, the cross-functional and cross-hierarchical nature of the teams will cause all employees to believe they were represented in the process. Second, because the teams are made up of "the best and the brightest" employees who have high credibility within the organization, others in the organization will readily accept their ideas. Finally, as a result of their positive experiences in the parallel organization, the chosen team members will champion the process and convince the excluded employees of the value of the proposed changes.

Why Change Management Needs Changing

Although revolutionary at its inception, the change management paradigm produces four outcomes that are not tolerable in today's business environment. They are increased bureaucracy, increased cynicism and resistance, more top-down management, and failed implementation.

Increased Bureaucracy

The parallel organization was designed to be temporary, but in actual practice the sponsor team, steering committee, and design groups often become permanent over time. This increases bureaucracy, creates a resource burden, and engenders an artificial separation between "change work" and the "real work" of the regular organization.

Increased Cynicism and Resistance

It is ironic that a process designed to increase employee participation in many instances actually ends up increasing cynicism and resistance. Here are some reasons why: The emphasis on picking the "best and the brightest" for the three teams leads many to believe that management is stacking the deck with people who will readily agree with its predetermined course of action. Because excluded employees feel that their voices don't count, they become cynical. Even when team members interview employees, most do not provide adequate feedback. And those people not selected for an interview are left to believe that their opinions are really unimportant. Is it any wonder that cynicism and resistance increase?

More Top-Down Management

Even though it has fewer layers, the parallel organization reinforces top-down management by requiring the solutions of the design groups to be passed along to the steering committee for approval and then ultimately to the sponsor team. This means that the design groups often spend as much time and effort preparing to present their proposals to the steering committee as they did developing the proposals in the first

The Flawless Consulting Fieldbook and Companion

place. During the presentation, when steering committee members raise concerns, the designers suspect them of pushing for predetermined solutions. They go back and revise their proposals according to the steering committee's recommendations, but their trust is shaken. After a number of iterations of this process, a decision is developed that the steering committee supports. Then the process repeats itself when the steering committee presents the proposals to the sponsor team.

Failed Implementation

Because it relies on the few developing solutions for the many, the change management paradigm guarantees that the implementation process will be difficult. People develop a negative bias toward change when they do not feel that their voices are being heard. Minimal information about proposed changes causes the rumor mill to operate over-time. Catastrophic scenarios fill the hallways. Separating change development from change implementation is a critical mistake.

How Change Management Lost Its Way

Originally, the goal of change management was to create shifts in organizational culture while simultaneously improving systems and/or processes. In the early 1980s, these dual goals fit nicely with the move toward greater employee involvement. But within a few short years some subtle shifts in implementation began to occur, causing change management to lose its way.

First, the teams within the parallel organization began to be consultant-led rather than consultant-facilitated. The purpose of the team members thus shifted from leading the change effort to providing information to consultants and organizational leaders, who then developed the new strategies independently. This was an unfortunate shift away from empowerment.

Second, the concept of changing the organization's culture began to take a back seat to the concept of changing the organization's structures and technology. Even though the development of new systems and processes required people to change the way they worked and who they worked with, these cultural aspects were ignored. People found themselves in new organizational configurations designed to produce cooperation, teamwork, and improved customer service. But cooperation, teamwork, and better customer service were impossible to achieve because the old hierarchical silo culture remained unchanged.

Third, although the goals of many change efforts were to reduce bureaucracy and improve teamwork, these goals were themselves introduced in an authoritarian fashion. Then, as Chris Argyris observes in *Overcoming Organizational Defenses,* the disparity between authoritarian leadership and supposed empowerment creates organizational defensiveness and resistance.

Finally, the change management paradigm assumes that people will resist change. In fact, the words "change management" are often seen as code for a process to manage resistance to change. Thus, change management treats employees as obstructionists who must be won over, rather than as willing partners in creating a new and better organization.

Toward a New Paradigm

For over a year, Detroit Edison followed the traditional change management paradigm to improve its supply-chain process. Despite the hard work of many people both inside and outside the organization, there was little to show for it. The sponsors and steering committee were frustrated by the lack of progress, and the design groups could not understand why they couldn't get the organization to support the changes they were proposing. In spite of its importance to the organization, most people greeted the supply-chain improvement process with disinterested yawns.

Deciding that this situation was no longer tolerable, Detroit Edison adopted a new strategy. In a few short months, one-third of the organization, over nine hundred people, were engaged in the supply-chain improvement process with a series of conferences attended by employees at all levels, customers, suppliers, contractors, and key union officials. Engagement quickly replaced disinterest. Today there

The Flawless Consulting Fieldbook and Companion

are over twenty-six active supply-chain improvement projects at Detroit Edison, with savings in the millions. Comments Joe Aresto, leader of the Supply Chain Improvement Process, "My personal experience is that I enter these processes with one mental model of how things should be and as a result of working with others my mental model shifts to one that is much better than the original."

How did Detroit Edison do it? By discarding an outmoded model based on change resistance and adopting a new one based on partnership. We call this new model the "engagement paradigm."

THE ENGAGEMENT PARADIGM: THE CONFERENCE MODEL

Throughout our twenty-five years of consulting experience, we and our partners have heard complaints from our clients that the change management paradigm is too slow and bureaucratic and does not create the necessary support for change. In response, we first developed a process called the Conference Model® to engage large numbers of people early on in the redesign of their organization. We were not alone in our thinking. Fred Emery and Eric Trist were the first to recognize the need to engage people deeply in change. Others such as Marvin Weisbord and Sandra Janoff, Kathie Dannemiller, Harrison Owen, and Robert Jacobs were notable pioneers in the creation of similar processes.

The Conference Model has two unique structures. The first is a series of linked conferences that create organizational momentum and allow issues to be addressed at increasing levels of depth; the second structure is a series of mini-conferences, called "walkthrus," that allow people who are unable to attend the conferences an opportunity to have input into the change process.

The Conferences

The conferences consist of meetings of the organization's stakeholders and employees at all levels (including important others from outside the organization, such as customers, suppliers, and community members).

The number of attendees ranges from small groups of thirty to large groups that number in the hundreds. Detroit Edison's supply-chain process involved more than nine hundred people (in both the conferences and walkthrus) from an organization of 2,500.

Conferences create an open exchange of information, increased understanding of the system under consideration, new agreements and actions, and enhanced relationships among participants. During a conference, people meet and discuss issues in a variety of formats. Sometimes they are in mixed groups representing all the people at a conference. Other times they meet in stakeholder groups representing a particular point of view. And sometimes they meet as a total community.

Conference participants engage in various activities to increase learning and understanding of the issues under consideration. Conference building blocks consist of three elements:

1. Creating a common visible database as participants post responses to questions on large butcher-block paper on the wall;
2. Analyzing the data in table groups and reporting findings to the whole group; and
3. Discussing it among the whole community.

The databases consist of a variety of formats to access auditory, visual, and kinesthetic learning styles. For example, participants may:

- Create visual maps to identify breakdowns in production processes;
- Use ropes that simulate organizational connections to really feel the tugs and pulls in the system;
- Bury dysfunctional norms and behaviors; and
- Create murals to symbolize a future state.

During a conference, activities build on each other, providing participants a common information base, facilitating analysis and decision making, creating new ways of working together, and stimulating action.

A key Conference Model feature is linking an integrated series of conferences usually spaced four to six weeks apart. Detroit Edison held two three-day conferences, while Hewlett-Packard held five two-day conferences. The number and content of the conferences are determined by the organization's needs. Participants meet in these conferences to understand their present circumstance and identify the future they want to create.

The Walkthru

Mini-conferences called walkthrus are held for organizational members who are unable to attend the conferences. In these sessions, participants are informed of the results of the conferences and are invited to provide input into the change process. This input is incorporated before the next conference. Both the conferences and walkthrus can successfully involve hundreds or even thousands of people, making it possible to involve every employee in the change process.

Six Assumptions of the Engagement Paradigm

We have used the Conference Model successfully to redesign organizations and processes in a variety of settings, such as healthcare, education, manufacturing, and government. We have also used it to create new organizational cultures and to support mergers and acquisitions. Once we saw that our model was successful, we examined the assumptions that guided it and other similar processes such as "future search" (Weisbord & Janoff), "open space" (Harrison Owen), "participative design" (Fred & Merylynn Emery), "real time strategic change" (Robert Jacobs), and "whole scale change" (Kathie Dannemiller). Our goal was to determine—and put into practice—the underlying principles that produce an organization in which everyone is engaged in the change process.

The engagement paradigm is based on the following six essential assumptions.

1. When You Know Your Voice Counts, You Become Engaged

In the outmoded change management paradigm, if you are chosen to participate in the parallel organization, your voice counts more than the voices of excluded employees. Even if the teams interview many people, only team members make the final decisions.

In the engagement paradigm, you know your voice counts because you are intimately involved in the debates that develop recommendations and courses of action. You are actually able to influence the decision-making process.

When people know that their voices count, they invest time and energy to create a future together. For example, I recently asked a group of people why they were putting in so much time and energy on a product development/redesign effort. They responded, "This feels like one of the few times in our working careers that we really believe that we can make a difference."

2. Collaboration Occurs When People Connect with One Another

In the outdated change management paradigm, some connection occurs within each of the teams that make up the parallel organization, but little is done to produce collaboration in the rest of the organization. And yet, most of us feel that collaboration is easier with people with whom we have some form of connection. In contrast, people connect with each other in the engagement paradigm. Consequently, they become known to each other not as stereotypes, but as human beings with real issues and concerns. Connections begin with matching a name to a face, and they evolve into understanding who these other people are, how they think, and what matters to them.

3. Envisioning a Positive Future Encourages People to Take Action

A fascinating study by Ron Lippitt found that when people discuss problems and try to fix them they become depressed. But when they identify the type of future they want to create, they become energized. The engagement paradigm spurs action by asking people to envision the future they want.

4. Democratic Principles Increase Trust, Commitment, and Creativity

Democratic principles can make a huge difference in organizations, helping to increase trust, commitment, and creativity. These principles include information sharing, public decision making, equity and fairness, and the use of democratic voting procedures to reach decisions.

When people work within the engagement paradigm, all the information is shared with everyone and decision-making processes are open to all. There are no executive sessions, no subgroups making decisions for the whole. People base their conclusions on facts they have observed, not on rumors or innuendoes.

Although some participants are specifically invited to take part in conferences, such as those with responsibility for the outcomes and those who have special knowledge, the engagement paradigm relies mostly on voluntary participation. When there are more volunteers than seats in conferences, participants are selected by lot to ensure equality. The fact that anyone can volunteer to participate and that everyone has an equal chance goes a long way in establishing credibility for the change process.

Equity and fairness come into play not only when deciding who participates in the conferences, and thus the change process, but also when responding to employees who may experience negative consequences of the change process. For example, one organization we worked with developed an equitable and fair process for meeting the needs of employees who would have to leave the company as a result of a change process. This included informing people of their status as soon as possible so that they could make necessary decisions, providing training for those who wished to pursue other careers, and offering financial packages for early retirement.

Finally, the engagement paradigm uses democratic, multi-voting procedures. When it comes times to make a decision, we give participants paper dots to place on the proposal of their choice. The act of physically placing a dot on the proposal of your choice is a powerful statement of equality.

The democratic principles that we have outlined produce trust and confidence in both the change process and those who are leading it. They are universal principles that speak to the desire to shape one's own destiny.

5. *Widening the Circle of Involvement from the Start Speeds Implementation*

In the outmoded change management paradigm, a few "best and brightest" develop plans and strategies for the many, and then face the arduous task of convincing others to buy into their decisions. In contrast, the engagement paradigm involves large numbers of people in the process from the very beginning. Hundreds, even thousands, of employees come together to create a critical mass for change. Engagement also includes new voices, such as those of customers, suppliers, and even community representatives. Bringing together as many people as possible in creating strategic initiatives builds ownership and commitment. As a participant in a recent change process said, "It may be an ugly baby, but it's our baby."

Furthermore, when using the engagement paradigm decisions are often made in real time. Because all those who have the relevant power and authority are in the same room, participants in conferences do not have to wait weeks or even months for their recommendations to make their way through the bureaucracy.

6. *Involving the Whole System Produces Creative, Integrated Solutions*

In his classic work on Theory X and Theory Y, Douglas McGregor stated that the ability to create solutions to organizational issues is widely distributed throughout the organization. It is not the sole province of an elite few, nor is it the province of the best and the brightest, nor does it reside in the hierarchy. Involving the whole system to address systemic issues is at the heart of the engagement paradigm.

When a rural hospital in Hawaii was faced with closing its doors, it involved doctors, nurses, patients, local residents, insurers, and even competitors in a large conference to determine the future of the organization. There were a number of surprising outcomes. For example, stronger hospitals offered to refer patients, and a doctors' group hired a gynecologist on the condition that this doctor would practice at the hospital. These solutions would not have been possible if the whole system had not resolved to save the hospital and developed a set of integrated solutions. As a result of these and other actions, this once-dying hospital continues to provide critical medical services.

The engagement paradigm also employs small groups and a planning team to add detail to the strategies, logistics, and initiatives developed in the larger sessions. But the cornerstones of the process are the large conferences and walkthrus.

ENGAGING YOUR ORGANIZATION

The best and the brightest minds can produce brilliant strategies, but without an engaged organization that is willing to implement them, these strategies are useless. The engagement paradigm provides leaders with a proven method for creating this critical engagement. When leaders employ its central principles and processes, they produce organizations where:

- People grasp the issues, become aligned around a common purpose, and create new directions because they understand both the dangers and the opportunities.
- Urgency and energy are produced to create a new future.
- Free-flowing information and cooperation replace organizational silos because people are connected to the issues and to one another.
- Broad participation quickly identifies performance gaps and their solutions, improving productivity and customer satisfaction.
- Creativity is sparked when people from all levels and functions, along with customers, suppliers, and important others, contribute their best ideas.
- Capacity for future change increases as people develop the skills and processes to meet not just the current challenges, but future challenges as well.

In short, through wider involvement, alternative structures, voluntary participation, and real-time decision making, the engagement paradigm helps you replace apathy and resistance to change with energy and commitment for a new future.

For More Depth

Further Reading

Argyris, Chris. *Overcoming Organizational Defenses: Facilitating Organizational Learning.* Boston, MA: Allyn and Bacon, 1990.

Dannemiller Tyson Associates. *Whole-Scale™ Change: Unleashing the Magic in Organizations.* San Francisco: Berrett-Koehler, in press.

Emory, Fred & Merylynn. *Participative Design for Participative Democracy.* Caberra: Centre for Continuing Education, Australian National University, 1993.

Faulks, Sebastian. *Birdsong: A Tale of Love and War.* New York: Vintage Books, 1997.

Goleman, Daniel. *Emotional Intelligence: Why It Can Matter More than IQ.* New York: Bantam, 1995.

Devi, Nischala Joy. *The Healing Path of Yoga: Time-Honored Wisdom and Scientifically Proven Methods that Alleviate Stress, Open Your Heart, and Enrich Your Life.* New York: Crown, 2000.

Jacobs, Robert. *Real Time Strategic Change: How to Involve an Entire Organization in Fast, Far Reaching Change.* San Francisco: Berrett-Koehler, 1994.

Kabat-Zinn, Jon. *Wherever You Go There You Are.* New York: Hyperion, 1994.

Lippitt, Ronald, Jeanne Watson, & Bruce Westley. *The Dynamics of Planned Change: A Comparative Study of Principles and Techniques Under the General Editorship of Willard B. Spalding.* New York: Harcourt Brace, 1958.

McGregor, Douglas. *The Human Side of Enterprise.* New York: McGraw-Hill, 1960.

Owen, Harrison. *Open Space Technology: A User's Guide.* San Francisco: Berrett-Koehler, 1997.

Remen, Rachel Naomi, & Dean Ornish. *Kitchen Table Wisdom: Stories That Heal.* Universal City, CA: Riverhead Books, 1996.

Schlink, Bernard. *The Reader.* New York: Vintage, 1999.

Turkel, Studs. *Working: People Talk About What They Do All Day and How They Feel About It.* New York: New Press, 1997.

Thompson, Kay. *Eloise.* New York: Simon & Schuster, 1969.

Weisbord, Marvin, & Sandra Janoff. *Future Search: An Action Guide to Finding Common Ground in Organizations and Communities.* San Francisco: Berrett-Koehler, 1995.

Whitely, Suzanne. *Appel Is Forever.* Detroit, MI: Wayne State University Press, 1999.

Websites and Schools

Somantic Learning, Rancho-Strozzi Institute, Petaluma, California. www.ranchostrozzi.com.

YouCanWrite.com.

School for Managing and Leading Change, Association for Quality and Participation. www.aqp.org.

www.abundantwellbeing.com

About the Contributors

Dick and Emily Axelrod's organizational development consulting firm, The Axelrod Group, Inc., is based in Chicago. Dick's latest book is *Terms of Engagement: Changing the Way We Change Organizations* (Berrett-Koehler, 2000); he and Emily co-authored *Collaborating for Change: The Conference Model* (Berrett-Koehler, 1999).

Chapter 31

Caring about Place

Peter Block

In one way or another, we are all trying to make the transition from the industrial era of predictability and control to the service/information era of choice and participation. One obstacle is that most of the rooms in which we come together were designed for the industrial era. It is almost impossible to find a room in an office building or a hotel that is suited for dialogue and participation. They, at best, are mostly suited for instruction and persuasion. At worst, they are well designed for eating.

To begin with, most of the tables are rectangular. If you sit on either side of a rectangular table, you cannot see most of the people on your side of the table. It's hard to engage people you cannot see. Putting the tables in a U shape or a square still blinds us to a third or a fourth of those in the room. Boardrooms are the worst. The tables are fixed and monumental. It clearly was never expected that real conversation would be required.

Each time the room is arranged for people to interact with the speaker rather than with one another, we reinforce passive contact and the values of the industrial culture. It doesn't matter much, then, what is said; the arrangement of the room carries its own message.

And it's not just the furniture. The architecture and design of training and meeting rooms are primarily intended to promote persuasion and display, either with the speaker

Earlier versions of this chapter appeared as "Caring About Place," November 1998, and "What a Difference a Space Makes," December 1999, in *News for a Change*, published by the Association for Quality and Participation, Cincinnati, Ohio.

in the room or a speaker in another location. Most of the new money spent on meeting spaces goes into electronics and projection equipment. A recent article in *Training* magazine identified the ten best conference rooms in the country. Why are they the best? Because they have spent the most money on electronic technology. In some cases, rooms designed to accommodate fewer than thirty people have over $250,000 in the walls, floors, and ceiling. With this kind of investment in the walls, you are not about to have the seats facing each other.

THE MARRIAGE OF INNER AND OUTER SPACE

What does this say about our beliefs about connecting and communicating? Maybe that in this electronic age in which we pay so much attention to the use of technology for learning we forget that people still want to meet to talk to each other. Maybe that we are oblivious to how hostile our meeting and common spaces are to building community and supporting learning. We will spend a fortune on talking to someone we cannot see, and in the process arrange the room so that we all face the front and face the wall. These rooms are artifacts of an industrialized and electronic culture. We are in love with technology in a way that far exceeds our interest in connecting with one another. To say that the technology connects us is a myth. It confuses information exchange with human interaction. There is nothing wrong with the technology; we just exaggerate its usefulness.

In a broader sense, we are culturally blind about the power of the physical place. We are willing to meet in rooms without windows, to look at walls without color or pictures and doors with no moldings. Windows, color, art, and architectural detail bring life and humanity into a setting. If you are in the business of training, running meetings, convening people, it is almost impossible to find a room in this country that is designed to have people really talk.

The symbol for participation is a circle. Round tables put us in sight of everyone else. Chairs arranged in a circle do the same. Even a room full of round tables has an interactive effect. Don't worry about

having some people with their backs to the front. The action is not in the front of the room—it is at the tables. We are now starting to appreciate this, and I believe eventually we will have whole rooms and buildings designed to hold the circle.

Saturn and Harley-Davidson have already understood the importance of the circle in the design of their buildings. Other organizations are also experimenting with new communal space. The Boeing Company has "visibility" rooms designed to display the goals, values, and progress of large projects. John Warner, a senior executive at Boeing, started to experiment with the structure of his visibility room in order to achieve deeper participation. First he got rid of the large table and had only chairs with a few low coffee tables to put stuff on. Then he brought in plants, to add some life to the environment. They then noticed that the neon lighting was cold and institutional, so they brought in floor lamps. This, however, was going too far. It started to feel like a living room. Out went the lamps, but the chairs, the plants, and the intent to design a room for open dialogue and human encounter remain.

The point is not that there is a right design for a room; it is about our consciousness. As we become more conscious about the impact of how we physically come together, we will start to redesign our common space. This will require the joint effort of furniture designers, architects, hotel executives, organizational real estate people, and those of us who convene the meetings.

To put it succinctly, we meet all the time but rarely in a place that fits the purpose of our coming together. I assume that we usually meet to learn from one another, to speak and listen to each other, to create something that did not exist before we came together. If we are not meeting for these reasons, then we are wasting our time and let electronics have their day.

WHAT A DIFFERENCE A SPACE MAKES

To state the issue more dramatically, our real task is to infuse more life and vitality into our workplaces. We defeat this intention when we think lifeless rooms are fine. We too often meekly surrender to rooms with no windows, where the tables and screens are the figure and people are the ground. Chairs lined up in classroom style, frozen without wheels. If it is a large group meeting, the chairs are often locked together, theater style, indicating no movement is allowed, no circles permitted. This arrangement answers the question: "How do you fit the maximum number of people into the smallest amount of space?" Wrong question.

Lifeless rooms seem to have been designed under a kind of architectural anesthesia. Their walls are dead. Blank, industrial, painted in cold tones of gray or blue or colorless in white. Few pictures. If there are pictures, they were bought at a Howard Johnson's going-out-of-business sale. There is nothing to remind us that art, the aesthetic, the images and imagination of who we are have for centuries been a means of shifting our consciousness. A lifeless, blank wall reflects the institutionalization of the human spirit, and this reminder is most often at odds with why we are coming together.

Our meeting rooms also lack a view of the outside world. Usually they have no windows to allow us to be connected to nature or to see that there is a larger world out there. Are we afraid that if we were distracted by a view of the outside world it might remind us that what we are doing in here may not be so important? And if there are windows, they don't open. So much for fresh air, a gentle breeze, the sounds of nature. When did nature become the enemy of productivity?

These rooms were clearly designed for efficiency and presentation. And if we meet in a hotel ballroom, we are in rooms created for the presentation of food. The hotels now call these spaces convention centers so they can rent them out between meals. Maybe that is where the phrase "food for thought" came from—us attending conferences in rooms designed for eating.

The cost of these spaces is that they create a tension within us. We are living, breathing souls trying to work with other human beings. These rooms deny our humanity, and civility becomes difficult in such an uncivil space. The only meeting rooms really designed for human occupancy are the ones for top management. They have art, windows, wet bars, wood-paneled walls, and carpet thick enough to sleep on.

The Flawless Consulting Fieldbook and Companion

And the ruling class does not go off-site to mere hotels; they go to royal retreat centers. But enough about them. Back to the working class.

WHAT TO DO

Here are some thoughts about how to overcome the limitations of the space we have been given for our meetings.

No Tables

If you must use tables, round ones are better than rectangular ones, but not much. Better to just cancel the tables. Even a round table keeps us apart, rigidly structures the distance between us, and makes rearrangement a labor-intensive art. People will whine that they have no place for their water bottles and notebooks or anything to lean on. Put a sheet on the wall labeled "Whining" so they can document their complaints, and then go ahead and bag the tables.

Chairs on Wheels

Chairs with wheels carry the expectation that change is possible—that there is no single, permanent way to be in relation to one another, that in the course of an hour, or a day, or a lifetime, our relationships to one another are going to change. Use chairs that want to move rather than be locked together.

Bright Lights

If nature is not going to provide the light, make sure the house does. Low lighting is depressing, and in larger meetings it puts all the attention to the front of the room, where the electronics preside. Stop organizing the space around overheads, PowerPoint,® and videos as a substitution for reality. The most valuable "power points" will come from the audience. Shine the lights on the participants, because this is generally whom the meeting is for. Low-lighted rooms make us feel as though we are meeting at sunset, the day is slipping away from us—not good conditions for optimism.

Amplify Every Voice

Make sure all voices are equally amplified. Colorado Wildlife Commissioner Chuck Lewis convenes volatile hearings involving ranchers, farmers, hunters, fishing enthusiasts, and environmentalists. They don't all really get along that well. He decided to invest in amplification equipment that would make everyone's voice equally heard. He reports that once he did that, the differences the groups had with one another remained, but the contentiousness went way down.

Equally amplified means that each person is always amplified. Not the typical way, where the leader has a permanent mike and the audience has to share a roving one. Wrong message. Either let all share the one mike or you'd better find the technology so all can be heard.

Graphic Recording

If you can't get pictures on the wall, create them. There are people who can create a visual and enlivening picture of a meeting as it progresses. They are graphic recorders, and they create images from our words on large paper that can be taped around the room as the meeting progresses.*

Graphic images not only bring life into the room, but they retain the history of the meeting. They offer a visual memory and give insight when the words being spoken fail. If you cannot use a graphic recorder, get participants to draw symbols and images of the meeting. Their graphics can represent anything: Their present state, their cultural history, their wish for the future, or even their worst doubts and concerns. This may take a little courage on your part and theirs, but try it. When people say they can't draw, tell them that is exactly why we want their

---

*Mae Kim, who works for the National Education Association, is one of the best. As this is written, her e-mail is *mkim@nea.org*. If she can't do it, she can help you find someone.

images. Intuitive, untrained art tells a much more powerful story than the sophistication of academically trained talent.

THE POINT

The point of space is to raise our consciousness about the presumably "small" dimensions of life that in fact are much more decisive than we imagine. The room and its life-supporting capacity give much-needed balance to all of our attention to rational thinking, presentation, getting the story straight, and being persuasive. It is the depth and quality of our experience that is in the end compelling. Despite the conventional wisdom, it is our relationship to our peers, and not to our leaders, that finally drives commitment and makes us act like owners of the place. The physical space can make all this easy or difficult.

Perhaps if we remember this the next time we construct space for coming together, we will design rooms that we want to inhabit. If we spend today in a room we want to inhabit, then chances are better we will spend tomorrow in an organization we want to inhabit.

Chapter 32

Unleashing the Spirit

Kathie Dannemiller, Sylvia James, and Paul Tolchinsky

Kathie, with her associates Sylvia and Paul, is among the founders of large-group methodologies. In this article they describe the planning and change process they invented that brings large numbers of people together to create a new future. In this planning and commitment-building process are the ingredients of the "one brain-one heart" spirit that Kathie, and her Dannemiller-Tyson Associates partners, have created. Their work captures some of the emotional impact that truly democratic processes can have on our world.

It was the evening of day two in a three-day meeting, which involved all two hundred fifty employees of a plastics manufacturing company in upstate New York. At the end of that day, the ten-member planning team for the meeting, together with the plant leadership and us consultants, read the two hundred fifty evaluations from the participants to understand what were the most significant learnings from the day and advice for tomorrow. We discussed the key themes we heard and tweaked the agenda based on the meeting purpose that the planning team had created.

We went to dinner with Ivor, who was coordinating the logistics for the meeting. When asked, "How do you think it's going?" Ivor responded, "It's not going anywhere; it's still the same old stuff. As I move around the room putting papers on the tables, I keep hearing the same conversations going on, the same dissatisfactions being expressed. I don't think it's going to work this time."

"That doesn't sound too good," Kathie said. "Would you do me a favor and around 10 or 11 o'clock tomorrow morning, report back to me whether the same thing is occurring?" The next morning, around 10 o'clock, his message came back, "It is as though someone has thrown a switch! Everybody is suddenly focusing on the main themes around their table that they have been sharing across the room. I can hear the energy in the room. It's obvious that nothing is going to stop that energy, the interactions. All of a sudden there's a ground swell of energy, manifesting a ground swell of activity all directed at common goals. It's like magic!"

And so it was: The paradigm shift moment! The magic! The spirit of all two hundred fifty people seeing the same things, feeling the same things—and all knowing that we know, connected in a truly different way.

What Ivor is describing is the moment we have come to know well in our work with clients. It is a moment when all of the people in the room are connected around what we call "one brain" (everyone seeing and knowing what each person sees and knows) and "one heart" (everyone connected around combined yearnings for the future, for each person individually and around the organization as a whole). We came to realize that that moment signals a "paradigm shift" on the part of each and every person in the room. When the paradigm has shifted, everyone sees the world anew, sees new possibilities unfolding, and cannot go back to where they had been before the shift. All of us as consultants doing this kind of work can literally FEEL the difference in the room, just the way Ivor felt the difference.

ONE-BRAIN, ONE-HEART BELIEFS

We believe there are key consulting beliefs that cause the spirit to get loose in this way. Ron Lippitt, from his work in the 1960s and 1970s, taught us that purpose drives every intervention in a system. The first step always is to identify and agree on "What needs to be different in the world because this group of people met?" The answer to this question will tell us what the purpose of this intervention is. Once we have a compelling answer to that question, Ron taught us to ask and answer two more questions: Who needs to be gathered together in a room in order to achieve that purpose? and What conversations need to take place to ensure that we have the "right" answer? Our consulting is always driven by these questions.

What we have been learning as we plan and implement change in this fashion is that the answer to all three questions needs to be developed by the system itself, not by the consultants alone. What we have discovered is that there needs to be a process for answering these questions in a way that will be representative of the whole system. We do this before we risk bringing together a critical mass of the system. Therefore, we start every intervention by getting the client system to convene a true microcosm group of fifteen to twenty people who will be an accurate representation of the organization. The group needs to represent all of the diverse organizational levels, geography, longevity, cultures, and attitudes of people who have come through acquisition as well as people who have been there forever. We think of that group as a DNA representation of the whole organization. We ask to have these people work with us in a two-day planning meeting. We design their meeting to unleash the spirit of that group and combine their knowledge and yearnings. As part of their meeting, we ask them to tell their stories—something that could touch on the following topics:

- Why I joined this company/organization;
- Why I stay;
- What I've done that makes me proud;
- What's been frustrating this past year; and
- What I believe needs to change in the ways we work together in the future if we are to become winners again.

We urge people to listen to one another in a way that will enable them to see what the other sees. For this process, we owe a debt to people at the National Training Labs, for example Ron Lippitt and David

Cooperrider, who developed the concepts of preferred futuring and appreciative inquiry. This microcosm group, which we call an "event planning team," then identifies common outcomes and reaches consensus on a purpose for the intervention: "What needs to be different in the world because we engaged in this effort?" From that agreement, we are able to move together into planning the "conversations" needed to accomplish it.

We are aware that what happens to the event planning team in the two days is that they connect around the head and heart in significant ways that foretell what will happen in the larger system as we move forward. Beginning with the event planning team, others will also experience that paradigm shift, leading to new hope and new empowerment in the organization.

WHAT SPARKS THE MAGIC

When we are working with the event planning team to decide on the conversations that must take place in the intervention, we are reflecting Meg Wheatley's and Myron Kellner-Rogers' concepts for systems thinking. Together with the event planning team, we decide on what needs to occur to deepen our common understanding *of information, identity,* and *relationships* in order to make the paradigm shift happen. We believe that it is the interplay of those three things that releases the spirit and sparks the magic.

Information

We know that a common database is essential to create real community. We generate data by moving continually from the views of the individual to the shared views at a maximum-mix (microcosm) table in the room to the combined views of every person and all people in the room. Each of us and all of us will begin to see things we've never seen before and will be able to influence further because we see farther. Combining our information unleashes broader possibilities and an expanded world view.

The Flawless Consulting Fieldbook and Companion

Identity

Identity of the individual, of a table, and of the whole room comes from the new thinking, the new insights. We are people joined together to bring about a change in the way we do our business, and this gives us new identity. As a colleague of ours, Barry Camson of Israel, describes it:

> People are fulfilling the need they have to have their voices heard and to belong to a community in which they believe. The processes start with existing perspectives. It moves beyond that to a collective knowing, a new ordering of old and new wisdom. It expands what people know as individuals into a common database of what people know collectively. This becomes the basis for their new identity.

It matters, in new ways, that we are all together working toward common goals. Each of us sees himself or herself in a different light, and who we see in that light excites and energizes us.

Relationships

The processes we use for the intervention work are based on the central importance of each person and then of each person connected with the whole. The magic of the moment is when people experience themselves in "true relationship." They see themselves in relationship with their co-workers and feel themselves connected to their organizations. Conversations have an important role in re-creating relationships and reconnecting people to their purpose and to the meaning in their lives and in their work.

THE TACO CABANA INTERVENTION

Perhaps a story from a client journey might help. We were approached by a former client, who had become the human resources vice president for a restaurant chain in Texas. He asked if we could do some Whole-Scale™ work of the type we had done for him on his previous job. We agreed to work with one hundred fifty managers for three days in February 1999. He was accustomed to our way of working toward "one-brain and one-heart" and understood the need for a microcosm planning team. In January the consultants met with a maximum-mix group of sixteen managers from different locations and different levels who were all part of the organization called Taco Cabana, a wonderful Tex-Mex restaurant chain in Texas and Oklahoma. We worked for two days with this group, bringing them together around a compelling purpose for the three-day event:

To work together to:

- Develop a shared picture of the Cabana experience for customers and employees;
- Create a common purpose that would unite each of us and all of us in knowing how important we are to its success; and
- Agree and commit to how we get there.

We then agreed on which conversations had to take place, which stakeholder voices had to be heard, and what strategic direction had to be developed and enriched in order to achieve the purpose. During the actual meeting of the one hundred fifty in February, we invited real customers of the operation to describe what they particularly liked about the Cabana experience and what they would change if they could. We shared a video of front-line workers in various locations, talking about their work, what problems they saw, and what they would like to see changed. That video, only ten minutes long, turned out to be honest, insightful, and compelling, as real people often are when they are asked to speak from their own hearts.

The participants had an opportunity to interact with the customers and connect with the workers' story. Using what they learned from those interactions, they worked at maximum-mix tables to enrich the leadership team's draft of the mission, vision, principles, and "99 imperatives" (the strategic goals for the year). In addition, everyone created a first draft of characteristics of the "Cabana Experience." Overnight, a combined group of executive leaders and the event planning team engaged

The Flawless Consulting Fieldbook and Companion

in transformational leadership that allowed everyone's voices to be joined in a common picture of both strategy and a visceral description of success from both the customers' and employees' eyes.

The "magic moment" came the next morning when that overnight group reported out, both verbally and in writing, the "Cabana Experience" and the shared mission, vision, principles, and "99 imperatives." The response from the whole group was immediate and electrifying. Actually, they shrieked and hollered in a standing ovation! In that moment, people clearly were seeing themselves in it, feeling connected to others, and knowing they would succeed. We believe that was the paradigm shift moment, like the one Ivor described in upstate New York.

The rest of the day, the participants identified first-step action plans for the system as a whole and for their back-home groups. We finished with the individual evaluations summarized in Exhibit 32.1 on pages 322 through 326.

This moment was the beginning of a journey. No one who was at the event will allow it to slip through his or her fingers. Additional work will continue through the next year.

And so, the most important message we'd like to leave ringing in your ears is that it does not take magic to create the magic. It takes focus on purpose and the belief that the wisdom is in the people. The magic is in combining and releasing the wisdom in the organization.

Taco Cabana's
"Break on Through" Leadership Conference

Held February 16 through 18, 1999

Purpose and outcomes were developed by the Event Planning Team prior to the February session.

Purpose: To work together to:

- Develop a shared picture of the Cabana experience for customers and employees.

- Create a common purpose that would unite each of us and all of us in knowing how important we are to its success.

- Agree and commit to how we get there.

Outcomes: The intended outcomes of our Leadership Conference are:

- A commitment to put fun into our processes.

- Make "Guest Centered" the heart of the Cabana experience.

- A commitment to make the Guest Experience mirror the Employee Experience.

- A commitment to make internal and external peoples happy.

- Feeling part of a closer knit family where we know each other well and can be resources for each other.

- Knowing help is available and who can provide it.

- Improved communications among upper management and lower management and corporate and field.

- A shared picture of the Cabana experience and an expanded definition (in concrete terms) of what it is, e.g., "hassle free" in every facet of business.

Exhibit 32.1. Break on Through: A Leadership Conference

The Flawless Consulting Fieldbook and Companion

- Take ownership in the destiny of one's circle of influence and enable others to do likewise.

- Understanding and appreciation for other people's perspectives, including my own.

- To learn new ways from each other and to improve consistency and quality of restaurant operations and be able to make it happen.

- Know that each one of us is important to the success of the company and feeling proud of it.

- Walk out with a common commitment to the importance of our own roles and responsibilities.

- Know you can evolve individually, affecting the company as a whole (creative visualization).

- Be able to demonstrate, transmit, and sustain our commitments and passions.

- A commitment and ownership of our enriched Vision, Mission, Operating Principles, and '99 Imperatives that we all own.

Summary of Final Evaluations from Participants

What Were the Most Significant Outcomes from These Three Days for You?

Summary of Responses Written Most Often

We have a better understanding of where the company is, how others perceive it, and where it's going. Great to see everyone focus and understand their roles in this business. Lots of commitments made. Great to have input/be part of the process on new Vision, Mission, Operating Principles, and Business Imperatives for '99. Finally the Cabana Experience is clearly communicated for us

Exhibit 32.1. Continued

and our Team Members. Great chance to meet the rest of Taco Cabana face-to-face/make new friends in the company. Great teamwork! Favorite sessions: Customer panel, Leadership panel, Board Member, and Stock Analyst, commitments by each team.

Actual Quotes

"I have new faith in Taco Cabana and the leadership."

"The fact that we were all united seeing things the same way and committed on the same Vision and End Results. . . ."

"We were allowed to speak out, not hold it back, and let it burn in our minds and hearts."

"We are a family."

"The great stuff we've learned and can now share with our people back at home. . . ."

"We are not divided as a division, a city, a market, a region; we are a WHOLE COMPANY."

"Feeling proud about the accomplishments of '98 and getting ready to move ahead in '99. . . ."

"The uniting of our Company. . . "

"Our voices are heard by top management."

On a Scale of 1 to 10, How Confident Are You That We Will Carry Out Our Commitments to Each Other?

Answers ranged from one person marking a low of "5" to 73 people marking a high of "10." The average answer was 9.27!!!!!

Exhibit 32.1. Continued

The Flawless Consulting Fieldbook and Companion

Why Did You Mark It Where You Did?

Summary of Responses Written Most Often

Be careful to follow up and hold people and groups account-able to their commitments. We are all working together now. We are enthusiastic and committed. Teamwork will make it happen/everyone had a part in the decision making. Let's be realistic about what some people can accomplish (guarded optimism). We're eager to get back to work and make all this happen. Follow-up must start at the top and will then work down. Some evaluators said that they "don't believe in scoring a 9 or 10 to anything."

Actual Quotes

"We have laid out a great road map to follow. . . ."

"Because I always keep my commitments!"

"We are united with the same new Vision and Mission."

"I saw moods change once upper management let us make changes and listened."

"I think 80 percent achievement would even be great."

"We have the Desire, Knowledge and Skill to DO IT!!"

"I see the passion to make change."

What Specifically Do We Need to Do from Here to Maintain Our Momentum?

Summary of Responses Written Most Often

By far the most repeated comment was "COMMUNICATION." Lots of responses suggesting more meetings like this one, even

Exhibit 32.1. Continued

if done regionally. Keep delivering the Cabana Experience to our Guests. Lots of follow-up to make sure we do what we said we would. Keep the commitment and support from upper management. We need to be consistent in service and quality for our customers. Commitment to development of our people. Take this excitement and commitment back to our restaurants and departments (don't forget Spanish version of some materials).

Actual Quotes

"Walk the Talk!"
"Follow-up, follow-up, follow-up!"
"Keep the unity built up between Corporate and Field."
"Believe in MAGIC and execute!"
"Stay focused, have input, be heard, be flexible."
"Keep pumping up the balloon we created."
"KEEP THE COMPANY UNITED!"

Exhibit 32.1. Continued

The Flawless Consulting Fieldbook and Companion

For More Depth

Bunker, Barbara, & Billie Alban. *Large Group Interventions: Engaging the Whole System for Rapid Change.* San Francisco: Jossey-Bass, 1997.

Cooperrider, David L., Peter F. Sorensen, Jr., Diana Whitney, & Therese F. Yaeger (Eds.). *Appreciative Inquiry: Rethinking Human Organization Toward a Positive Theory of Change.* Champaign, IL: Stipes Publishing, 1999.

Daft, Richard, & Robert Lengel. *Fusion Leadership.* San Francisco: Berrett-Koehler, 1998.

Dannemiller Tyson Associates. *Whole-Scale™ Change: Unleashing the Magic in Organizations.* San Francisco: Berrett-Koehler, in press.

Dannemiller, Kathie, et al. *The Whole-Scale Change Toolkit.* San Francisco: Berrett-Koehler, 2000.

Holman, Peggy, & Tom Devane (Eds.). *The Change Handbook: Group Methods for Shaping the Future.* San Francisco: Berrett-Koehler, 1999.

Jacobs, Roger W. *Real Time Strategic Change: How to Involve an Entire Organization in Fast and Far-Reaching Change.* San Francisco: Berrett-Koehler, 1994.

Wheatley, Margaret J., & Myron Kellner-Rogers. *A Simpler Way.* San Francisco: Berrett-Koehler, 1996.

About the Contributors

Kathleen Dannemiller and Sylvia James of Dannemiller Tyson Associates LLC and Paul Tolchinsky of Performance Development Associates are frequent consulting and writing collaborators. Kathie is a founding partner of Dannemiller Tyson and co-inventor of Whole-Scale™ change.

Chapter 33

Nancy's Checklist

Nancy Sanchez

Nancy has brought consulting skills into some of the business world's most difficult environments. I can't tell whether her success comes from her skill as a consultant, educator or from her resolute and deep commitment to a set of values and beliefs that she courageously lives out, or both.

As an external consultant who has made *Flawless Consulting* a focal part of my work, I would like to offer the following eight pieces of advice. They are based on years of learnings about what has worked and what has not worked when interacting with my clients.

1. Begin with the whole in mind. *Share the entire flawless consulting model with your clients before you contract and negotiate with them. This is similar to the well-known reporter adage: "Tell 'em what you're going to do. Do it. Then tell 'em what you did."*

2. Do not forget to use any of the flawless consulting tools. *Check and re-check to be sure that you are applying all of the tools.*

3. Admit when you are wrong.

4. Admit when you need to adjust your course.

5. Maintain some distance. *If you are too close to the work, enlist the help of a colleague in auditing your work to see whether it is on track.*
6. Be open to learning. *Keep learning and transfer the knowledge to your client.*
7. Be humble and let your clients teach you.
8. Have fun!

For More Depth

Arrien, Angeles. *The Four-Fold Way: Walking the Paths of the Warrior, Teacher, Healer, and Visionary.* San Francisco: Harper San Francisco, 1993.

Block, Peter. *Flawless Consulting: A Guide to Getting Your Expertise Used* (2nd ed.). San Francisco: Jossey-Bass/Pfeiffer, 1999.

Chaleff, Ira. *The Courageous Follower: Standing Up to and for Our Leaders.* San Francisco: Berrett-Koehler, 1998.

Veary, Nana. *Change We Must: My Spiritual Journey.* Waipahu, HI: Booklines Hawaii, 2000.

About the Contributor

Nancy Nielsen Sanchez is the consulting services manager for Netigy Corporation, a pre-IPO firm in Manhattan.

The Flawless Consulting Fieldbook and Companion

Chapter 34

Anonymous Data Collection?
Definitely Yes and No

Neale Clapp

Effective organizations seek trust and authenticity. In this article, Neale addresses this issue through the question of whether consultants should promise anonymity when conducting interviews. The article demonstrates his belief that every step of our work with clients should model the organization we hope to create. Some of Neale's gifts are his intellectual integrity and his willingness to question what is considered standard practice among consultants.

Since the publication of the first edition of *Flawless Consulting* and its wide professional acceptance, the emphasis on the process of consulting has raised our consciousness on a host of issues, ranging from requisite interpersonal skills to the sequence of each phase of consultation.

Despite this attention and growing consensus regarding good consulting practice, consulting remains an elusive art, subject to as many interpretations as there are practitioners. This article addresses one small, but hardly minor, aspect of today's collected wisdom in process consulting: When to, and when not to, make your data collection anonymous.

THE APPEAL OF ANONYMITY

The notion of collecting data anonymously has obvious appeal and rationale.

1. It provides the opportunity for greater candor and disclosure from the people providing the data. Anonymous sources are comfortable knowing that they can freely express unpopular controversial or judgmental points of view. This candor is in short supply in the types of situations OD consultants usually encounter. After all, we wouldn't be called in if a free exchange of valid information had been forthcoming.

2. Confidentiality assures that blaming and scapegoating can be avoided. Furthermore, identifying the source is frequently an opening for feedback recipients to discount the data with dismissive statements such as "Joe is a chronic complainer" or "Miriam has her own axe to grind."

3. No matter how benign management has been in the past, there is always the creeping suspicion that they have something up their sleeves. Or, to quote my own law of organizational dynamics: "You can never overestimate the extent of paranoia in an organization."

4. Anonymous data collection gives the veneer of objectivity and impartiality, which helps to demonstrate both the alleged rationality of the process and the professionalism of the consultant.

5. There are certainly occasions in OD practice when it doesn't matter who the sources of the data are. For example, anonymous data collection makes obvious sense when the goal is to "take the pulse" of an organization in a way that yields quantifiable results, such as in employee opinion surveys. In these instances, the data may be analyzed at multiple organizational levels, such as subunits or departments, to reveal different perspectives, while still cloaking the individual responses in confidentiality.

So where's the problem? The logic of anonymity has become part of the conventional wisdom of OD practice. Efforts to examine this

practice with an open mind are met with skepticism and puzzled frowns. Why challenge a practice with such established legitimacy?

In my experience, and that of many others, the unexamined acceptance of this logic has resulted in consulting nightmares and ethical dilemmas for the following reasons:

- The promise of anonymity may give license to a source to make false allegations;
- The recipient of anonymous data may attribute it to an innocent source; and
- Not knowing the source of negative information may create an environment of distrust. For example, the consultant may gather information that suggests dishonesty, sexism, or racism. These are allegations or insinuations, not established facts. In such cases, anonymity may be used as a cloak for character assassination, and the reputations of innocent individuals can be tarnished. Furthermore, keeping sources anonymous causes both the sources and recipients of unfavorable data to become distrustful of one another. Sources may fear that they will be identified and sanctioned, and with good reason: Receivers of unfavorable data have a strong tendency to try to identify the source. Whether the identification they make is accurate or erroneous, their disapproval or retribution can permanently damage others' careers.

So the question is not *whether* to collect data anonymously, but *when* to do so. The consequences of either choice need to be fully explored with the client in the initial contracting session, although the decision ultimately resides with the consultant, because it is our area of expertise.

WHEN AND WHEN NOT TO COLLECT DATA ANONYMOUSLY

Here are three brief examples, based on my experience, that illustrate when it is and when it is not appropriate to use anonymous data collection.

Case 1: Intergroup Conflict

The clients were the vice presidents of marketing and manufacturing operations. Their respective units had a long history of conflict, replete with mutual recriminations, stereotyping, and "fighting dirty." Approximately fifty people of various levels were engaged in this ongoing tug-of-war. Both vice presidents had high stakes in the resolution of this conflict, as their primary objectives for the year were to demonstrate improved relations and coordination between their units.

I collaborated with the clients to write a detailed questionnaire to be used in individual interviews. We agreed to interview all fifty people, who were about equally divided between marketing and operations. The data feedback was identified only by which unit it came from. No individuals were singled out. To no one's surprise, when the data were displayed, each side of the conflict thought itself more willing to work toward resolution than the other side. Each thought its own behavior exemplary, while seeing the other's behavior as purposely destructive.

On reflection, both units were struck by their own bias and self-serving construction of reality. With good humor, both acknowledged their contributions to bad inter-unit relations and engaged in action planning toward improvement.

In this instance, the presenting problem was intergroup conflict. There was nothing to be gained by revealing individual responses to the questionnaire. In fact, anonymity helped the participants to recognize the extent to which group norms and peer pressure influenced their judgment.

Case 2. Externalizing the Problem

The five managing partners (the client) of a medium-sized law firm were at their wits' end in coping with the attrition of senior associates, just at the time these associates were to be considered for partnership. In a group discussion, the partners revealed very contradictory ideas as to the source of the problem. Some were furious with the associates, accusing them of having a "suicide syndrome"—in other words, engag-

The Flawless Consulting Fieldbook and Companion

ing in self-destructive behavior. Other partners were puzzled and could offer no explanation. Only one partner suggested that the partners themselves might be partly responsible. He was denounced all around by his colleagues.

I reached agreement with the clients to interview roughly half (twenty) of the current associates, whom the office manager and I selected jointly. We had a clear understanding that names would not be shared with anyone—even with the other associates. All interviewees were told at the beginning of the interview that their words were totally confidential. Although quotes might be used in the feedback session to the partners, no attribution would be included. Further, specific examples that might lead to identification or misidentification of individual associates would be scrupulously avoided. The interviews proved to have surprising depth and candor.

The feedback session to the partners was difficult and perilous. Essentially, the associates revealed that there was a total lack of consistency in their treatment by the partners. The plain fact was that each associate was at the mercy of the whims of each partner. Some partners saw their responsibility to steward associates and provide developmental opportunities. Others used associates as lackeys or "gophers." And, in fact, associate attrition was directly attributable to punitive behavior by partners.

Of course, many partners were angered by these findings, and the threat of retribution to associates was obvious to all. In this case, anonymity was necessary to assure the associates' futures and to preclude vindictive behavior. Furthermore, this method forced the partners to relinquish externalizing the problem and to seek solutions that were directed at curtailing destructive partner behavior.

Case 3. Building Team Effectiveness

In a classic case of team building, a vice president and his six direct reports sought assistance in coping with their interpersonal problems. I made it clear that the entire team, not just the vice president, was the client. Furthermore, efforts would be made to improve team effective-

ness, rather than to focus on individual deficiencies. I explained in the contracting session that everyone would be expected to "own" all that he or she said in the interviews, which were to be conducted separately with each individual. There would be no confidentiality.

As expected, the first response from the team was that a great deal of data would be lost in the self-censoring process. However, I pointed out that information taken anonymously was of little use because no one would know the source and might misattribute it, and everyone would be free to deny any responsibility for the unidentified information, creating mutual suspicion in the team. The team reluctantly agreed, but felt that the interview would be weakened by the absence of the "real stuff." I countered by indicating that I would be put in the bind of colluding with one or more of them if I took data about another team member.

Each interview was prefaced with the reminder that the decision to respond to a particular question during the individual interview sessions was up to the interviewees. No judgment would be made if they chose not to answer, but any answer they gave would be attributed to them. All team members had to decide the extent to which they wanted to disclose and ultimately confront those issues that were inhibiting the team.

When the team got back together after the interviews, the working sessions established several key points. Members learned that they could successfully address difficult issues with one another. As that happened, their confidence in the process rose significantly. Many of the concerns they had avoided in the individual interviews were disclosed freely in the team session. They became increasingly aware of the subversion and loss of trust caused by talking behind one another's backs. Eventually, they all went on record as supporting the idea that all team members would discuss their concerns or confront other members with whom they had problems, rather than relate problems to a third party hoping to gain an ally.

For me, it's critical to model the behavior that leads to effective teams as we work together. This is a component of the authenticity that makes for an effective consultant. When consulting with a team, taking

The Flawless Consulting Fieldbook and Companion

data in confidence builds distrust and puts the consultant in the unfortunate and inappropriate position of playing God with the findings. By so doing, the consultant condones the very behavior that effective teams deplore. The justification for this lapse is the wish to surface more data. The aftermath may be more destructive than any potential gain.

Also, if the consultant feeds back anonymous findings, there is every reason to expect that the team will reject the threatening items, deny the accuracy of the data, and take no responsibility.

After thirty years of team-building experience, I haven't seen the "owning" of an interviewee's own feelings, attitudes, and interpretations have negative consequences. The one time that interviews revealed deep animosity and a planned "ganging up on" the boss, I canceled the session, for it would have been a lynching, not team building.

The decision about whether to collect data in confidence should not be automatic and unthinking. It should be a function of the context, the appraisal of the client's situation, and the planned intervention. Primarily, one must consider how anonymous data collection will affect the trust level in the organization, as well as the organization's ability to solve problems in the future.

About the Contributor

Neale Clapp of Essex, Connecticut, has consulted to organizations and groups in a variety of business settings for more than thirty-five years.

Chapter 35

Toward a More Participative, Productive Workplace

Marie McCormick

One of the most traditional ways to initiate change is through an employee survey. This has been called "action research," because it can be a data-based, logical way to structure new conversations about improvement. What attracts me to Marie's survey instrument is that the questions keep the responsibility for improvement in the hands of those filling out the inventory.

Too many questionnaires focus on management behavior, as if management were cause and employees the effect. This becomes a sophisticated form of whining that implies that management is responsible for the employees' experience. This reinforces the role of boss-as-parent, which breeds the kind of control culture that the questionnaire is supposed to be changing.

Marie's inventory is mostly free of this management-as-cause bias. The construction of most of the questions places the locus of change clearly in the hands of the employees. I am also grateful to Marie for placing this instrument into the public domain. It is an act of immense generosity.

Most change efforts fail. We all know that. What we don't know is why. In order to begin to understand the why, consider the following. You are a CEO or any manager leading a change effort. You basically have three ways in which you could go about attempting to transform your organization, or in fact bring about any desired change.

Scenario 1: Leadership by Mandate.   You lock yourself in your office for a week. Develop a vision of the new future that you want for your organization. Document the vision and mandate the changes that you think are required.

Scenario 2: Leadership by Representation.   You select the best and the brightest from around the firm and create a cross-functional "expert" team. Use the team to interview, come up with their version of what is best, and then sell/mandate the vision and associated changes to the rest of the organization.

Scenario 3: Leadership by Engagement.   You create the opportunity for people from throughout the organization to come together to discuss the issues, opportunities, and interconnections in your business. Have them create an ideal future that you can all agree on and action plans to accomplish that vision.

Consider three questions concerning these scenarios:

1. In your experience, which of the three leadership models do most CEOs and/or managers employ? Why?
2. Which of the three do you believe lead to the best business results? Why?
3. What impact does each have on the people involved? Why?

I believe that the answers to these questions provide insight into the reason most organizations fail to bring about true transformation. Let's focus on re-engineering as an example of the "leadership by representation" model to gain some insight into the answers. In the last

The Flawless Consulting Fieldbook and Companion

decade, organizations around the globe have used this method and spent billions of dollars and many hours in an attempt to improve outcomes. How successful do you believe that they were? What results did they achieve or not achieve? What impact did they have on people in the organizations that sponsored them? Why?

From my point of view, some of the positive results were that a number of improved processes and structures were developed and a cadre of energized change agents were spawned by being on the work teams. But, most re-engineering efforts had a critical flaw; most didn't involve enough of the people who would be impacted by, and could impact, the change. The short-term focus on efficiency of process overrode the most critical element: engagement of all people who could ensure enduring and successful change. Rather than engaging and empowering employees whose jobs would be affected, they chose to include only a few who could represent the whole because this seemed easier to manage. Thus, although better processes may have been outlined, the desired results were never realized. Most people really didn't care or they felt threatened by the required changes. The improved structures and processes were not *their* better structures and processes. Most people didn't feel a part of the effort. Rather, they felt that the change had been done *to* them.

In my experience, most leaders use "leadership by mandate" or at best "leadership by representation," whereas the model that creates the best-sustained business results is "leadership by engagement." My research suggests that the methods you choose to bring about change greatly impact the overall success of the effort. How people feel about their role in the organization influences how people do their jobs. If change or work is mandated, people become hapless worker bees. If transformations are driven by representation, representatives become charged up change agents and the rest of the organization remain as hapless worker bees. If change is by engagement, everyone in the system knows more about what is going on, believes that he or she has a voice in how the work is done, and feels valued for contributions. This kind of engagement leads to better-informed solutions and, in turn, to better bottom-line results.

The underlying reason why change efforts fail is that success, financial or otherwise, cannot come about *solely* through process and structure changes. Enduring success comes about through process and structure changes that are part of a common vision of the people—people with energy, commitment, and a sense of ownership of the new reality.

The great majority of change efforts do not consider what it is that they are really attempting to change. It is not just "processes" or "functions." It is, in fact, people's work. People want to have a voice in "how things are going to change around here," how their work is going to be different. They know their jobs better than anyone, and together they can figure out almost anything if given the chance. The role of leaders becomes to give them that chance and to remove any barriers that are in the way. People want to contribute what they know and what they can do. When truly committed, they can move mountains. People want to be engaged. People have to be engaged for their own sake and for the sake of the business. I am not suggesting that we include people solely for the sake of making people feel valued. I am suggesting that it is only when people are truly valued for what they know and can do that real change can happen.

Improved results will only be sustained on a long-term basis if we create healthy workplaces, places in which people feel connected, knowledgeable, and empowered to get the job done. Places in which people find meaning and value. Places in which people feel part of a community that they care about. So if we are tired of failed change efforts, we need to rethink the processes used to create change. It doesn't mean we eliminate process redesign or any other technical tool at our disposal. It *does* mean that we must incorporate the best of these tools with change methodologies that include as many contributors in the process as possible. It is only in this way that we can create the most productive and successful solutions.

THE EMPLOYEE ENGAGEMENT INVENTORY

I developed the McCormick Employee Engagement Inventory (MEEI) (Exhibit 35.1 beginning on page 349) to measure the impact change efforts have on the people involved. The MEEI looks at changes in the level of employee engagement that result from any change initiative. Its goal is to help your organization create a healthy work environment, one in which people really want to work, be accountable, and be productive.

The inventory has two fundamental components: (1) a pre-intervention assessment, aimed at establishing a baseline and providing insight to establish change strategies, and (2) a post-intervention version designed to assess the impact that the process, and indeed the ongoing operations, have on employee engagement. The pre-intervention version asks questions that are rarely asked, such as: Do the employees know what's going on in the entire organization? Do they feel appreciated? Do they hold hope for the future success of the organization? The post-intervention version, given at critical intervals throughout the process, asks the same questions, plus a few more directly related to the change effort itself.

The questionnaire measures employee engagement as defined by six elements:

1. The employee's understanding of his or her role and how it fits with the whole organization;
2. The climate of the workplace;
3. Organizational and business knowledge;
4. The quality of relationships with clients/customers and suppliers;
5. Leadership style; and
6. Perceived goal achievement.

In the post-intervention survey, participants are asked on a five-point scale how strongly they agree or disagree with a number of items in these six categories, such as: "There is a greater feeling of community at work," "There is an increased level of trust in the organization," and "I hold more hope for the future success of this organization." The inventory measures changes in the workplace that have to do with issues at the core of employees finding meaning and value in the workplace—and ultimately being committed to future goals.

WHY WE NEED SUCH A TOOL

The pre-intervention inventory provides informative feedback about employees' attitudes about the organization's status quo. It also offers the organization an opportunity to start talking about issues such as "personal empowerment," "community at work," "hope," and "trust" in a concrete and useful way. The post-intervention survey indicates whether the actions being taken are moving the organization in the right or wrong direction in terms of the kind of workplace that will both support change and increase employee fulfillment. This powerful combination of before and after measurement can help the organization succeed in its change initiative.

I have used the post-test version of this inventory in several settings and would like to share with you some of the more intriguing results, because, I believe, they challenge our traditional thinking.

One example involved participants in a democratic, high-interaction, system-wide change initiative at the INOVA Health Care System in Virginia. This initiative focused not only on "hard" changes, such as substantial cost reductions over a five-year period, but also on targeted goals in the area of culture change, as defined by increased accountability, partnership, and commitments to both service and learning. Traditional business wisdom says that leadership commitment and follow-through to a change effort like this are critical to success. But my research showed a minimal relationship between leader involvement and the participants' perceptions of the success of the change effort.

So if success was not related to leader commitment, what was it related to? In fact, success seemed to be related to dynamics of a very different nature, such as changes in the participants themselves. The statement that was most highly correlated with success was, "I feel a greater sense of personal empowerment." Other statements that were correlated highly with success were: "There is an increased commitment among members of the organization"; "I hold more hope for the future success of the organization"; "I feel more supported by other departments"; and "There is a greater feeling of community at work."

The Flawless Consulting Fieldbook and Companion

These results suggest that we redefine what contributes to success to include the creation of a workplace in which employees feel committed, have a sense of personal empowerment, feel more supported, and even have more hope. Clearly, this research challenges some dearly held assumptions and provokes us to rethink what is critical to a successful change effort.

A second example involved administration of the post-intervention inventory to two hundred fifty participants of a series of conferences aimed to develop a future vision for a school system in Nevada. Again, this intervention was highly participative and based on principles of respect for each voice and emphasis on the whole system. One especially interesting finding involved the statements that were agreed with most often by participants. Some of these statements were: "I know more about what's going on in the entire organization"; "Our organization has a better understanding of clients/customers"; "I have a better idea of how my job relates to other people's jobs"; "My understanding of industry issues has increased"; "We gained much in terms of better working relationships"; and "There is a greater feeling of community at work." Not only was a future vision created for the school, but also participants gained an increased knowledge about the industry, the organization, its customers, and their roles. Additionally, participants walked away with better working relationships and an increased feeling of community at work. Also provocative is the fact that there was an unmistakable relationship between all of these items and the employees' perception of the success of this intervention.

HOW TO PUT IT TO WORK

My inventory supports an organization in crafting a successful change effort. If you want to increase your potential for a successful change effort, factor in and measure employee engagement issues along with whatever your other organizational goals might be.

Here are the steps involved in putting this inventory to work for your organization:

1. Make Sure That Your Change Effort Incorporates Employee Engagement Factors

When you are developing the goals of your change effort, consider the items in the inventory. Include items that reflect these goals, along with the other objectives that your organization has set. Realize that the more tangible deliverables that have been outlined for your change effort are intimately tied to the engagement goals that we're talking about here. Whatever your organization is working to achieve, a more fulfilling workplace must be part of it.

To become clear on what your employee engagement goals are, imagine the kind of workplace you want to create. Ask employees what they believe a "community at work" would look and feel like and how the organization might begin to move in that direction. What would it take to have people feel "accountable for the success of the whole organization"? What would people be doing if they were feeling "more supported by other departments"? What would make people develop a "greater sense of personal empowerment"? Be explicit not only around tangible goals and strategies that outline the why's and what's of business, but also clearly articulate the how's of business. And make sure to include a wide range of employees in the process. Then communicate these goals, along with goals such as increased efficiency or reduced cost. Make them equal partners.

2. Administer the Pre-Intervention Survey

You can even customize it to better fit the environment you are seeking to create. Omit an item or add several others. Adapt the tool to align with your organization's vision of an engaged workplace. Get a handle on where your organization is in terms of the kind of workplace you want to create, through either the instrument as is or your customized version. Appreciate your strengths—celebrate and communicate them. And target the weaknesses as areas that deserve special attention when refining the change effort.

3. Build a Change Process That Models the Environment You Want to Create

Remember that any change process is itself a training ground for the new world you are creating. Design a change effort that models the vision of the organization the way it can be. There are many models that I think incorporate issues of employee engagement. These include "Future Search," "Whole-Scale Change," "Open Space," and the "Conference Model." Use one of these, tailor it to meet your specific needs, or develop your own. But whatever you choose, make sure that your change effort is explicit about the kind of workplace you are working to achieve. The importance of doing this is the reason the Employee Engagement Inventory includes items such as, "The experience of the change effort was reward enough" and " I am more optimistic about the next change effort." These items speak to the power of participative processes in the workplace.

4. Administer the Post-Intervention Inventory

Assess changes after your intervention. What areas have improved? Are there other areas that in fact have gotten worse? Talk about results with employees and use this information as the foundation for your next undertaking.

5. Use the Tool Again and Again, Because Change Is Not a One-Shot Deal

Supporting the kind of workplace you want to create involves more than creating good change efforts. It means living the values of employee engagement every day. It's a good idea to periodically re-administer the inventory to feel the pulse of the organization:

- At mid-point in change efforts that exceed six to nine months;

- At major milestones during implementation; and
- Any time you need to get a grip on the level of engagement.

Have brown bag lunches to discuss various aspects of creating community and bringing meaning back to the workplace. Stay in the game. Let's be clear about this: *The process of creating workplaces that support growth and engagement is certainly more an art than a science. It commands constant attention and nurturing.*

WHAT'S NEXT

I believe that the next frontier will hold new ways to relate improvements in employee engagement and bottom-line results. If you are a profit-making business, your bottom-line results may be financial. If you are a non-profit organization, they are the measures you use to define success—number of clients served, client satisfaction, or whatever. But if you believe as I do that creating a more fulfilling workplace will lead to better results, then marrying employee engagement and bottom-line goals is the only way to make success happen.

The McCormick Employee Engagement Inventory

1. Name of your organization _____

2. Industry:
   _____ Health Care
   _____ Education
   _____ Telecommunications
   _____ Criminal Justice
   _____ Other (Please specify)

3. Did you participate in an organizational change effort in your organization?   _____ Yes   _____ No

4. If "Yes," on a scale of 1 to 9, with 1 being "not successful at all" and 9 being "tremendously successful," how would you rate the success of the organizational change effort? (Please circle correct response.)
   1   2   3   4   5   6   7   8   9

5. Would you recommend doing this organizational change effort to another organization?
   _____ Yes   _____ No

6. Gender: _____ Male   _____ Female

7. Age:
   _____ Less than 25
   _____ 25 to 35
   _____ 36 to 45
   _____ 46 to 55
   _____ Over 55

8. Are you in a management position?   _____ Yes   _____ No

9. Are you a supervisor?   _____ Yes   _____ No

10. If "yes," how many people do you supervise?
    _____ Fewer than 5
    _____ 5 to 9
    _____ 10 to 19
    _____ 20 to 29
    _____ 30 to 39
    _____ 40 to 49
    _____ 50 to 99
    _____ Over 100 people

11. Are you the organizational leader who sponsored the organizational change effort? (For the purposes of this study "organizational leader" will mean the person highest on your organizational chart who was involved in the organizational change effort.)   _____ Yes   _____ No

Exhibit 35.1. The McCormick Employee Engagement Inventory

Please answer the following questions, using as your time reference the time that has passed since you participated in an organizational change effort. If you did not participate in a change effort, use the last two years as your time frame. The questions are grouped according to key topic areas. Please circle the category that most closely matches your level of agreement with each statement where:

SD = Strongly Disagree   A = Agree   D = Disagree   SA = Strongly Agree
N = Neither Agree nor Disagree   NA = Not Applicable

Communication

12. I know more about what's going on in the entire organization.	SD	D	N	A	SA	NA
13. Our organization leader's communication on important issues has increased.	SD	D	N	A	SA	NA
14. Our organization leader's communication is more honest.	SD	D	N	A	SA	NA
15. I see more sharing of information across departmental boundaries.	SD	D	N	A	SA	NA
16. We developed a new common language related to the change effort.	SD	D	N	A	SA	NA
17. This new language is very helpful in bringing about desired outcomes.	SD	D	N	A	SA	NA
18. My understanding of our business and its issues has increased.	SD	D	N	A	SA	NA

Customer/Supplier Relationships

19. Our organization has a better understanding of clients/customers.	SD	D	N	A	SA	NA
20. I have more frequent interactions with my clients/customers.	SD	D	N	A	SA	NA
21. I have more frequent interactions with my suppliers.	SD	D	N	A	SA	NA
22. My understanding of my customers' requirements has increased.	SD	D	N	A	SA	NA
23. I define my clients/customers differently.	SD	D	N	A	SA	NA
24. My definition of clients/customers includes internal customers.	SD	D	N	A	SA	NA
25. Our customer satisfaction level has improved.	SD	D	N	A	SA	NA

How I Do My Job

26. I tend to do less problem solving and more exploring "possibilities."	SD	D	N	A	SA	NA
27. I have a greater appreciation for the contribution that I make.	SD	D	N	A	SA	NA
28. My understanding of my role is clearer.	SD	D	N	A	SA	NA
29. I am more confident in my own abilities to do my job.	SD	D	N	A	SA	NA
30. I have a better idea of how my job relates to other people's jobs.	SD	D	N	A	SA	NA

Exhibit 35.1. Continued

The Flawless Consulting Fieldbook and Companion

SD = Strongly Disagree   A = Agree   D = Disagree   SA = Strongly Agree
N = Neither Agree nor Disagree   NA = Not Applicable

31. I take more risks at work.	SD	D	N	A	SA	NA
32. I feel a greater sense of personal empowerment.	SD	D	N	A	SA	NA

Goals and Outcomes

33. I understood the change effort objectives before beginning the process.	SD	D	N	A	SA	NA
34. Our organization met stated goals the change effort set out to achieve.	SD	D	N	A	SA	NA
35. The most important outcomes of the change effort were unexpected.	SD	D	N	A	SA	NA
36. We gained much in terms of better working relationships.	SD	D	N	A	SA	NA
37. A few initiatives resulted from the change effort. Nothing else changed.	SD	D	N	A	SA	NA
38. The experience of the change effort was reward enough.	SD	D	N	A	SA	NA
39. We have seen improvement in the bottom line related to the change effort.	SD	D	N	A	SA	NA
40. There was little or no follow-up to our implementation plan.	SD	D	N	A	SA	NA

Work Climate

41. There is a greater feeling of community at work.	SD	D	N	A	SA	NA
42. There is an increased level of trust in the organization.	SD	D	N	A	SA	NA
43. I feel more supported by other departments.	SD	D	N	A	SA	NA
44. Morale seems better.	SD	D	N	A	SA	NA
45. Our organization is more prone to action.	SD	D	N	A	SA	NA
46. I hold more hope for the future success of this organization.	SD	D	N	A	SA	NA
47. There is an increased commitment among members of the organization.	SD	D	N	A	SA	NA
48. I am more optimistic about the next change effort.	SD	D	N	A	SA	NA

Leadership

49. Our organizational leader truly believed in the change effort.	SD	D	N	A	SA	NA
50. This leader was committed to seeing change effort outcomes through.	SD	D	N	A	SA	NA
51. Our organizational leader is more collaborative in his/her approach to work.	SD	D	N	A	SA	NA

Exhibit 35.1. Continued

SD = Strongly Disagree   A = Agree   D = Disagree   SA = Strongly Agree
N = Neither Agree nor Disagree   NA = Not Applicable

52. New leadership talent became obvious during the change effort.   SD   D   N   A   SA   NA

53. Our organization is less bureaucratic than it used to be.   SD   D   N   A   SA   NA

54. People not involved in the change effort were made to feel included.   SD   D   N   A   SA   NA

55. I realized that we didn't need the support of top management to
make changes that make sense.   SD   D   N   A   SA   NA

COMMENTS

Reflecting on the questionnaire, please provide additional comments that you think are important to this research.

THANK YOU FOR YOUR PARTICIPATION IN THIS STUDY!

Exhibit 35.1. Continued

The Flawless Consulting Fieldbook and Companion

For More Depth

Further Reading

Weisbord, Marvin. *Productive Workplaces: Organizing and Managing for Dignity, Meaning, and Community*. San Francisco: Jossey-Bass, 1992.

Wheatley, Margaret. *Leadership and the New Science: Discovering Order in a Chaotic World* (2nd ed.). San Francisco: Berrett-Koehler, 1999.

Further Training

Appreciative Inquiry Workshop

Future Search workshops. Contact Future Search Network at (215) 951-0328 or www.futuresearch.net.

Senn Delaney Leadership Consulting Training. www.senndelaneyleadership.com.

About the Contributor

Marie McCormick's organization development and training firm is the Pearce-McCormick Consulting Group, based in Philadelphia.

Chapter 36

Co-Creating a Community's Future
Once upon a Time in a Place Called Home

David and Carole Schwinn

Here is a vision of hope and optimism written by two people who consistently see the promise in the world around them and have a deep faith that we keep moving toward a more caring and forgiving universe.

This mostly true story of Jackson, Michigan's CommUnity Transformation Project is offered as a lesson in the redesign of very large-scale social systems. The story represents the work of a small, diverse team of people who committed to "being themselves what they wished to bring forth in their community" and to engaging increasing numbers of citizens in a process of:

- Creating shared understanding of their community's current condition;
- Designing their community's desired future;
- Taking action to realize the design; and

The Jackson CommUnity Transformation Project is a learning partnership of Jackson Community College, the Jackson Area Quality Initiative, and the W.K. Kellogg Foundation. Members of the "consulting" team include Delvin LaMont Williams, Sue Justian, Brian Cook, David and Carole Schwinn, Bradley Smith, Mary Beers, Kathleen Conley, William Morrison, and Sandra Jimenez. The primary external consultant to the project is Jamshid Gharajedaghi, INTERACT: The Institute for Interactive Management. The project has engaged over five thousand citizens and two hundred organizations since its launch in June 1995.

- Sustaining a process of citizen participation in community development.

The story is offered as an opportunity for readers to reflect on their own practices, rather than as a model or a set of recommendations for how they might improve their own consulting. As you read the story, imagine that you and your colleagues are members of the small, diverse team responsible for the process. Then ask yourself:

- What beliefs and assumptions are the basis for your actions in the community?
- What theories or mental models about large-scale social systems are informing your work?
- What "consulting" skills or tools and techniques are most critical for your work?
- How are they the same or different from common approaches used in organizations?
- What are the implications for your own work?
- What lessons from working in a "place called home" can be transferred to large-scale redesign work in organizations?

ONCE UPON A TIME

We shall not cease from exploration
And the end of all our exploring
Will be to arrive where we started
And know the place for the first time.

T.S. Eliot, *Gerontion*

Once upon a time in a place called home, people poured out of their homes, their offices, and their schools to know themselves again for the very first time. They gathered in deep conversations, citizen to citizen, Catholic to Protestant, manager to worker, young to old, black to white, rich to poor. Sometimes conversations were difficult, sometimes exuberant, even sad and angry, but they always led to better understanding and deeper connections.

Their purpose was to create a "developing" community, in which

The Flawless Consulting Fieldbook and Companion

everyone would be able to meet his or her own needs, the needs of others, and the needs of the larger world of which they were a part. They organized their work around the principle that all citizens should:

- Have reasonable resources to meet their own needs;
- Share in decisions that affect their well-being;
- Find meaning in their lives, experience belonging in the community, and enjoy a clean, healthy environment;
- Have the means to shape the values and ethics of the community and have access to resources for dissolving conflict; and
- Be able to learn and develop their unique talents, skills, and abilities.

As they talked, they imagined the first settlers arriving near the Grand River and the generations-long journey that led Jackson, Michigan, to become the home of the world's largest concentration of auto suppliers, the world's largest walled prison, the Republican Party, Cascades park and waterfalls, and more golf courses per capita than just about any other community in the country.

They asked themselves, "What do you suppose our history has to do with who we are now, how we think, and how we interact with one another?" Someone wondered whether the city fathers' choice to locate the state prison instead of the University of Michigan in Jackson was still influencing the community. Another remembered that the decision was made because the prison provided cheap labor. Another observed that the prison still provided a large number of jobs. Still another wondered how having a large number of people employed in a prison impacted the community and whether those were the jobs the community would choose if they could have any kind of jobs at all. Not everybody agreed about these issues.

Still more citizens came to the table, especially when food was served and the setting allowed for family participation. Talk turned to the community's dependence on "The Big Three" and how citizens suffered when the auto industry took a downturn. They wondered where and how decisions were made that influenced how Jacksonians made a living. They wondered how those decisions and the types of jobs available influenced how the schools worked, how healthy people were, and how much money was available for important things such as water, fire and police protection, home building, and cultural activities.

Often, conversations turned to the world outside Jackson and the changes that people were seeing. They saw that computers and the global marketplace and changes in climate and in demographics could all affect the lives of people in Jackson. Some things they saw were troubling, but others created exciting possibilities. As the people told their stories of Jackson and how it came to be, they talked about things they would just as soon leave behind. There were many other things, though, that they wanted to keep in the new community they would create together.

LEAVING THE OLD, EMBRACING THE NEW

After several months of talking together, the people sat back and noticed patterns in the stories they had been telling. They noticed patterns of thinking that might not serve the community well in the future. They worked together to agree on a list of the "old assumptions" that they thought were best left behind. Their old assumptions were as follows:

- We need strong leaders to take care of us and make decisions for us;
- Citizens are powerless to change the main systems that affect their lives;
- Citizens outside our personal circles need to take care of their own problems by themselves;
- If we had enough time and money, new laws, and better enforcement, we could fix any problems; and
- If citizens gained the right job skills, they could have long-term security.

The Jacksonians saw that the community's future was not very pretty unless something took the place of the old ways of thinking and acting. They decided to generate a set of "more valid" assumptions for

The Flawless Consulting Fieldbook and Companion

the "ideal" Jackson they would create. Their more valid assumptions were as follows:

- Leaders can be developed everywhere to create the conditions for citizen responsibility and democracy;
- Citizens can make and influence choices, take responsibility for the consequences, and learn;
- Citizens can use their talents and work together to vastly improve the whole community for all citizens;
- Citizens can be deeply motivated to understand and take action on complex problems with very little money; and
- The changing nature of work requires the resources and availability of lifelong learning for all citizens.

As the Jacksonians turned their attention to their dreams and desires, they imagined an empty space where Jackson once was. The land and the river were still there and the trees still stood, but everything else had disappeared. They wanted to use the space as a giant canvas to begin to paint a picture of the community they would have today if they could have any community at all.

THE COMMUNITY'S VISION

First, they talked of creating neighborhoods and communities in which people would live together in harmony. In centers all over the county, they would join with others around them to define any problems they had, to create solutions, and to work together toward their common goals. Community guides would be available to help them learn how to dissolve conflict. Advanced technology would connect the centers so that they could work with other neighborhoods and the larger community on common issues and concerns. They would call this unit of organization "Citizen Participation."

The people knew that important decisions and actions had to be made about how the whole community would work. Some people and organizations would have to decide how land and resources would be used, what rules would govern behavior, how all citizens would come to understand those rules, and how the community would respond to those who broke the agreed-on rules. This unit of organization they called "Planning and Justice."

Conversations turned to how people would make a living. In a unit called "Enterprise Development," they decided, people would come together to create the kind of work in which citizens could find meaning, provide for their own and the community's needs, and provide products and services needed in the larger society. New kinds of work, civic participation, and planning would require new kinds of learning in the "new" Jackson. A community learning unit would organize itself to provide lifelong learning experiences that people and organizations needed for their ongoing development.

In the "new" Jackson, citizens, organizations, and neighborhoods would still need services that helped them to provide for their own health, safety, and security. Should they need help during times of illness, loss, or other stressful conditions, special services would need to be in place. Another unit of organization, "Community Support," would provide for those needs.

The people realized as they created this "ideal" community that they needed to have strong connections to the rest of the world. They would need to have new information and resources and ideas coming into the community all the time. They would also want to tell their story to others and to provide others with information, resources, and ideas. A unit of organization called "External Connections" would serve as a "window to the world."

The evolving vision of the "new" Jackson began to look pretty complex to a lot of people. They wondered how everyone in the community would stay connected, keep informed of what was going on, and learn together about how the community could move closer and closer to its "ideal" over time.

A unit called the "Community Council" would be organized to help manage the "white spaces" between the other units, to create many pathways for connection, to work on a set of community quality indicators, and to regularly convene the community to reflect on what they were learning.

The Flawless Consulting Fieldbook and Companion

FROM IDEAS TO ACTION

These conversations, as you might imagine, were taking a very long time. As more and more people came to the table, more and more ideas flowed. Some people were very tired of talking and said, "When are we ever going to just *do* something?" Someone else said, "Don't you know that talking and understanding one another *is* how people get their important work done?" Many others, seeing a different way of working together and a new set of possibilities, simply set out to take their ideas to action.

One group of people created an organization called "Youth, Education, and Athletics," bringing together many organizations concerned about the well-being of young people and finding new ways and new resources for working together. Another group created the "Minority Economic Development System" to provide all citizens with the opportunity to participate and contribute to Jackson's economy. Still another group formed the "Jackson Area Neighborhood Council" to engage citizens in taking increasing responsibility for the well-being of children, families, and neighborhoods. Others began to build support for the CommUnity Network, a community-owned and operated "information infrastructure" that would be an ongoing source of knowledge, a vehicle for internal and external connections, and a new source of funds for community development.

The "new" Jackson began to attract attention from other people interested in creating a different future. They asked whether the same design would work in their communities and whether the same principles and methods might also work in organizations. Jacksonians said, "Those are the questions we're asking, too. What we know is that this is very hard work and that it takes great patience and persistence. No community or organization should try this unless it is willing to be guided by strong theory, purpose, and principles; to develop and adopt the right methods for their own environment; to ask for help when needed; and to keep learning all the time."

"Working in a 'place called home,'" they said, "requires new ways of bringing people to the table, framing conversations, surfacing

and challenging assumptions, designing large social systems, managing momentum and inclusion, taking vision to action, and reflecting on learning. We're beginning to think of the people who do this work as 'web-workers' and 'pathfinders,' who are systems thinkers, pattern makers, and visionary, action researchers all at the same time.

"And it really helps if they are compassionate, mindful, trustworthy, authentic, and optimistic relationship- and community-builders, too."

Well, for now, that's about as far as we can go with the "new" Jackson story. We sure would love to say that Jacksonians lived happily ever after and that all their dreams came true. But that would be a fairy tale, not a pretty true story of one community's adventures in transformation. We do feel quite comfortable, though, in telling you that Jacksonians are asking different questions, coming together in different ways, making a difference in their own lives, and beginning to believe that they really can co-create their own future.

For More Depth

Gharajedaghi, Jamshid. *Systems Thinking: Managing Chaos and Complexity—A Platform for Designing Business Architecture.* Woburn, MA: Butterworth-Heinemann, 1999.

Hubbard, Barbara Marx, & Neale Donald Walsch. *Conscious Evolution: Awakening the Power of Our Social Potential.* San Rafael, CA.: New World Library, 1998.

Levoy, Gregg Michael. *Callings: Finding and Following an Authentic Life.* Pittsburgh, PA: 3 Rivers Press, 1998.

Roberts, Elizabeth J., & Elias Amidon (Eds.). *Prayers for a Thousand Years.* San Francisco: Harper San Francisco, 1999.

Schorr, Lisbeth B. *Common Purpose: Strengthening Families and Neighborhoods to Rebuild America.* New York: Doubleday, 1998.

Senge, Peter M. *The Fifth Discipline: The Art and Practice of the Learning Organization.* New York: Doubleday, 1994.

Wheatley, Margaret. *Leadership and the New Science: Discovering Order in a Chaotic World* (2nd ed.). San Francisco: Berrett-Koehler, 1999.

Wilber, Ken. *Sex, Ecology, Spirituality: The Spirit of Evolution.* Boston, MA: Shambhala, 1995.

Williamson, Marianne. *The Healing of America.* New York: Simon & Schuster, 1997.

About the Contributors

David and Carole Schwinn work with individuals, families, neighborhoods, organizations, and communities to create system-wide, large-scale change. Their organization, The Webworks Alliance, is located in Brooklyn, Michigan.

Chapter 37

How Am I Doing? How Am I Doing? You Like Me! You Really Like Me!

Peter Block

> How am I doing? How am I doing?
>> Ed Koch, former Mayor of New York City

> . . . you like me! You really like me!
>> Sally Field, on winning her second Academy Award

We spend a lot of effort in meetings, conferences, and training sessions designed to initiate or sustain changes. Most of our traditional planning for communication meetings and conferences is about the actions of the presenters, what we want to present, and how we want to present it. We think power is the point. We seem to ignore that it is people's active experiences in the room that will affect their emotional response to change, and ultimately the quality of action.

Three elements of experience that we most undervalue are: (1) The questions we ask of participants, (2) the design and structure of the room, and (3) the evaluation of the event. Choosing the right questions and picking the right room are touched on elsewhere. Our business here is evaluation.

Earlier versions of this chapter appeared as "You Are the Audience," May 1998, and "How Am I Doing?" January 2000, in *News for a Change*, published by the Association for Quality and Participation, Cincinnati, Ohio.

The way we evaluate what we do can either reinforce passivity or push people into a more accountable position. Change happens when we take traditional activities and construct them to capture the new, larger purpose. Evaluation is another opportunity to use powerful questions to confront people in support of strategy.

SPOTLIGHT ON PARTICIPANTS

Nowhere is the mechanical age more deeply honored than in our love of evaluation, and this is not an argument against it. The argument is about how we think about evaluation, what we evaluate, and when we evaluate it. As an example, every conference I have ever attended has an evaluation form and they are all alike. Every one of them implies a relationship between how well the material was presented and the value received by participants. One set of questions is about the presenters:

- Were they dynamic?
- Were they well-organized?
- Did they present what was promised?
- Did they know their stuff?
- How good were the audiovisuals?
- Were the handouts useful?

The second set of questions is about value received:

- What did you learn?
- Was it useful?
- What will you do differently tomorrow?

These measures are based on the belief that *cause* is in the front of the room and *effect* is in the audience. We think that if people like the presenter and if the presenter is doing well, is clear, and on target, the meeting will be a success. It is our elitist, leadership compulsion reinforced by an entertainment-and-spectator culture that leads us in

The Flawless Consulting Fieldbook and Companion

this direction. If we seek accountable employee action, we need to move the spotlight from the stage and into the audience.

O'Henry begins his book *Four Million and Other Stories* with the statement:*

> Not very long ago some one invented the assertion that there were only "Four Hundred" people in New York City who were really worth noticing. But a wiser man has arisen—the census taker—and his larger estimate of human interest has been preferred in marking out the field of these little stories of the "Four Million."

O'Henry understood that the character of a city was better defined by the story of its citizens than simply by the story of its leaders. Same with our meetings, training events, conferences, and change efforts— the character of the event is better defined by the story of the participants than the excellence of the presenter.

HOW WE EVALUATE CARRIES A MESSAGE

The act of evaluation has a power. The same goes for whom we evaluate. Next time you evaluate a meeting or workshop, keep these thoughts in mind.

1. *Evaluation is not a benign event.* It carries as clear a message of our intentions as anything else we do. It says more by the way its questions are composed than by the answers it provides.
2. *Evaluation takes a stance on who is responsible for learning and outcomes, even for culture.* Is it the leader/trainer or is it the citizen/participant? If a meeting or training event does not go well, the evaluation questions imply that the leaders may have to do it differently next time. Our questions rarely indicate that next time the participants will have to change the nature of their participation.

*O'Henry. *Four Million and Other Stories.* New York: Airmont Publishing Co., 1963.

3. *Evaluation also takes a stance on how engineer-able or predictable the world can be.* It most often reinforces the illusion that change is predictable and knowable in advance, and the ones who know are the leaders and trainers. If we find out that the event was characterized by surprise, chaos, or confusion, we consider that a failure of leadership. But maybe surprise and confusion are the essential ingredients to learning and change. Maybe if everything goes as planned, the meeting failed.

4. *Evaluation is not a neutral, "objective" inquiry.* It is an active element in learning and changes what it touches. Tim Gallwey, author of the *Inner Game* series of books, commented recently that we are always ready to evaluate the effects of training, but we never measure the effects of the evaluation.

HIGH-ACCOUNTABILITY EVALUATION

Here are some ways to use evaluation as a powerful means to confront participant accountability. As a start, we might design our evaluation around the following questions:

- *What was your purpose in attending this event? What are you doing here?* Even if you were sent, you decided to come and brought expectations that were solely yours. In asking about purpose, we start with the belief that each of us is creating our own experience, even if we did not ask to be born.

- *How well are you achieving what you came for?* This raises the question of whose conference or change process this is. Are we active in seeking our own outcomes or are we waiting for room service?

- *Where in the room did you place yourself?* The place we choose to sit is a physical fact and an expression of the initial nature of our engagement, commitment, and willingness to be present. We will rationalize our seating by saying, "It was close to the door," "I need to make a call," "I don't want them to call on me," or "That was the only open seat." All of these are thin reasons to defend ourselves against engagement and accountability. The right question serves to

confront people with their choice and their willingness to care for the whole. Use every chance we get, including the evaluation form, to push back on passivity and entice people into the fray.

- *When during the day have you been bored or disappointed, and how are you dealing with this?* This question confronts the issues of energy and relevance. Whose job is it to maintain interest, to be relevant? When energy drains, where does it go? Why is it the leader's job to keep the power plant running? This does not let the leader go free, but it reduces the role to that of one player among many, not the only player.

- *What change on your part, during this event, might give you different results?* The idea that we are continually co-creating our world is implied in this question, as in the others. This takes the questions we ask ourselves as leaders and trainers and places them equally on the shoulders of the audience.

Asking these exact questions is not really the point; your questions will change with the purpose of the event. What is key is to have evaluation be a means of real-time reflection, done for the purpose of creating accountable communities and used to carry the message that self-evaluation is at the essence of change and learning.

NOW IS THE HOUR

In addition to *what* we evaluate, *when* we evaluate is also critical. We typically evaluate an event after it is over, filling out the forms on the way out of the room. Or we send in evaluations a month after the event. That implies that the feedback will help us do better next time. Well, in fact, there won't be a next time. Even if we hold the same event again, the same people will not be in the room, their purpose will be different, the reality of the world will have shifted somewhat.

Evaluating an event at the end has us care only about the past and misses the opportunity to confront how we are doing while there is still time to do something about it. To complete an evaluation as we leave the room also makes it too easy for people to express their frustration as a parting shot, avoiding any engagement or responsibility.

We also abandon the leader/trainer when we evaluate at the end. In my own case, I usually am furnished participant reactions after an event. Some thought I exaggerated, that my humor and cynicism were distracting, or that I consistently finished other people's sentences for them. Well, where were these people when I needed them? When did I lose them? Why did they believe the situation was unsalvageable? There is truth in what they said, but now the opportunity to do something about it is forever lost.

If evaluation is intended to improve our performance and not just judge it (big if!), it has to occur in the middle of things. Kathie Dannemiller, goddess of large-group methodology, understands this and takes a "pulse" reading at key points along the way—and then makes it public information. Smart strategy. We shouldn't wait until the end of our life to evaluate it—same with our meetings, training sessions, and conferences.

Key Point.   Have evaluation done early, in the middle, and often.

One More Point.   Evaluation is not about ratings, it is about learning. It should be a conversation among participants. Get it in writing first, but then make it the beginning of a conversation, make it public, invite people to own their response to the event. It gives people information they can act on, engages the people who are drifting away, and thus reinforces the belief that we can shape our destiny, not just observe and remember it.

YOU ARE THE AUDIENCE

There is a fine line between education and entertainment, and we have crossed the line and chosen entertainment. We soften the reality by calling it "edutainment," thinking we are learning while we are being entertained. When we do this, we are abandoning learning for the sake of stimulation, an outside stimulant—like better living through chemistry.

The Flawless Consulting Fieldbook and Companion

Here are some signs that we would rather be entertained than do the work of educating ourselves:

- We attend conferences based on who the keynote speakers are. We will spend a lot of time and money to listen to some well-known speakers talk for an hour.
- When we evaluate the conferences we attend, we evaluate the quality of the presenters. Did they meet their objectives and fulfill the promise of the brochure? Were they knowledgeable about the subject? Did they hold our interest?
- We want our learning to be effortless. Where are the handouts? Show me the slides. Did the handouts track the presentation? Is the talk being taped so I can get it later if I missed it now?

We are so easily satisfied. Our demands are so small. We are willing to settle for a fast-food experience, preferably with a drive-through window so we can purchase the insights as quickly as we can hear them. We want to learn effortlessly, to be transformed without having to bite or swallow.

I know this world because I am a beneficiary of it. I am paid celebrity fees to show up and talk for an hour. And I am on the lower end of the food chain. Tom Peters and Colin Powell were paid $60,000 for a one-hour talk in 1999.

We should stop mistaking listening for learning. Learning demands something of us. We cannot receive value for something we have not invested in. Sitting quietly is not an investment. Sitting passively in a large, dark room simply reinforces our willingness to be a spectator to life—to let life happen to us.

I once attended a Willie Nelson concert and a friend I was with said she thought it took him the first half of the show to get us warmed up. She enjoyed the second half better. I said, "Why do we enter the hall expecting Willie to warm us up? If we came for a good time, maybe it was our job to warm Willie up?" She gave me a strange look.

Later I heard a music group begin their set by saying, "We are the Southern County Rounders . . . and you are the audience." That

made sense to me. They were telling us that we, the audience, had a role to play and a job to do that evening. For them to be the singers, we had to be the audience. Something was required of us.

CONFRONTING THE WISH TO BE PASSIVE

If we care about learning, then we need to confront the passivity inherent in the speaker-listener connection. Learning comes from moments of engagement, from finding our voice, from putting energy into the moment. The solution is not to eliminate the speaker/entertainer. It is to activate the listener.

Here are two simple ways to engage people, even when they come with the expectation to sit and listen.

Start Early and Ask Different Questions

Here are some questions to ask early in the presentation. Ask each person to answer:

1. How valuable an experience do you plan to have over the next hour or few hours? Rate it from lousy to great.
2. How engaged and active do you plan to be?
3. How much risk are you willing to take?
4. How much do you care about the quality of the experience of those around you?

Have people answer these questions and then share their answers with two people sitting near them.

By people simply answering the questions and then having to say the answers out loud, the culture in the room is changed. The process communicates to everyone that something more than just "being there" is required of the audience. Even if a person does not want to engage and wants to be quiet and listen, at least it becomes the person's choice and not a constraint of the setting.

Each time I ask these questions, something always shifts. There is more life in the room. People ask more questions, some people get

irritated, some would rather keep talking to their neighbor then return to the speaker. All are signs of life.

Change the Form

A second way to confront the wish to be passive is to change the evaluation form for the event. Instead of focusing exclusively on the speaker, add questions about the way each person chose to get involved. Include on the evaluation form questions such as:

1. How participative did you choose to be in the session you just attended?
2. How many questions did you have and how many of them did you ask?
3. If you were not getting what you wanted from the session, to what extent were you able to influence its direction?
4. How much did you learn from other participants?

Asking questions like these makes a statement. The statement is that learning comes from engagement and activism. It does not come from celebrity speakers or sophisticated platform skills. Plus, if we had more faith in the learning capacity of the audience, we could reduce the cost of the speakers and get them back to earning an honest living.

7

No Masks No Bargains

In her poem that appears at the front of this fieldbook, Meg Wheatley writes the lines:

> Naked in dirt
> No masks
> No bargains

To be clothed, clean, masked, and making deals is so tempting that when we allow ourselves to be naked, transparent, and without an angle, it is almost a state of grace. This grace comes with time and age, but also

375

with a willingness to understand ourselves as eagerly as we wish to understand our clients. The challenge in knowing our "Self" is to face the shadow side with an open curiosity. Because there is no shadow at noontime, we must wait until the coming of night before we get a glimpse into what is normally hidden. It is at the end of the day, when we are away from others and have time to reflect on our experience, that we begin our real wondering. This is where our failures, our fears, our dreams in the night can become our ally.

This section is about our becoming more transparent, at least to ourselves. This takes us briefly into dreams, stories of some failures, and finally to a short road map of traps that I have fallen into, over and over. The purpose of all of these reflections is to again remind ourselves that we are not in this alone, especially when things don't work so well, and that our work is always to go deeper into understanding our expertise and to be willing to swim beneath the surface.

WRONG CITY, WRONG GROUP

Our dreams are the way our unconscious and the collective unconscious speak to us. We think that our dreams belong exclusively to us, but when we begin to share them, we realize that our culture and all who came before us speak through our dreams. Our dreams bring into our minds the anxiety and fears that we do not create room for in the light of day.

Thinking that maybe by sharing our dreams we would achieve a deeper understanding of what it means to be in the consulting role, I asked the contributors to this book to share their recurring dreams. Here is a sample, all from external consultants.

Dreamer 1

One woman who wanted to be identified only as "distinguished and quite glamorous" has this recurring dream:

I show up at a business meeting in a conference room. There are twelve to sixteen people seated around a large table. The chair at the head of the table is larger than the others, which is good, because I show up naked above the waist. I stand behind the chair and conduct business as usual. As I muddle my way through, I try to appear calm. The setting of my dreams is always business.

Some Thoughts

These are strong images. Twelve to sixteen people is a nice number of disciples, like the small group that will change the world, according to Margaret Mead. The table carries the image of a meal to be eaten, and the consultant is at the head of the table, holding the largest chair, feeling the weight of making it all worthwhile, as if they came for her sake alone. Or that success rests solely in her hands. Naked from the waist up expresses vulnerability or the innocence of a child who is allowed to appear without a top. And we go on with the business as if everything is fine.

Dreamer 2

I am working with a client and one critical piece of information is missing. I cannot find out what it is. Sometimes it's one piece of a work process. In my dream I miss that one step every time—except that I cannot remember what it is. Just as I am about to remember, I wake up. Sometimes the missing information is how I am doing in the client's eyes. They all know the feedback, but they won't tell me. It usually is information that everyone has but me.

Some Thoughts

We are always ultimately dependent on our client to find out what is real. They know the reality of the situation much more than we do; they have the final control over their learning and future. There is so much we will never know about the places where we work, and they often do not want us to know, because if we did, the client would lose some protection. The missing information is an indication of our powerlessness. What we don't know *does* hurt us. And that is just the way it is, and maybe should be, for it is their lives in the balance, not ours.

Dreamer 3

My recurring dreams are the good old standards: Naked in public, unprepared for school, driving off the end of a bridge.

Some Thoughts

I love the statement "the good old standards . . . driving off the end of a bridge." As though it isn't even noteworthy. The nakedness is more indication of our openness and vulnerability, the images about school always touch the part of us that is convinced that we are never enough, no matter how we perform. And no amount of recognition will erase this.

Dreamer 4

I am working with a group. They start to lose interest. They start talking to each other, moving around, leaving the room. I try to get them interested, move toward them, but to no avail. I've lost them! I finally stop trying when I have lost critical mass. At the point of dissolution, there are generally forty to sixty in the room. In another recurring dream, I am on my way to work. It is getting later and later. I am lost. Then it is past time.

Some Thoughts

We carry the wish to be relevant and central. In this dream we are reminded that we often are not relevant enough to join the conversation, and they go on without us. As they go on without us, we are no longer visible, let alone central. And finally, we are not only too little, but we are too late. This dream may also be an opening to the idea that we can give up our concern about being so relevant and central, and the world will get along just fine.

Dreamer 5

> I am late for a talk in a strange room. I cannot find the room, I get there six minutes late, and they have already begun. Someone else is talking, and no one cares that I have arrived. Other dreams place me on airplanes going to the wrong city and in elevators not stopping on the right floor. Even when I know the number of the floor, I cannot get to it.

Some Thoughts

This dream is mine: Searching for what seems unattainable. Looking out there for the meaning that resides only inside. Constantly looking in the wrong places, seeking a floor where the elevator does not stop. This dream is a call to rediscover my humility and to remember the fact that others can have meaningful conversations without me.

DREAM ALONG WITH ME

These themes balance out the competent, orderly, almost cocky image the world has of consultants. They speak to the nature of the burden that we carry as educators and facilitators. It is no small thing to stake your work on the learning and development of other people. The dreams touch the essence of the overarching theme of consulting, which is to try to have influence when you have no control. When people are thinking of becoming independent consultants, they should not be blinded by the seeming freedom of the role; they should be aware of the emotional costs that choice entails, and these are expressed in a brief summary of what I think our dreams are saying:

- We are outsiders, and somewhat lost. We become like gypsies, pitching our tent at the edge of the city. Although the community is fascinated with us at first and comes to us for readings and some entertainment, after awhile they begin to ask us when we will be moving on. Any wish we have to find the place where we belong goes unfulfilled. We do not belong, despite all our talk of community. And so we are destined to wander from place to place, reassuring ourselves that it is interesting, varied, and challenging.

- We are very vulnerable, standing naked before the world, despite the fact that we seem to be running the meeting. We have moments of great visibility, often in front of groups, despite the fact that many of us are introverts. The work requires a capacity to connect with people very quickly and then leave them before we are ready. There is some pain, as well as relief, in these whistle-stop relationships.

- We fear we are irrelevant, and that everyone knows it but us. The question of whether our work made a difference is permanently hard to answer. Even in the face of reassurance from our clients, even when they continue to pay to bring us back, the nagging question remains about our impact. It is a question no amount of measurement can fully answer.

These and other costs are of course balanced by the joys of the work—the endless variety, the chance to see a larger world, the challenge of the ideas and nursing them into reality. The costs associated with consulting, though, are still there and need our attention for the sake of our own wholeness. Living with less of the familiarity of place and language that most people take for granted is a constant source

The Flawless Consulting Fieldbook and Companion

of anxiety. The pressure to be good and useful every time is constant. The space to fail is small because we are so disposable.

The point is the need for more open dialogue among consultants about the difficult emotional life inherent in the role. I would someday like to attend a conference for consultants at which we only talk about what did *not* work. The more aware we are of our own shadow side, our own struggles, the less likely we are to project them onto our clients. This allows us to see our clients for who they are, and are not, rather than who we want or fear them to be.

Chapter 38

My Worst Consulting Nightmare

Amy J. Katz

Our worst nightmares (especially the ones that occur during the day) are opportunities for learning and remind us of our humanity and vulnerability. This story shows the risks we run when we collude with our clients and delude ourselves that we are managing the business of each phase of our consulting work. It also shows that our failures are important teachers, if we have Amy's kind of courage to see them clearly.

My worst consulting nightmare had to do with a situation involving sexual harassment. My client was the head of a twenty-person department who asked me to investigate complaints that one of his high-level employees was making inappropriate sexual overtures to some of the women in lower level positions. The central personnel department of his organization had advised him that it was his job to document behavior of this kind and that, without documentation, it would be difficult to build a case. While describing the situation, my client gave me the impression that he wanted the problem solved quickly, because there could be significant legal ramifications.

I did not feel comfortable with this client. In our initial meeting he seemed to diminish the importance of the alleged violations. He was also flirtatious with me, and I felt immediately thrown off guard, trying to be social and professional at the same time. I had considerable difficulty keeping the discussion on track, and the conversation went on for far too long. Also, he made several negative references to his secretary throughout the meeting. She had initially told him of the concerns of the women in the department. He indicated his doubts about her view of the situation, and he also made disparaging remarks about her work in general. He seemed to elevate my status while demeaning hers, which made me feel very uncomfortable.

Feeling self-conscious and uncertain, I quickly agreed to his suggestion that I interview the women in his department and the man under investigation and then report back to him.

The interviews with the women were strained, to say the least. The interview with the man was useless. I felt very foolish after asking questions along the lines of "When did you stop beating your wife?" while he sat back, looking amused.

I dutifully reported back to my client that the women did indeed have concerns about the man's behavior. I suggested that he go back to the personnel department and tell them. Then, because a number of the women had voiced general concerns about the way the department operated, I suggested we all meet as a group to talk about how to improve communications in the department. The session was a disaster. People were silent in response to questions about how to improve things, and I felt as if the temperature in the room had dropped thirty degrees.

I never met with the group again, but I learned that a few days after the meeting a young female assistant to the man suspected of harassment contacted my client's boss and gave him explicit, detailed examples of how the man had treated her. Her accusations were vivid and damning, and the man was immediately fired.

THE LESSONS

This was by far my worst and most embarrassing consultation. I couldn't deal with my client and I couldn't deal directly with his problem. I allowed him to suggest the approach, and I lost my professionalism in the process. Perhaps at some level, just knowing I was involved helped the assistant turn the man in, but that remains small comfort to my sense of shame about how I handled things.

The Flawless Consulting Fieldbook and Companion

I wish I could have thought about the situation in clear and simple terms. My client had a problem—he had heard complaints from his secretary about the way a high-level member of his staff treated women in the department. They had complained to her. He knew from his contacts with the personnel department that it was his job to document the problem and to talk to the staff person. So he hired me to investigate. I don't typically think about a consultation in this kind of step-by-step fashion, but in this situation it might have helped me to avoid becoming derailed. I wish I had seen that my problems with the consultation had to do with other things as well, with challenges in the consulting relationship that are hardly unique to this client: The entry process, the boundaries of the contract, and the depth of the intervention. So in retrospect, what have I learned?

First of all, my client clearly had difficulties with women—a significant issue, given the request for consultation. Unfortunately, I was so accustomed to trying to be "helpful" to my clients and to have them like me that I focused on building a relationship with him and basically ignored his behavior. Had I paid more attention to his style as a part of my assessment, I might have concluded that he wasn't taking the complaints against his staff person seriously, and that he probably wasn't taking me seriously either.

Second, my client was obviously uncomfortable with having to handle the situation. I should have known and respected that, whether or not his own behavior was questionable. He had gone to the personnel office, and that department had given him a directive that he could not easily fulfill. He was not sure how to raise the issue with his staff person, although apparently he had tried. My hunch now is that their conversation was superficial, that "just between us guys" they mocked the complaints, and that my client made it easy for his employee to deny any wrongdoing. But I could and should have asked him how it went and probed for the details of the conversation. The details could have provided both of us with a way to think about next steps.

Third, I made a big mistake in conducting the interviews. It should have been clear to me that my client needed some help in directly confronting the problem. Instead of acting like a consultant, I became his subordinate, taking on the role of a hired hand to do detective work.

I should also have realized that the interviews were bound to fail. With some hesitancy, the women spoke to me, trusted me, and confirmed my own feeling that my client was a difficult boss, demanding and harsh with women. I heard as much about my client as I did about his staff member when I conducted those interviews. And in the process I started to view my role as an organization development consultant, looking at the whole system, a role my client had not asked me to play. I also got scared. I wasn't sure how to handle the things I was hearing about the staff person. It seemed to me that there were certainly grounds for the harassment charges, but what was I supposed to do with them? So, not having been too careful about what I asked for, I avoided the specific issue and focused on the more general problem of "improving communications in the whole department."

Fourth, I learned how tough it is when you don't like your client. It is very hard to help someone you don't like, although if the person is willing to learn, it can be enormously satisfying. That was not the case here, but I'm not sure I gave him the chance to really be a client.

NEXT TIME

So what would I have handled differently? I would have paid acute attention to how I was feeling during the interview. This would have given me an enormous amount of data about how my client was viewing the problem. I'm learning that clients often ask for help assuming that other people are the problem, and I tend to collude with that. I need to probe for other views. Rather than interviewing other people, I can take a "devil's advocate" approach, and raise questions that challenge his (or her) opinion, observing where that leads. My own reactions to what the client is saying can in all likelihood provide clues to other viewpoints within the system.

I would have been supportive of my client and of his problem, but I would not have agreed to solve it for him. I would have indicated that confronting an employee about such a problem would be difficult for anyone, but I would have asked him to talk about what was specifically difficult for him. I might have told him that it seemed to me that he doubted his secretary's viewpoints, but that would have been risky.

I would have confined my role to the problem at hand, and helped him develop an approach that he could feel comfortable with. I would not have suggested the interviews, and certainly not the large-group meeting. In time, I may have reached the point at which my client could look at his own behavior and understand how it affected his department. But given the intensity of the issue, he needed a coach who could help him move quickly, not a therapist.

Finally, I could have asked for help! When client situations feel scary, or when I start to feel inadequate, it's a good sign that I should bring someone else in to work with me or ask a colleague to serve as a shadow consultant. There are so many dynamics to manage in OD, and another person's perspective and support, even in relatively manageable situations, can be invaluable. Undoubtedly I have forgotten, repressed, or distorted some of the features of this particular consultation, but I don't think that takes away from the learning. I continue to believe, as many others do, that the best learning comes from the most difficult situations. For me, this one certainly qualifies.

For More Depth

Further Reading

Chernow, Ron. *The Warburgs: The Twentieth-Century Odyssey of a Remarkable Jewish Family.* New York: Vintage, 1994.

Hegi, Ursula. *Stones from the River.* New York: Simon & Schuster, 1997.

Websites and Schools

The Center for Applied Research, Inc. www.cfar.com.

The Family Firm Institute. www.ffi.org.

The International Society for the Psychoanalytic Study of Organizations. www.ISPSO.org.

The publications available through these websites are excellent.

About the Contributor

Amy J. Katz consults with organizations in the private, public, and not-for-profit sectors within the Greater Cincinnati area.

Chapter 39

Three Nightmares
A Conversation with Henry Johnson

At one time or another, all of us have felt as though we are living a bad dream in our consulting work. In this article Henry shares three daytime nightmares and in so doing offers us a good example of the healing power of telling our stories publicly.

Although I do not have any nightmares about being a consultant, I have had more than one consulting experience that I consider a nightmare. The first occurred while I was involved in a whole-scale change event in which a national volunteer organization was reviewing a draft of its strategic plan with the goal of reaching a consensus. The meeting appeared to be going smoothly until I noticed a trickle, then a flood, of people walking out of the room.

At the end of day, we interviewed some of the people who left the meeting. When we asked what the problem was, they were surely eager to tell us. We discovered that they felt their voices were never heard and that they therefore had not been represented when the draft was developed.

That evening my colleagues and I invited everyone who was not previously included in the draft of the strategic plan to join together to redesign the draft so their voices could be heard the next day. During this meeting we noticed that they initially felt a need to vent all of their concerns. Only after airing their frustration did they focus their concerns on the strategic plan.

The next day we presented the revised draft of the strategic plan. It passed.

This nightmare could easily have been averted if my colleagues and I had known that the client organization had included only selected regions of its national offices in the development of the strategic plan. Unfortunately, we were substituting for another consultant who, as it turned out, was also unaware of this shortcoming. We learned an important lesson: Don't assume that clients intuitively know the importance of including a true microcosm of the system when soliciting representatives to draw up plans that require organization-wide consensus.

My second consulting nightmare occurred because I agreed, against my better judgment, to conduct a half-day meeting for a client who was undergoing organizational change. I should have guessed that this was just a token meeting and that the client really did not want to change. I either didn't think about or didn't realize the negative impact that a half-day meeting could have, given the circumstances.

I was under the impression that the client wanted to help the group understand fiscal accountability. My colleagues and I did our piece in the morning, and we felt it went well, as did the participants. We stayed for the afternoon program and noticed that it was not related to our presentation. Even worse, people were bored out of their minds and walked out. They were insulted by the other consultants' simulation, which did not take into consideration the wide range of financial acumen of people in room. It was a debacle!

The damage was done. There was no way to recover what people had gained from our morning session. Furthermore, my consulting firm's reputation had been tarnished because some of the people in the meeting assumed that our group was responsible for bringing in the boring group. We never worked with this client again.

Looking back, I can clearly see my culpability in this fiasco. First, I should have known that we could not achieve our purpose in one day, never mind one half. Second, I did not ask in advance for the client's full agenda. Now I realize that when you share the stage with another group, you have to know how your part fits into the whole puzzle and how the process will flow, in order to achieve your desired outcomes.

My third consulting nightmare occurred when I did not frame an activity in the right way and it fell apart. It was my first whole-scale change event. I got the sequence of an activity backward in front of a group of four hundred. It was my first facilitation of such a large group and I was nervous. I asked the group to do the activity before I explained its purpose, so of course they did not have a rationale for engaging and became confused. My colleague, Kathie Dannemiller, rescued me by coming to the podium and saying, "Hold it!" Then she clarified the purpose and rationale of the activity for the group. With time and experience I'm now comfortable enough to say to the groups with which I consult, "Whoa, I missed something!" and to reframe the activity and then proceed.

Now I'm very careful about where I am in training and how I'm doing it. Sometimes I'll write out my framing process on 3 x 5 cards. I've learned to listen more carefully to the activity that comes before mine and to be better at making a smooth segue between them, because it's important to have meeting activities move in a seamless fashion. Framing is important and should be forward-looking, and it should be so clear that people understand the connection between the previous activity and the one you are about to get them engaged in.

For More Depth

Further Reading

The *Bible*

Block, Peter. *Flawless Consulting: A Guide to Getting Your Expertise Used* (2nd ed.). San Francisco: Jossey-Bass/Pfeiffer, 1999.

Bunker, Barbara, & Billie Alban. *Large Group Interventions: Engaging the Whole System for Rapid Change*. San Francisco: Jossey-Bass, 1997.

Jacobs, Roger W. *Real Time Strategic Change: How to Involve an Entire Organization in Fast and Far-Reaching Change.* San Francisco: Berrett-Koehler, 1994.

Waldinger, Thomas P. *The Wisdom of Life Through My Patients.* Dearborn, MI: Thomas P. Waldinger, 2000.

Wheatley, Margaret J., & Myron Kellner-Rogers. *A Simpler Way.* San Francisco: Berrett-Koehler, 1996.

Workshops, Schools, and Websites

Dannemiller Tyson courses. www.dannemillertyson.com.

Association for Quality and Participation, School for Managing and Leading Change. www.aqp.org.

The Berkana Institute. www.berkana.org.

The Fielding Institute. www.thefieldinginstitute.org.

University of Michigan. umich.edu.

About the Contributor

Henry Johnson is a former university executive and now a consultant with Dannemiller Tyson Associates, Inc., in Ann Arbor, Michigan.

Chapter 40

Twelve Questions to the Most Frequently Asked Answers

Peter Block

ere is my version of the "one-minute consultant." It lists twelve presenting problems that are generic to the work. They all deal with the human system, which is a challenge no matter how technical the assignment. They are best thought of as "presenting problems" because if we take the client statement at face value, we will become as frustrated as the client is. We will end up frozen in a room with no exit. Like Stephen Wright, the comic who quipped that he lived at the end of a one-way, dead-end street.

Even though it is a mistake to accept any problem as defined, we still have to remember that clients are giving their best understanding of what they are up against. The problem is, though, with the way the problem is defined or the question is framed. This is, in fact, where they are stuck and what we can help them with. Here are some recurring and classic problem statements and some ideas on reframing the question.

Helpless and Distressed Team with Tyrannical Boss

The number one complaint, even in the new economy, is "The Boss." The problem is presented as a boss behavior problem. The boss is too controlling, plays favorites, doesn't communicate enough, controls too much—you name it.

If You Acted on This Definition.   You would coach the boss, do 360-degree feedback, and pray that the boss changes.

To Reframe It. Remember the inmates run the prison. The deeper problem is that the members of the team do not support each other. If members of a team support each other in public, they can handle any boss. If one member confronts the boss in a meeting, the others have to affirm their support verbally—no staying silent and giving support after the battle is over.

The team has to overcome its middle-class caution and meet independently, decide what it needs to get the work done, and then bring it up to the boss when all are around. Knowledge workers hate to do this; it feels like mutiny. So help them get over it. Bosses are created by those who work for them. If the boss isn't bossing well, then the team is teaming well.

A Summit Conference of Organizations or Groups That Want to Improve Cooperation

A meeting is planned to get interdependent organizations to build trust and better cooperate and communicate with each other. They could be units within an organization or agencies dedicated to the same end, such as education, community development, or at-risk children.

If You Acted on This Definition. You would have them share their programs and purpose with one another. Have them agree on common goals, common projects, develop a strategy of cooperation, work out a schedule and milestones, and agree on the next meeting.

To Reframe It. Communication and defining common goals are not the problem. If they were the problem, they would have been solved long before now. The problem between groups is territory, territory, territory. They have defined their boundaries tightly around their own organization and think their mission is to do a good job within those boundaries.

For change to happen, each will have to yield territory and control. They have to be confronted with this question: "What are you willing to give up for the sake of the larger purpose?" They have to be

The Flawless Consulting Fieldbook and Companion

willing to give up projects, budget, and a piece of their identity if anything new is going to happen for their citizens or customers. Trust is built from telling the truth and from acts of surrender.

Don't buy the aspirin that better communication will be a good start. It will be the start that leads to a lot of motion and no movement. We have to face the usually unspoken belief that if the *other* organization would change, cooperation would improve. If they do not decide *they* are going to change and accept that they are going to lose something in the process, then we become a pawn in their negotiation strategy

We need to take a firm stand on this early, when we have the most leverage.

Civil Service Obsessed with Elected Officials

A government agency wants to reinvent or reform itself. It thinks the way to do this is to build more support and be more effective dealing with elected officials and also to reduce cycle time and costs.

If You Acted on This Definition.   You interview elected officials or their staff and ask them how they could be better served. You involve employees in designing better processes.

To Reframe It.   The agency has got the wrong customer. Government agencies are not in business to better serve elected officials. They too often demonize them, making them more powerful than they need be.

Shift the attention to citizens and community. Talk about the question of whom the agency is there to serve. Help them withdraw emotional energy from the legislature or city council and aim it at the community.

Postpone the redesign of new processes until they are clear on purpose. The voice of the community has to outweigh the voice of the elected officials before any new process will make a real difference. Too many public servants have drifted from the dream that brought them into the work in the first place. This passion has to be rekindled before operational questions can be addressed.

The discussion of purpose has to begin with personal purpose, which can then be connected to agency purpose.

Helpless and Political Manager

Manager wants a better strategy to deal with difficult employees, peers, or bosses.

If You Acted on This Definition.   You coach the manager on strategy. Do a stakeholder analysis and figure out how to approach key people, define what their needs are, what style is most effective, how to time the enterprise. You become involved in managing the client's visibility and stature.

To Reframe It.   Helpless managers have surrendered their own freedom and have lost their own sense of purpose. They have forgotten that they have choices that are independent of the response of others. We are asking them to reclaim what they have given away. The working of this theme is key; make the point with your client in words to this effect: "You are reclaiming your own freedom. This is something you can do without permission. You are taking back what you have given away, not what was taken from you."

If we fail to understand that we have given away what we might have held onto, we stay forever chained to the whims and shifts in those around us. Becoming more political and tactically clever won't help, because people always know what you are up to and will quite effortlessly defend against it.

The Deadwood Dilemma

Early in every discussion of accountability and institutional reform, someone will ask what to do with the "deadwood." How do we handle low performers under this new world order? Same thing when working with teams: Someone will identify one team member who is not pulling his own weight.

If You Acted on This Definition.   You work on performance management questions, making accountability a central element of your work. You might develop competency models so that evaluation of the deadwood will be more objective and improvement targets for these people will be more self-evident. You might even talk about exit packages to aid in the housecleaning.

To Reframe It.   Deadwood is not the problem. The focus on low performers takes the attention off of us. If we were performing well and together, we could bring along some free-riders without even noticing their weight. And who is to say that the ones worried about the dead weight are not in that category themselves?

We hear all the time that we need to get certain people "on board." Well, why do we think that we are the ones on board? Often it is a lone voice that knows where the boat should be headed, while we are the ones free floating in a cold, wet sea. The problem person is likely to be the victim of our projection. We project onto the most vulnerable member of the group the problems we do not want to face in ourselves. In family therapy the child that gets all of the negative attention is called the "identified patient." And that "patient" carries the symptoms of what is really a family problem.

Wanting Proof Positive

They want measurable, hard data that the change will improve the operations.

If You Acted on This Definition.   You include an evaluation research component in the project and bring in independent evaluators to do a pre- and post-intervention study.

To Reframe It.   You can measure the impact of a project to the extent that the organization can measure itself, which is a very elusive proposition in a human system. It is a management task to know how we are doing. If you bring in a third party to evaluate, the evaluation has its own impact, and this may bring more interference than enlightenment. Plus, I have almost never seen anyone's mind changed as a result of social science research.

The wish to measure tightly is an expression of our doubts. It is the recognition that every project has its own risks. Why not deal with the doubts and risks directly by naming them carefully right from the beginning? We cannot engineer human development, nor can we know it with the precision we might wish for. We can generate some data about the change, but most of it will be putting numbers on people's feelings—that's what surveys do. Why not just convene people every once in awhile and ask them how it is going? Ultimately, we will know how we are doing by assessing the quality of our experience. If experience is such a good teacher, maybe it also knows how to measure.

Taking It to Scale

When we have done a pilot project that has been successful, someone wants to do the same thing on a large scale. It worked in one place, so let's make it work in every place. And let's do it in a hurry.

If You Acted on This Definition.
We will standardize the elements of the pilot and then obtain support from the top. Then we'll turn it into a program, hold a bunch of meetings, conduct training programs, set system-wide standards, and all the rest that has become stock in trade in change management.

To Reframe It.
Pilot projects work largely because those involved in one site engaged in creating it. It is the act of engagement and creation that leads to high performance. When we take something to scale and do it fast, the imaginative life is drained out of it. What once was choice becomes coercion. Nothing can be taken to scale. The success record of proliferation is poor.

The way to think about it is that, like politics, all change is local. What you *can* proliferate is the possibility of local invention following

The Flawless Consulting Fieldbook and Companion

some rough guidelines and statement of purpose. The wish to do something quickly is really a defense against local choice. It is the argument that we do not have time to engage a lot of people.

Don't buy speed as an argument. Speed is a defense against depth and meaning. Nothing important happens quickly. Choose quality of experience over speed. The world changes from depth of commitment and capacity to learn.

Fix Those People

How do we get those people to change their behavior? How do we get them to adopt the new mission, the new business or institutional reality? How do we give them the skills they need for the new world?

If You Acted on This Definition.   You start communicating and training in a big way, spend time defining the desirable behaviors, then design or purchase programs to meet these competencies. You train managers to conduct the programs and get the top to endorse them.

To Reframe It.   "Those people" are not the problem, and wide-scale training will cost a lot and not really help. Plus, focusing on people's deficiencies only reinforces them. Change is more likely to happen when we capitalize and bring to bear people's capacities and gifts and strengths.

Despite the claims of consultants and their intimate organizational champions, large-scale training has had a poor record of changing organizations. As the economic beneficiaries of the training movement, consultants are reluctant to be accountable for the fact that most large change efforts have led to little change. We hold on to the belief that if we had had more top management support things would have been different.

Resist the "fix" mentality. Local groups deciding what change and learning they need—with an emphasis on their underutilized capacities—is a faster and cheaper path to learning. We are in the community-organizing business: Bringing local groups together, engaging them in questions of purpose, allowing for local variation whenever possible. Make the bet that this engagement effort will lead to a level of accountability that will make up for any fixing benefits that might accrue from the traditional strategy.

Fighting Peers

Tom and Jerry don't work well together. Help them resolve their conflict.

If You Acted on This Definition.   You meet with Tom and Jerry separately to hear their viewpoints, then bring them into the same room and use some mediation process to help them come together.

To Reframe It.   Conflict resolution is very valuable; that is not the question. The one caution is to be careful to test whether Tom and Jerry want to work it out. Too often the boss wants resolution, but the combatants do not. The simple question is to ask each one whether he wants to *win* or *work it out*. If one or both are so entrenched that they just want the other to die or disappear, then don't move ahead. Resolution strategies depend on a certain level of good will. If it does not exist, then surgery may be required.

I have made the mistake of believing that all conflicts are resolvable. They are not, and we lose our credibility, especially in our own eyes, by taking on a task that never had a chance.

Sometimes confronting the players with the belief that you cannot help them raises the stakes and wakes them to the cost of their conflict.

One other thought: What seems to be a problem between two is often a problem among three. The person who asks us to get involved is often a player too. Be open to the possibility of a dysfunctional triangle and try to understand the role of the sponsor of the mediation, who might be unknowingly keeping Tom and Jerry at odds. If this is the case, Tom and Jerry will feel it. Ask them what role your sponsor plays in their relationship and what impact that has.

Where Are These Ideas Working?

We are all caught in the paradox of wanting to innovate and at the same time wanting the reassurance that what we are contemplating has been tried before. So the question of where else this is working is inevitable.

If You Acted on This Definition.   You will research examples of where what you propose is working. You will look for organizations in the same business as the client. You might arrange site visits and references.

To Reframe It.   Even if it is working somewhere else, there is no assurance that it will work here. Every new idea has to be customized locally. We risk making a false promise if we support the idea that a change can be imported with little risk into our client's workplace.

We can help the client understand that behind their question of where it is working are doubt and anxiety. There is a wish for a guarantee that this will be successful. As consultants, working in partnership, we cannot make this guarantee, because so much depends on the energy and investment of the client. This is the difference between selling and consulting. We are doing both, but lean toward the consulting. Selling means our goal is to make the sale; consulting means the goal is to help the client make a good decision.

Clients will make a better decision if they understand all that is required to make a change. The field of consulting carries the shame of promising too much so soon. The search for what is working elsewhere might be useful, but can't be a substitute for a willingness to try something new, with little more than our own faith as proof we are making a good decision.

Define What You Mean

We need a clear definition of what we are moving toward. How do you define the difference between change and transformation? How do you define leadership, empowerment, the new economy, or the role of a middle manager? What is the new role for human resources?

If We Acted on This Definition.

We would spend a lot of time trying to define what is new in terms that people will understand. We'd write it down. We'd produce manuals and short brochures to put in "lay terms" what is essentially a change in consciousness. The ultimate attempt at definition is the competency model. This is a comprehensive listing of the skills needed to be fully proficient at a job or role. I have never seen one that any human being could achieve.

To Reframe It.

The request for definitions is not a problem in clarity, but an expression of disagreement. It is fine to make one attempt at definition, but most of the time we have already done that, and the question persists. The request for *us* to define the terms is what I would focus on. If a definition is necessary, let those who ask the question struggle with the answer.

For years middle managers have wanted to know what their new role is. Well, if they can't figure it out, maybe there is no new role. We each have to translate language into our own setting and our own experience. Others can help a little, but they cannot do it for us. Dennis Bakke, head of AES, a very enlightened company that produces electrical power around the world, likes ambiguity in language. He says that if people are unclear about what something means it forces them into a conversation about it, and that conversation leads to learning. Hearing a definition from another leads to memorization, not learning. The only definition that endures is the one that I, myself, have created.

Also, the wish for a clear definition is another form of the wish for safety. I want to know where I am going before I go there. It is a longing for safety that does not exist. Defining terms is an academic diversion from the more fundamental questions involving risk, purpose, courage, and adventure. Real safety comes from the experience of discovery, acting in the face of our fears—not waiting to act until our fears have disappeared. It is not until I try something that I will realize that I will survive it.

Standards and Measurement

There is the belief that, for change to occur, we must set high standards and develop clear measures against that standard. These standards must be consistent across the culture and approved by the top.

If We Acted on This Definition. We set new standards. We create universal measures against those standards. We believe that unsatisfactory performance was caused because the standards were not high enough and the measures were sloppy. An example is the proliferation of high-stakes testing in public education.

To Reframe It. We need standards and measures. We all want to know what is required and how we are doing. The shift is about who sets the standards and measures and how they are used. Too often they are used as a control device, not as a mechanism for learning. It is the engineering mind that elevates standards and measures to the level of dogma and ideology. This is fine for engineering projects, but the idea that we can engineer human development is more mythology than fact.

Standard setting has become part of the class struggle, where one class of people is setting standards for another—legislators set them for teachers, management for workers, professional guilds for their members. They may start with sincere intent, but they soon become exclusionary. They become a way to limit access to membership and keep those who were first through the door in power.

The solution is to have people close to the teaching, the work, or the service struggle with proper standards for the local environment. Ask people to define the measures that will have meaning for them. Then have them talk about how they want to hold themselves accountable. This reduces the possibility that standards and measures will become punitive. Once measures become punitive, people will work to outsmart them; learning diminishes and energy that should be going toward achieving the work is replaced by becoming maze bright in beating the system.

Postscript

Jerzy Kosinski, a famous writer, was asked how he knew when a book was finished. He said the book was never finished, he just stopped writing. So it is with consulting and with our attempt to understand it. I am not sure we should even think of consulting as a profession, for that puts a boundary around it and commercializes it. Better to think of it more as a calling or an invitation to learning.

What is demanded of us is to make the work something that transcends fashion or the latest response to customer requirements. We can then keep the work highly personalized and recognize that there are a thousand ways of doing it, all of them bringing value. That is why I like the idea of a book like this, written in a variety of voices, structured as a circle of experiences. There is no clear beginning or end; you can come and go as you please.

This is the experience we want to give our clients. We become just one way for them to improve their lives and organizations. They are going to keep learning whether we are around or not—and sometimes more when we are not. Framing our consulting work as a practice rather than as a profession leaves it more open-ended. It may be an advantage when we tell someone that we are an internal or external consultant and they do not know what we do. It keeps us from getting lost in our own ideology and trapped in a model that works. It is our success that limits us, because we are tempted to keep reaping its rewards.

If we ask our clients to let go of their past and try a different future, then we will do the same, for we are forced to take the same journey that we advocate. The work is also much broader than improving organizational functioning, or developing people's skills. We are trying, especially these days in which balance remains a distant longing, to bring some sense of wholeness into the world. The real work is to shift our consciousness so as to embrace community, the environment, greater economic and social justice, and the well-being of the next generation—all into our every act, into our workplaces and our relationships, and into our own way of thinking about ourselves.

This has always been the purpose of the humanities and the arts, but we have become strangers to them. I think this will start to change and that we will rediscover the value of thinking and reflection, especially in the face of an electronic and website world. This love of speed and efficiency and automated living at some point will take us too close to the sun, but we will still survive, and it will all melt into its rightful proportion.

No modern technology can awaken our sense of purpose or care as powerfully as a person's story honestly told, whether told through literature, a picture, or music, or by one individual standing up in a large group and finally speaking the truth. It is we as consultants who have the opportunity to convene the group, pick the room, create the context, and give the assignment that eases these moments into being. This is the possibility that makes it all worthwhile.

Thanks to Contributors

More than most books, this one is the creation of a community of people. The more visible ones are those listed below. What they write about and what they list as their resumes are small abbreviations of the work they have engaged in over their lifetimes. I want to thank them for the generosity they offer to the world, and to this fieldbook.

I want to also thank Matt Holt, Jossey-Bass acquiring editor, whose determination forced me into putting this book together. Also a special thanks to Andrea Markowitz, a delightful soul, who worked with the other contributors and added her own energy and insight into some of the chapters. Leslie Stephen, whose editing always speaks for the reader, is so essential that I could not imagine doing this project without her. She has reassured me that she will outlive me, so I won't ever have to write a book without her.

My thanks also goes to Maggie Rogers, a friend and colleague, who sees that the commitments I recklessly make actually happen.

Finally, thanks to all the people who believe in these ideas, so much so that they are committed to live them out in their own lives. Any time any one of us has the courage to act with some authenticity and faith, all of our lives are changed.

Here are the contributors. Contact them . . . they love to talk.

Dick and Emily Axelrod

Dick and Emily Axelrod's Chicago-based Axelrod Group, Inc., specializes in creating customized, large-group change processes that engage people at all levels in the organization to address critical business issues. Their areas of specialization range from start-ups to organizational and process redesign, and from cultural shifts and transformations to mergers, alliances, and the introduction of new technology. They are equally proficient at working with traditional organizations and the new dot-coms.

Their work is founded on a set of principles that integrate the needs of the individual, the small group, the large group, and the client, giving them the flexibility to engage a critical mass of people to achieve a common purpose.

Dick and Emily can be reached at:
    The Axelrod Group
    723 Laurel Avenue
    Wilmette, IL 60091
    Phone: 847-251-7361
    Fax: 847-251-7370
    E-mail: *Dick@AxelrodGroup.com*
    E-mail: *Emily@AxelrodGroup.com*
    Website: *http://www.AxelrodGroup.com*

Rosemarie Barbeau

Rosemarie Barbeau is fundamentally a designer and facilitator of conversations at the interpersonal, small group, and organizational levels. Her work is centered around helping clients clarify direction and strategy, implement strategy, and build the relationships required to do all of this well. Rosemarie also focuses on supporting organizations in balancing the competing needs, values, and concerns of multiple stakeholders to create solutions that work the most powerfully for "the whole."

In addition to her independent consulting practice in northern California, Rosemarie serves as a senior associate with the Axelrod Group, an internationally recognized organization development firm that pioneered the use of large-group processes to create large-scale, sustainable organizational change.

Rosemarie can be reached at:
E-mail: *Rbarbeau1@aol.com*

Clifford F. Bolster, Ph.D.

More than twenty-five years of work experience from the shop floor to the top floor taught Cliff Bolster a great deal about teamwork, dialogue, courage, and learning. Cliff's work history covers all areas of human resources, including hands-on experience in organization development, training, and industrial relations. As a private consultant, he now designs and conducts training programs in personal and organizational empowerment, interpersonal skills, negotiations, analytical skills, leadership, learning, and coaching skills. Cliff also works with leadership teams to help them have more productive conversations and meetings about difficult and complex issues. He currently specializes in the application of sound learning principles and practices to improving leaders' and organizations' performance.

Cliff's consulting firm works with organizations of all sizes and in many industries, including: Procter & Gamble, Rhone Poulenc Rorer, McKinsey & Company, Texas Instruments, The GEON Company, and Reebok International.

Cliff can be reached at:
Bolster and Associates, Inc.
203 Hillside Road
Brunswick, ME 04011
Phone: 207-729-7464
E-mail: *cbolster@ime.net*

Neale W. Clapp

Neale Clapp has consulted to organizations for more than thirty-five years. Neale's career started in the fields of delinquency and the war on poverty, which contributed to the sociological bias with which he looks at organizational issues. His ideas about group norms and information systems have been applied in a variety of settings. In recent years he has focused his attention on intergroup conflict.

A former senior vice president at Block Petrella Weisbord, in 1980 Neale left the firm to return to private consulting. For many years he was the dean of Team Building and Process Consultation for the National Training Laboratory in Bethel, Maine. Neale continues to serve the Master of Science in Organizational Development program at Pepperdine University, where he was a member of the original faculty. Now retired, he still can be lured back to work by challenging projects.

Neale can be reached at:
    7 Captain's Walk
    Essex, CT 06426
    Phone: 860-767-2201

Lou Ann Daly

Lou Ann Daly incorporates the arts, learning, and a variety of disciplines in her organization, which is called "O! LAD," an acronym for Life Architecture and Design. O! LAD is designed to support individuals, families, teams, and whole organizations in clarifying what is really important to them and then using architectural principles to create a life tailored to their unique values, beliefs, desires, and needs.

O! LAD helps clients to develop an appreciation for the art of working with personal and organizational structures to achieve the results they want. Clients not only develop an architectural blueprint that they can follow, but they also develop their capability to design their lives and organizations continuously, based on purpose, vision, and changing needs.

Lou Ann can be reached at:
    O! LAD
    Phone: 617-549-1116
    Fax: 781-631-4147

Kathleen D. Dannemiller

Kathleen D. Dannemiller, founding partner of Dannemiller Tyson LLC and co-inventor of Whole-Scale™ Change, is a passionate advocate of empowerment, systems theory, and whole-system change. Her work as a consultant, coach, and mentor is recognized worldwide for Kathie's ability to move entire organizations forward with speed, depth, and spirit by giving all people a voice in shaping their futures.

Kathie's work in Whole-Scale™ Change with Sylvia James and Paul Tolchinsky is described in *Large Group Interventions: Engaging the Whole System for Rapid Change* by Barbara Bunker and Billie Alban (San Francisco: Jossey-Bass, 1997) and in *Fusion Leadership* by Richard Daft and Robert Lengel (San Francisco: Berrett-Koehler, 1998). *The Change Handbook: Group Methods for Shaping the Future*, edited by Peggy Holman and Tom Devane (San Francisco: Berrett-Koehler, 1999), describes her concepts about Whole-Scale™ change. The partners of Dannemiller Tyson Associates authored together *Whole-Scale™ Change: Unleashing the Magic in Organizations* and the *Whole-Scale Change Toolkit* (San Francisco: Berrett-Koehler, 2000).

Kathie can be reached at:
Kathie Dannemiller
3671 Eli
Ann Arbor, MI 48104
Office phone: 734-662-1330 ext. 112
Home phone: 734-971-0516
E-mail: *kathie@dannemillertyson.com*

W. Patrick Dolan

Pat Dolan specializes in labor/management cooperative approaches to large-system change. He attributes his success in this area to involving organized labor deeply in all of the work. Two of Pat's most gratifying large-scale change projects, in which he helped the union and management work together, were with a major aeronautical manufacturing company and with the teachers' unions of five Midwest states.

Pat heads his own consulting firm, W.P. Dolan & Associates, in Leawood, Kansas.

Pat can be reached at:
>   Phone: 913-385-5225
>   E-mail: *WpDolan@worldnet.att.net*

Phil Grosnick

Phil Grosnick is president of Designed Learning, Inc., a training and consulting company that specializes in organizational change. Phil focuses on developing staff consulting skills that are grounded in relationships and authentic interaction, based on the belief that organizations are only as capable as the individuals who work inside them. He helps clients increase individual and organizational capacity through building individual skills, business literacy, personal accountability, and exercising choice. These new skills encourage participation and discourage cynicism.

Phil's clients include executives and staff in some of the world's largest and most influential organizations. Yet his greatest rewards come from clients who find the courage to take on challenges they previously avoided. His favorite compliment came from a client who said that the workshop "helped me be 'me' better."

Phil can be reached at:
>   Home office: 904-519-5626 (usually gets the quickest response)
>   Designed Learning, Inc.: 908-889-0300
>   E-mail: *Info@DesignedLearning.com*

Joel P. Henning

Joel Henning's consulting and training firm, Henning-Showkeir and Associates, is committed to building the capacity of individuals and organizations to create real worth through the deliberate distribution of business literacy, choice, and accountability. Joel believes that success in the future depends on an organization's capability to create powerful new knowledge through the collaboration of very different people in rapidly changing circumstances.

Joel's approach to change focuses on the individual and the first-person perspective, changing the world one person at a time. His highly regarded book, *The Future of Staff Groups: Daring to Distribute Power and Capacity* (San Francisco: Berrett-Koehler, 1997), describes how to transform individuals in human resources, finance, information technology, and other staff positions into leaders of complex change.

Joel can be reached at:

Henning-Showkeir and Associates
Route 153
Rupert, VT 05768
Phone: 802-394-2420
Fax: 802-394-0034
Cell phone: 908-313-2297
E-mail: *joelphen@sover.net*

Sylvia L. James

Sylvia James has more than twenty-five years of experience as an internal and external consultant and is a pioneer of Whole-Scale™ processes. Her whole-systems approach uncovers the yearnings and focuses the wisdom, heart, and power of people in organizations and communities. Sylvia works with high-tech, service, manufacturing, government, and education systems around the world to "unleash the magic" in the power of participation throughout a whole-system change journey. She presents her work and ideas at conferences, and leads workshops on Whole-Scale™ processes.

A partner in Dannemiller Tyson LLC, Sylvia designs and facilitates interactive meetings that focus on strategy, mergers, culture change, and organizational design. She specializes in applying the Whole-Scale™ approach to organizational and work design, helping organizations make rapid, sustained change while creating a culture and structure that enables results and agility. Sylvia recently began applying her firm's "one-brain, one-heart" intervention to virtual environments.

Sylvia can be reached at:
 614 Crestwood Drive
 Seabrook, TX 77586
 Phone: 281-532-1999
 Phone: 734-662-1330 ext. 118
 E-mail: *sljijj@aol.com*
 Website: *www.dannemillertyson.com*

Jill E. Janov

Jill Janov is founder of Jill Janov Associates, a firm dedicated to the development of organizational capacity and the person at work. She consults internationally with a variety of *Fortune* 500 corporations, privately held companies, government agencies, educational institutions, and non-profit organizations. Jill's work engages the client system in discovery, design, and implementation of initiatives that align strategic intent, organizational structures, work processes, and competence.

Jill trains other OD consultants, serves as visiting faculty for the AQP School of Managing, the Gestalt Institute in Cleveland, the Gestalt Academy in Sweden, and the JFK/NTL University Taiwanese Program, and as a guest lecturer in the Stanford MBA Program. Jill is the author of *The Inventive Organization: Hope and Daring at Work*, published by Jossey-Bass in 1994.

Jill can be reached at:
 Jill Janov Associates
 343 Adams Street
 Denver, CO 80206
 Phone: 303-394-1444

Henry Johnson

Henry Johnson of Dannemiller Tyson Associates LLC helps people in industry, government, and education change for the better by creating the organization of their own choosing. Henry provides his clients with commonsense ways to tap people's wisdom, release their energy, combine their knowledge, and commit them to take action for change. He uses the Whole-Scale™ method of engaging large and small organizations that takes a microcosm (a cross-sectional cut) of the system to create critical mass and to tap the multiple views, opinions, and pooled wisdom in the organization. Together, each microcosm collects data, creates a vision of its preferred future (its yearnings for something better), and commits to action for change.

Before becoming an organizational consultant, Henry engaged in careers in psychiatric social work and higher education administration.

You can reach Henry at:
Dannemiller Tyson Associates
Suite 203
303 Detroit Street
Ann Arbor, MI 48104
Phone: 734-662-1330 ext. 204
Fax: 734-665-0295
E-mail: *h3516@aol.com*

Amy J. Katz, Ph.D.

Amy Katz consultants with a variety of organizations in the Greater Cincinnati area, including healthcare, educational institutions, social service agencies, and family businesses. Her work includes strategic planning, leadership development, and team building. Amy's work covers the entire range of organization development interventions. Her experience in multiple work roles and settings allows her to offer a wide variety of business perspectives.

Amy also assists with creating networks among clients who are from different settings, yet share similar concerns. She predicts that collaborative networking initiatives between multiple organizations with similar interests will make a significant contribution to solving shared problems.

Amy can be reached at:
Phone: 513-321-9636
E-mail: *ajkatz@fuse.net*

Peter Koestenbaum, Ph.D.

Peter Koestenbaum devotes his life's work to applying deep philosophical insights to the practice of business. He believes that understanding the human condition and reconciling it with the realities of business results in becoming a more effective businessperson. Themes of freedom, choice, paradox, ethics, and courage permeate Peter's teachings and many writings. Peter's philosophical approach pertains to both internal issues, such as team building and making difficult decisions, and external issues, such as strategic thinking and implementation.

Peter's Koestenbaum Institute develops products and customizes leadership processes based on Peter's own philosophy and model, the Leadership Diamond®. The Institute conducts consulting, training, seminars, and coaching, using its own resources and a worldwide network of trained and licensed partners. His philosophy is also accessible to everyone through his most recent books, *The Heart of Business: Ethics, Power, and Philosophy* (Dallas: Saybrook, 1987) and *Leadership: The Inner Side of Greatness: A Philosophy for Leaders* (San Francisco: Jossey-Bass, 1991).

Peter can be reached at:
E-mail: *pkipeter@ix.netcom.com*

Samuel P. Magill

Sam Magill works at the heart of organizations to promote organizational health and to create strong partnerships that take people into the future. His work ranges from steering entire organizations through large-system change to coaching individuals who want to move forward. For Sam, an organization is no less than a series of ongoing conversations and no more than a gathering of people with an array of talents. The challenge is to get people to work together to meet their commitments and create a future.

Sam's expertise in building and restoring relationships has helped many organizations resolve long-standing problems. He believes that *what* people talk about is the key. Sam also works to keep things as simple as possible, believing that humans are naturally good at this.

Sam can be reached at:
    11708 Clearview Drive
    Edmonds, WA 98026
    Phone: 425-787-0846
    E-mail: *magill@halcyon.com*

Andrea M. Markowitz, Ph.D.

With degrees in English literature, music, applied psychology, and industrial/organizational psychology, and careers that span from retail, advertising, and human resources to writing and editing, consulting, and teaching (pre-school through graduate school), Andrea Markowitz lives her beliefs that learning is everything and that everything is interconnected. She draws on all of her educational, workplace, and life experiences to develop creative and unique ways of communicating the rewards of learning and personal growth to others.

Andrea is an independent consultant and an assistant professor of industrial/organizational psychology at the University of Baltimore. Her consulting work includes customized surveys, training programs, and group interventions. Andrea believes the greatest contribution she can make is to help others become aware of their power to make change happen, within themselves, and within their organizations.

Andrea can be reached at:
OB&D, Inc.
2014 Mt. Royal Terrace
Baltimore, MD 21217
Phone: 410-225-9021
E-mail: *ammarkowitz@worldnet.att.net*

Marie T. McCormick, Ph.D., MBA

With a background that includes more than a decade of working in a major telecommunications firm in the operations, sales, marketing, and finance areas, Marie McCormick understands the importance of bottom-line results and believes the key to success is engagement of people in an organization. Her organization development and training firm, the Pearce-McCormick Consulting Group, is located in the Philadelphia area. Pearce-McCormick practices OD with a strong business slant, placing emphasis on measurement of both people engagement and business results.

Marie and her colleagues specialize in helping organizations develop and achieve strategy through the contribution of people, focusing on the role of the individual and work groups in creating change while finding meaning and connection to the whole in their work. Pearce-McCormick offers large-group interventions, culture change and culture building, executive and management coaching, and customer-focused initiatives.

Marie can be reached at:
Phone: 215-233-9113
E-mail: *pmccg@aol.com*

Elizabeth McGrath

As an affiliate of The Symmetry Group, Elizabeth McGrath provides consulting and training that bridges the gap between current reality and preferred futures. She is convinced that productive conversation is the most powerful tool to make the changes necessary for an organization to close that gap and fulfill its highest aspirations. Elizabeth sticks with the basics of productive conversation and convenes the right people to have the right conversations, using a level of intention and skill that moves people to take the right action.

Elizabeth considers one of her most significant accomplishments the work she has done with a marketing division of a high-profile, high-tech firm. The focus was on self-awareness and self-organizing to have productive conversations. The people took the fundamentals they learned and practiced, using videotape and feedback, until they were confident that they were communicating more effectively.

Elizabeth can be reached at:
>
> The Symmetry Group
> 507 Lake Court
> Wauconda, IL 60084
> Phone: 847-526-2251
> E-mail: *mczony@aol.com*

Kenneth F. Murphy

Ken Murphy is senior vice president of human resources for Philip Morris USA, the domestic tobacco unit of Philip Morris Companies, Inc. A significant part of his role is to help this unique organization through an unprecedented period of tumult and transition by helping to clarify its mission and values. Ken, who views the company as his client, is also working on changing how HR contributes to the company, its people, and communities.

Ken credits the Staff Consulting Skills workshop by Designed Learning, Inc., for changing the way he looks at the work and how he fits in. It helped him: (1) See why something worked or did not, (2) gain the courage required in a staff role, and (3) feel he could be himself in a corporate world and still do okay. That was more than fourteen years ago. He's still working on it.

Ken can be reached at:
E-mail: *kfmpcm2@aol.com*

John O'Connell

John O'Connell is director of Interplay Network, a San Francisco-based organization development firm specializing in process facilitation, leadership and team development, visioning, strategic planning, and conflict resolution. John is known for his work in action and experiential learning. He designs learning activities that draw on his knowledge of "planned change," which he studied with Ronald Lippitt, on the martial art "Aikido," and on his expertise in game design for experiential learning.

John's work ranges from "partnering" with other consultants to direct consulting with groups as diverse as union members and top-management teams. He also designs and leads large-scale meetings. John served as senior vice president of organization development for UCSF Stanford Health Care and is currently a faculty partner with the Center for Executive Development in Cambridge, Massachusetts, a partner with the Paragon Consulting Group in Vail, Colorado, and a faculty member of the Boston University Leadership Institute.

John can be reached at:
Interplay Network
Phone: 415-386-3752

Charlotte Roberts

Charlotte Roberts is a speaker, workshop leader, program designer, writer, and consultant who works with executive teams to increase their productivity and their ability and willingness to lead profound change. She believes organizational learning is a core competency and the heart of sustainability and competitiveness.

Charlotte promotes cultures of organizational learning by helping leaders of financial services, healthcare, utilities, and public education institutions have the conversations that they do not yet feel capable of having and by strengthening relationships through encouraging people to talk about what's really going on. She lives by the philosophy that truth seeking builds trust. Charlotte is a co-author of *The Fifth Discipline Fieldbook,* with Peter Senge and others (New York: Doubleday, 1994, 1999) and *The Dance of Change: The Challenge of Sustaining Momentum,* with Peter Senge and others (New York: Doubleday, 1999).

Charlotte can be reached at:
>   Phone: 828-478-5933
>   Fax: 828-478-5972
>   E-mail: *charlotter@mindspring.com*

Nancy Nielson Sanchez

Nancy Nielsen Sanchez is the consulting services manager for Netigy Corporation, a pre-IPO firm in Manhattan. By identifying and offering "Best Practices for Next Generation Service Providers," Nancy positions young companies and start-ups to compete effectively by optimizing service quality and operating efficiency while minimizing costs. She approaches quality and continuous improvement by providing mission-critical process definition and standards. Nancy performs analysis and problem solving for mature businesses as well, helping them "jump start" their business evolution and introduce mission-critical business solutions.

Nancy has worked on Wall Street, introducing process methodology at the working level within the telecom group of a multibillion-dollar corporation. She has also consulted with three publicly held wide area network service providers and a number of pre-IPO service providers.

Nancy can be reached at:
>   E-mail: *nancysanchez@home.com*

John P. Schuster

John Schuster, co-founder of The Schuster Kane Alliance/Capitol Connections and director of the Center for Leadership at Rockhurst

University, strives to create a sense of purpose and caring and to increase business literacy for all people in organizations. He relishes the challenges of consulting, such as working with colleagues in the new economy, with non-profits as they measure their impact and strive for excellence, and with supply-chain management as e-business takes over. John also enjoys coaching overly busy executives.

John's firm offers public workshops on leadership that yoke the business and the numbers to the soul and human will. He shares his philosophy of business literacy at work in *The Power of Open-Book Management: Releasing the True Potential of People's Minds, Hearts, and Hands,* with Jill Carpenter and M. Patricia Kane (New York: John Wiley, 1996) and in *The Open-Book Management Field Book,* with Jill Carpenter and M. Patricia Kane (New York: John Wiley, 1997).

John can be reached at:
> Phone: 816-753-7055
> E-mail: *skalliance.com*

David and Carole Schwinn

The theme of David and Carole Schwinn's work is to "lift the voices and mobilize the creative energy of all people." It permeates their work to foster "communities of place" with families, neighborhoods, communities, and organizations, including their own nonprofit organization, The Webworks Alliance, their local Citizen Center for the Common Good, and Carole's employer, Jackson Community College.

David and Carole help communities and organizations design their ideal futures and take action to realize their ideals through citizen participation. Their work uses a "whole systems" approach to bring about large-scale change in organizations and communities. Their methods are based on a synthesis of sound theory and practice, including leadership, reflective learning, systems thinking, continuous improvement, and community building.

Carole and David can be reached at:

The Webworks Alliance
14913 Oak Lane
Brooklyn, MI 49230
Phone: 517-547-6767
Fax: 517-547-4442
E-mail: *cdschwinn@dmci.net*

Leslie Stephen

Leslie Stephen has worked with Peter on four books, starting with the first edition of *Flawless Consulting* in 1980. Now an independent book and electronic content producer and editor, she is a veteran of more than twenty-five years in the publishing industry and has worked in editorial, marketing, and management positions for trade, professional, and educational houses. Today she works directly with authors, as well as with both large and small publishers and corporate clients, to help them create and produce their work in the fields of business and management, human resource development, and law.

Leslie can be reached at:
8605 Oakmountain Circle
Austin, TX 78759
Phone: 512-346-0247
Fax: 512-346-0239
E-mail: *lesliestep@aol.com*

Paul D. Tolchinsky, Ph.D.

Paul Tolchinsky has been consulting to major companies in North America for more than twenty-five years and has led numerous study missions to Japan. With an undergraduate degree in business administration and a doctorate in organization behavior and design, Paul's work gravitated toward applying sociotechnical and Whole-Scale™ design principals to his work. He manages and facilitates large-system change efforts, new plant designs, and start-ups and redesigns existing manufacturing facilities, particularly where unions are involved.

Paul's international consulting firm, Performance Development Associates, is dedicated to fostering highly successful workplaces by engaging everyone in creating a work environment of their choosing. Paul is known around the world as a pioneer in the development of Whole-Scale (Whole-System) approaches to change. He has authored a number of articles, and his work is featured in Bunker and Alban's *Large Group Interventions* (San Francisco: Jossey-Bass, 1997) and Daft and Lengel's *Fusion Leadership* (San Francisco: Berrett-Koehler, 1998).

Paul can be reached at:
> Fax: 440-349-0410
> and at conferences around the world

Nancy S. Voss

Nancy Voss is president of Voss Consulting and a senior associate of the Axelrod Group. As an organization development consultant, she brings people together to achieve desired results at the personal, group, and system levels, specializing in large-group, large-system change processes. Nan's work ranges from helping organic farmers collaborate in developing sustainable agriculture, to facilitating the redesign of large manufacturing, service, and healthcare organizations, to strategic planning with groups of executives. She also teaches consulting skills to graduate students and designs and facilitates many different workshops and seminars.

Nan's unique ability to foster personal and interpersonal development while addressing organizational and whole-system effectiveness grows out of more than twenty-five years' experience in teaching, counseling, and consulting to individuals, groups, and organizations.

Nan can be reached at:
> Voss Consulting, Inc.
> 109 South Evergreen
> Arlington Heights, IL 60005

Phone: 847-392-9980
E-mail: *VossNJ@Home.com*

Marvin R. Weisbord

Organization development consultant and writer of *Productive Workplaces: Organizing and Managing for Dignity, Meaning, and Community* (San Francisco: Jossey-Bass, 1991), Marvin Weisbord now co-directs the Future Search Network (with Sandra Janoff), an international non-profit firm that is dedicated to community service, colleagueship, and learning. Future Search offers planning conferences anywhere in the world, charging only what people can afford. Keeping with its mission to make Future Search accessible to everyone, its members carry out one pro bono service project a year.

Marvin describes the theory and practice of Future Search in two books, *Discovering Common Ground: How Future Search Conferences Bring People Together to Achieve Breakthrough Innovation, Empowerment, Shared Vision, and Cooperation* (San Francisco: Berrett-Koehler, 1992) and *Future Search: An Action Guide to Finding Common Ground in Organizations and Communities* (2nd ed.), with Sandra Janoff (San Francisco: Berrett-Koehler, 2000).

Marvin can be reached at:
Future Search Network
4700 Wissahickon Avenue, Suite 126
Philadelphia, PA 19144
Direct line: 610-896-7035
Phone: 215-951-0328
Fax: 610-658-0991
E-mail: *mweisbord@futuresearch.net*

Margaret J. Wheatley

Dr. Margaret Wheatley is a writer, public speaker, educator, and organizational consultant. She is president of The Berkana Institute.

She is eagerly engaged in helping a very diverse group of people from many different countries and types of organizations realize that there is a simpler way to organize human endeavor. She has been intrigued by how life self-organizes, and she spends her time describing the possibilities of human organizations in which freedom, creativity, and self-determination prevail. Her two books are *Leadership and the New Science* (San Francisco: Berrett-Koehler, 1992, 1999) and *A Simpler Way*, co-authored with Myron Kellner-Rogers (San Francisco: Berrett-Koehler, 1996). Her work, articles, favorite books, and dreams are at *www.berkana.org*.

About the Author

Peter Block has been a consultant and speaker to governments, businesses, and communities all over the world for more than thirty years. He is a founder of two well-known training and consulting firms, Designed Learning and Block Petrella Weisbord, and the author of three best-selling business books: *Flawless Consulting* (1981; 1999), *The Empowered Manager* (1987), and *Stewardship* (1993). Peter has received several national awards for outstanding contributions to his field, including the American Society for Training and Development Award for Distinguished Contributions and the Association for Quality and Participation President's Award, and was named to *Training* magazine's HRD Hall of Fame. For more information visit *www.PeterBlock.com* or e-mail Peter at *pbi@att.net*.

Peter is the creator of the Flawless Consulting Workshops, which are offered both as public seminars and internally by Designed Learning and have taught consulting skills to thousands of people in the staff role in areas such as engineering, systems analysis, finance, and personnel in the United States and around the world. Designed Learning can be reached at (908) 889-0300 or *www.Designedlearning.com* or *Flawless Consulting.net*.

Peter has also joined with the Association for Quality and Participation to create The School for Managing and Leading Change, a unique, nine-month program for public- and private-sector teams to learn how to redesign their workplaces. For information on the school, call (513) 381-1959 or visit the website at *www.aqp.org*.

Index

Orientation stage of team performance model, 279, 280
Orpheus, story of, 194–196, 197
Overcoming Organizational Defenses (Argyris), 296
Owen, Harrison, 297, 299
Oxymorons: constructive criticism, 237; context of, 7; definition, 9

P

Paradigm shifts, 316, 318
Paradigms: change management, 292–297; conflict management, 145; cross-functional nature of teams in change management, 293; engagement, 291, 299–300; future search, 145; partnership as consulting, 85–86
Paradox: in change, 177; of confrontational style, 191; examples of sitting with, 141–144; in future search, 139; inherentness of to consulting, 8, 9; as a tool, 10
Paradoxical intention, 191
Paradoxical nature of life, 121
Parallel organization, 292
Participative design, 299
Partners, definition, 168
Partnership: as consulting paradigm, 85–86; versus expert, 85; importance of, 234; relationships as, 234;
Passivity in meetings/conferences, 372–373
Pathological anxiety, 158
Patriarchal culture, 216–217
Patterns of female-to-female relationships, 212–213
Performance, improving consulting, 112–113
Performance through conversation, dealing with, 62
Personality, 8
Perturbers, consultants as, 126
Peters, Tom, 371

Pfeiffer, Bill, 74
Philosophy and business, marriage between, 153
Pidd, Colin, 140
Place questions, 132
Planning meetings, 144, 150
Plato, 155
Poems: "Flawless" (Wheatley), 5–6, 375–376; "The Midwife" (Barbeau), 180; "Untitled" (existential crisis), 162–163; "We Shall Not Cease From Exploration" (Eliot), 356
Point of view, openness to others', 115
Polarities of too much/not enough, 220–221
Policy, questions about, 132
Politics of Experience, The (Laing), 193
Positive envisioning of future, 300
Post-intervention surveys, 344–345, 347
Powell, Colin, 371
Power and competition, 218–222
Power of words example, 154
Powerful, presence of women as, 185
Pre-intervention surveys, 346
Preferred futuring, 318
Presence, women's, 185
Pride, of consultants, 105–109
Proactive theory, 128
Process for transformation, steps for, 193–194
Productive Workplaces (Weisbord), 139
Projection, 222–224
Promises, accountability and, 61
Properties of good questions, 151–152
Proposing change, 62
Provider-client relationships, 86
Purpose: awakening our sense of, 406; discovery questions about, 131; as driver of every intervention, 316

Q

Questionnaires, 339, 342–352. *See also* Evaluation forms; McCormick

Employee Engagement Inventory (MEEI)

Founded by Peter Block, **Designed Learning** is a full-service training and consulting organization existing to help organizations succeed at complex change. Through a variety of innovative ideas and technologies, we strive to help our client organizations support the transformation of staff people into effective internal consultants and consultant teams. **The Flawless Consulting Workshops** are a key element in our mission to help organizations build capacity and develop people for more successful, more meaningful work.

Flawless Consulting—Three hands-on, skill building workshops for internal and external consultants. These are the **only** consulting skills workshops developed by Peter Block, author of *Flawless Consulting* and *The Flawless Consulting Fieldbook and Companion*. To learn more about these workshops, call us today or visit our website at www.designedlearning.com.

Learn how to establish and maintain collaborative working relations with clients, which result in positive outcomes for the business. Learn how to have influence when you do not have control.

Flawless Consulting I: *Contracting*

- Develop commitment from your internal clients.
- Work more in a partnership role with client managers.
- Negotiate more effective and enduring working agreements with clients.
- Identify consulting phases and skills.
- Develop techniques for defining roles and responsibilities and clarifying expectations.
- Gain better use of staff expertise in the organization.
- Avoid no-win consulting situations.

Flawless Consulting II: *Discovery*

- Practice a data collection or discovery model.
- Conduct interviewing meetings to collect data around a business issue.
- Deal with client resistance.
- Gain skills in turning recommendations into a decision to act.
- Conduct a successful feedback meeting.
- Identify methods for mapping out action steps with the client prior to implementation.
- Increase line manager commitment and action.

Flawless Consulting III: *Implementation*

- Choose engagement over mandate and direction.
- Create a balance between presentation and participation.
- Break away from familiar refrains to create new conversations.
- Learn the eight steps that create meetings for greater engagement.
- Handle resistance and support public dissent.
- Develop authentic dialogue within the client organization.
- Focus on assets and gifts rather than weaknesses and deficiencies.

Other Designed Learning workshops:

The Empowered Manager Workshop: *Choosing Accountability—Making the Business Your Own*

The Stewardship Workshop: *Building Capacity—Deepening Customer Service*

The Conflict Workshop: *Managing Differences and Agreement—Making Conflict Work For You*

Staff Groups in the New Economy: *Transitioning from Staff Function to Consulting Service*

For more information contact:

Designed Learning Inc.
313 South Avenue, Suite 202
Fanwood, NJ 07023
Phone: (908) 889–0300
Email: *info@designedlearning.com*

Developing the Person at Work
Fax: (908) 889–4995
Website: *www.designedlearning.com*